IMAGES of America
AMERICAN INDIANS
OF THE PIKES PEAK REGION

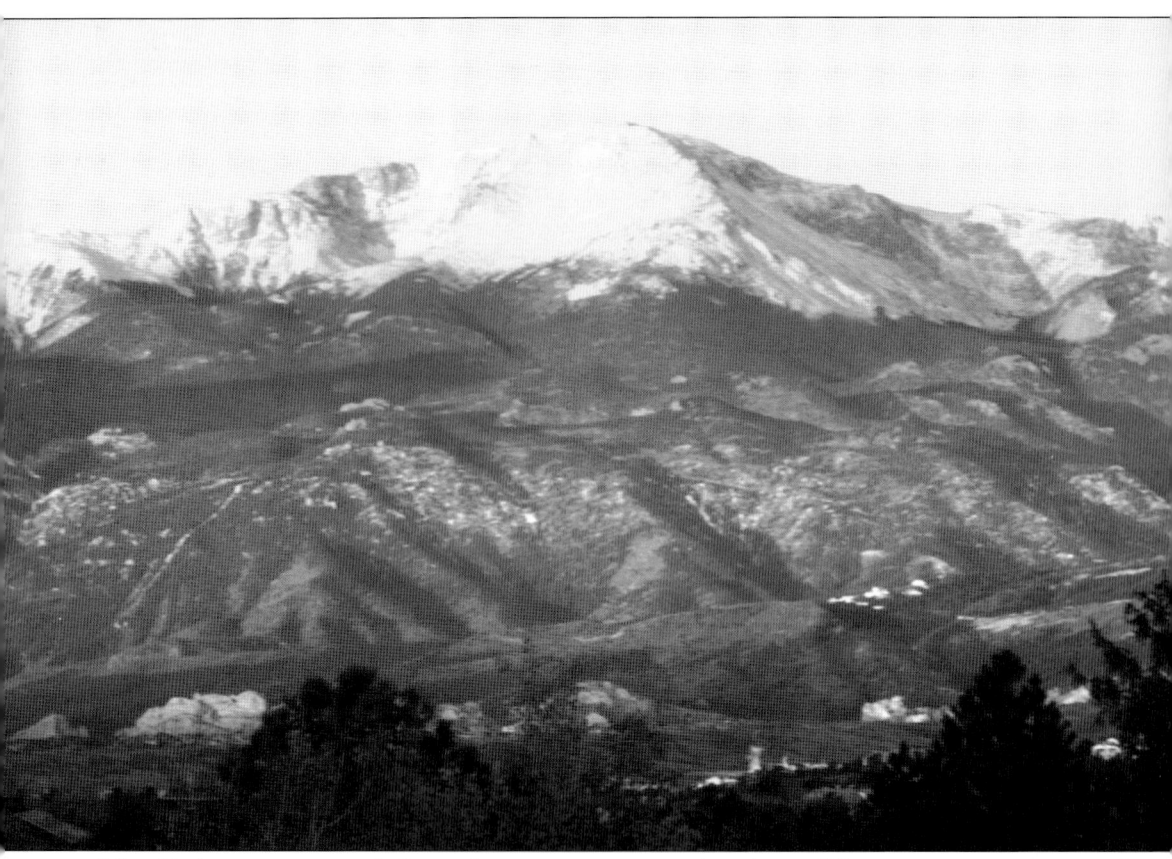

Pikes Peak appears on early Spanish maps as a *cerro*, or lone butte. This error was not corrected until Spanish expeditions to the area in the late 1700s. Its snowy pinnacle, clearly visible for hundreds of miles, beckoned First Nations from as far as the eye could see.

ON THE COVER: From left to right, John Deal, Cerette, and Ocapoor pose in 1911 while encamped with Buckskin Charlie's band in Garden of the Gods for Shan Kive. During the ceremonies, Buckskin Charlie sang the death chant, indicating the great sorrow the Ute people felt at being separated from the "dust of the grandfather's bones." (Courtesy Denver Public Library [DPL].)

CONTENTS

Acknowledgments		6
Introduction		7
1.	Prehistoric People of the Pikes Peak Region	11
2.	Nuche, the Ute Nation	17
3.	Tin-ne-ah, the Apache Nation	63
4.	Ne 'me Ne, the Comanche Nation	75
5.	Inuna-ina, the Arapaho Nation	87
6.	Dzitsi'stas, the Cheyenne Nation	97
7.	Tepki'nago, the Kiowa Nation	107
8.	Lakota, the Sioux Nation	115
Selected Bibliography		126
Index		127

Acknowledgments

I am deeply grateful to all those who helped make this volume possible, especially my husband, Harold. Hannah Carney, my editor, deserves great credit for her kind and expert guidance; Laurie Wagner Buyer for her editing; and friends Andy Weinzapfel, Ann Carlisle, Bill Arbogast, and Bridget Ambler for their support. Frank Ross of Coffrin's Old West Gallery in Bozeman, Montana, made possible the exquisite images from L. A. Huffman. Finally, I am sincerely grateful to all of my friends from the First Nations for their help with this work, including Loya Arrum, Clifford Duncan, Jimmy Arterberry, Ben Ridgley, and Wankiyan Sna Mani. Thanks also go to Neil Cloud, Gordon Yellowman, Lorene Willis, and Billy Evans Horse. Unless otherwise noted, images are from the author's collection.

INTRODUCTION

Pikes Peak commands the horizon of the Rocky Mountains along Colorado's Front Range, looming above Colorado Springs on the east, Pueblo and Cripple Creek on the south, Florissant on the west, and Woodland Park on the north. Its snow-capped summit has a numinousness that speaks to human beings from at least 12,000 years ago to our present time.

Archaeological surveys on the west slope of Pikes Peak, at Mueller State Park, and at the Florissant Fossil Beds National Monument reveal a number of ancient sites. In 1932, Etienne Renaud from the University of Denver's anthropology department and his survey team found sites in the Florissant Valley that included 12,000-year-old artifacts. A 1974 survey documented Plano artifacts from about 8,000 years ago. On the east side of Pikes Peak, around Colorado Springs, archaeologists have documented human presence from thousands of years ago at Fort Carson, the Air Force Academy, Garden of the Gods, and Pulpit Rock Open Space.

Who were these ancient people? Did they simply disappear, or did they evolve a unique cultural identity? In answer, the *Nuche* (Ute Indians) say that these ancient people were their ancestors. Age-old legends tell of their creation on Pikes Peak:

> Sunif and Yahowitz lived in a carniv, a cloud tipi, on top of Pikes Peak. One day, the Older Brother [Sunif, the wolf] wanted to put the people here and there, so he made a little bag and this he will pack on his back and as he moves to the north he will distribute these little people throughout the world. He did not tell anyone about what he was doing. But his brother Yahowitz [the coyote] was a curious animal.
>
> Yahowitz murmured, "*Ahat iya aqay?* What is he doing?" The Older Brother was breaking these small twigs to small size and putting them in a bag. But the Younger Brother watched without getting too close. Now the Older Brother, Sunif, decided to take a walk and when he was gone the curiosity got the best of the Younger Brother, Yahowitz. Because in the bag he could hear people talking. There's music going on in the bag. He'd listen real carefully and he would say, "*Niahook?* What's it saying, what is in there?" So he took his flint knife and he cut a little hole on the side of the bag.
>
> And when he looked in through the hole, the people saw him. There were people in there. The sticks had turned into people. And some jumped out, and about that time the Older Brother he's come back again. Not knowing what had taken place, he put the bag on his back. Every once in while he would stop and reach in the bag and put some people down on the earth and say, "You will live here!"
>
> Finally, when he got to the high place way up in the mountains, then he knew what was going on. There was a hole in the bag and all the people had jumped out. But they are still in there that he left in there and he talked to them. "You my people, you my children, I'm going to put you over here. You will be called the Yutica, Yuta, the Ute. You will live in these mountains for these shining mountains will be your home."
>
> And that's how the distribution was made and how the Utes were placed on the mountains.
>
> —Clifford Duncan, Northern Ute elder

Fortunately, Sunif placed the Ute people in the Rocky Mountains, their Shining Mountains, which abound in big game such as elk, bear, deer, and antelope. Plains Indians, jealous of this hunter's paradise, constantly disputed Ute possession of the Pikes Peak region. Their incursions began when Athapascans pushed down through the Great Plains and into Ute territory about 1400 CE. Ute Indians have an oral record of these invaders, who "were big and red, and they fought the little people and killed many of them, and those they did not kill they drove away to the south. The big people followed to the south, and they were the fathers of the Navajo, Apache, and Kiowa." These aggressors from the north named the people they found in the Southwest *Anasazi*, "ancient enemy," providing lasting documentation of this conflict.

Some bands of these Apaches continued southward until they settled in western New Mexico, where they took up farming. Local Tewa Indians referred to them as *Navahu*, "cultivators of large tracts of land." Other bands like the Jicarillas established villages along the Arkansas River. Spanish maps and documents show their presence in the Pikes Peak region from the early 1500s. However, conflicts with the Comanche Nation forced the Jicarillas out of the Pikes Peak area by the 1700s. From there, the Jicarillas established a homeland in northwestern New Mexico.

Comanches, Shoshones, and Utes share the same dialect of the Aztec (Numic) language, and were one people long ago. Scientists theorize that the Shoshone culture first appeared in the late 1600s. Shoshones probably separated from the Utes after the introduction of the horse. A note on a 1778 Spanish map tells us of Comanche origins.

The mapmaker writes that the Comanches split from the Ute Nation after an altercation at Abiquiu, New Mexico, in the early 1700s. Spanish authorities corrupted the Ute word *Komantcia*, which means "anyone who wants to fight me all the time," leading to historic use of the name Comanche. Comanches were forced from the Pikes Peak region in the late 1700s.

In the domino-type displacement of First Nations after the European invasion, the Cheyenne and Arapaho Indians flooded into the Pikes Peak region from the northeast in the early 1800s. Their ancestors, the Lenni Lenape (the Delaware), kept a record of their migrations from the Bering Strait on wooden tablets called *Wallam Olum*, or "Red Record." After acquiring the horse in the mid-1700s, the Cheyenne and Arapaho Nations ranged into South Dakota and Wyoming. In the 1830s, they were drawn to the lower Arkansas for trade at Bent's Fort.

This predominately peaceful era of the Southern Cheyennes and Arapahos ended abruptly in 1864. On November 29, Col. John Chivington and a force of 700 soldiers attacked a sleeping village on Sand Creek (near Bent's Fort), killing 150 to 160—mostly women and children. Spurred to action by this tragedy, the Cheyennes and Arapahos went on the warpath. Peace finally came with the Medicine Lodge Treaty of 1867, and the Southern Cheyennes and Arapahos were assigned to a reservation in Oklahoma, ending their presence by Pikes Peak.

We first learn of the Kiowa Nation in the Kootenay region of British Colombia. As the European invasion forced the tribe southwestward, members formed an alliance with the Crow. The Cheyennes and Arapahos later pushed them along the South Platte and then down to the Arkansas River. They finally made peace and became allies with these enemies in 1840. Eventually, the Kiowa people also made an alliance with the Comanches, raiding deep into Mexico. Again with the Medicine Lodge Treaty of 1867, both the Comanches and Kiowas were placed on a reservation in southwestern Oklahoma.

The Siouan-speaking Lakota people ranged sporadically into the Pikes Peak region, probably in search of buffalo. These hunting forays left little evidence of Lakota presence for future generations. We have only a passing reference by pioneer Irving Howbert: "In 1859, a battle between the Ute on the one side, and the Cheyenne, Arapahoe, and Sioux on the other, was fought six miles north of Colorado City, in the valley now occupied by the Modern Woodmen's Home." However, Pikes Peak is linked indelibly with Lakota culture by the vision of medicine man Black Elk. His prophetic 1873 vision was immortalized in Neihardt's *Black Elk Speaks*. Although his vision took place on Pikes Peak, Neihardt changed its location to Harney Peak when he wrote his book. Fortunately, transcripts of Neihardt's interviews with Black Elk have been preserved in Raymond DeMallie's *The Sixth Grandfather*.

Throughout recorded history, these three ethnic, or linguistic, groups fought for possession of the Pikes Peak area. Through all of the fierce battles of the Algonquians, Athapascans, and Uto-Aztecans, in the end it was the Nuche who preserved their hunter's paradise. Yet all of these First Nations evinced a deep respect for the sacredness of Pikes Peak. Friend and foe revered the bubbling waters of "Creator's breath" at Manitou Springs and the "dust of the grandfather's bones" found in the red soil of Garden of the Gods. Moccasins, beads, strips of red cloth, and other treasured items were left as offerings to the Great Spirit at these places.

Hundreds of medicine trees (scarred ponderosa) and prayer trees (bent ponderosa) still stand as living artifacts of the Nuche presence in Pikes Peak. Dozens of medicine wheels, stone cairns, and rocky fortifications hold the spirit of the Nuche ancestors who built them. Mossy sleeping platforms and conical wickiups encircle the ancient Sundance grounds of the Nuche on Pikes Peak. The nation was dispossessed of its sacred mountain by the Ute Agreement of 1880 and forcibly relocated to reservations in southern Colorado and northeastern Utah. Sunif had placed his people well, but broken treaties prevailed in the end.

In July 1911, Colorado Springs invited Utes to a celebration of the city's 40th anniversary. Gen. William J. Palmer dispatched a Denver and Rio Grande train for the guests, and soon Utes, tipis, and horses spread throughout South Cheyenne Canyon. Their contingent joined a grand parade of pioneers who marched through Colorado Springs for the celebration. In August, a delegation of Utes returned to Colorado Springs to inaugurate a new annual event, the Shan Kive. Over 30 years after forced relocation, the Nuche performed sacred dances once again in the "dust of the grandfather's bones."

One

Prehistoric People of the Pikes Peak Region

We have no way of really knowing what language was spoken. They left no written record other than mysterious, pecked images on well-weathered stone. These are the ancient people of the Pikes Peak region, occupying the area from at least 12,000 years ago. Maybe they were created here. Or maybe they were an ancient migration of the Olmec culture from Central America. Or maybe they came by sea, island hopping along the Bering Strait.

Whoever these first people of Pikes Peak were, they left many intriguing mysteries. In the 1930s, famed anthropologist E. B. Renaud performed the first scholarly study documenting Paleo-Indian presence in the Pikes Peak region from about 10,000 BCE. Meanwhile, on the west slope of the peak, an ethnological survey at Mueller State Park included finds of Paleo-Indian and Archaic stone tools. A little farther west, near the Florissant Fossil Beds National Monument, Renaud's team found Yuma and 12,000-year-old Folsom points, as well as tipi rings, stonework shops, and campsites.

On the east flank of Pikes Peak, archaeologists found evidence of human occupation from 5,000 years ago on Turkey Creek at Fort Carson. At the Air Force Academy, scientists uncovered a prehistoric stone circle with charcoal dating back 830 years. They also found a brush structure with 310-year-old charcoal. At Garden of the Gods, prehistoric etchings from at least 1,000 years ago mark the presence of these first people. They also left a fire pit in an arroyo about 3,500 years ago.

Finally, east of Colorado Springs, near Jimmy Camp Creek, there is evidence of numerous prehistoric occupations. Among these, one is dated from 665 CE, a second from 1400, and a third from 1650.

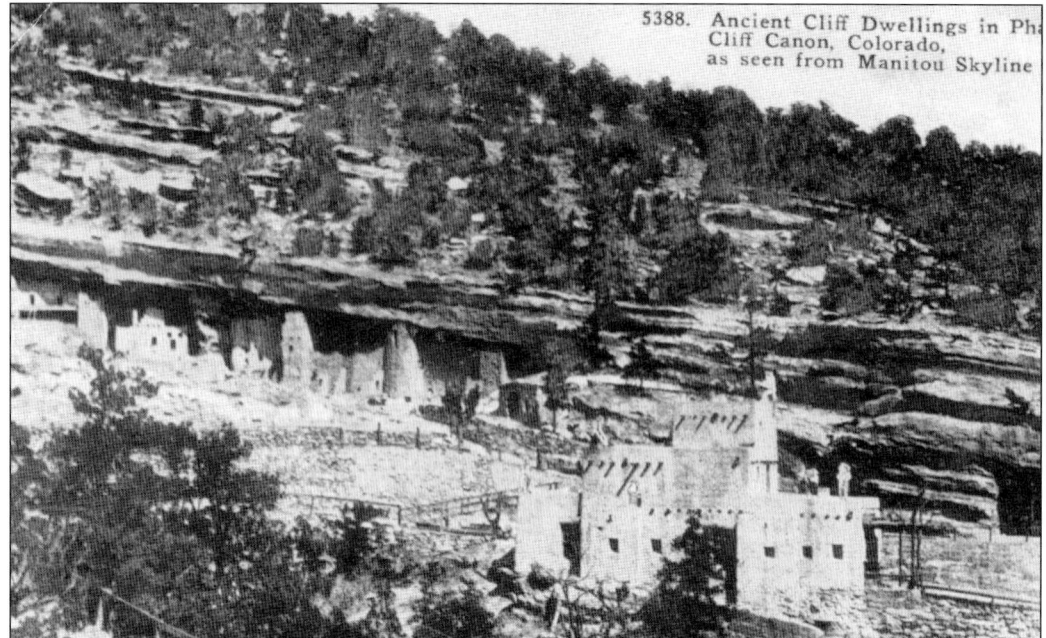

These cliff dwellings off Highway 24 north of Manitou Springs are authentic of prehistoric people, though not authentic to their location. In the early 1900s, some enterprising residents moved these Anasazi dwellings from the Mesa Verde area and had them reconstructed at their current site. (Courtesy Ute Pass Historical Society.)

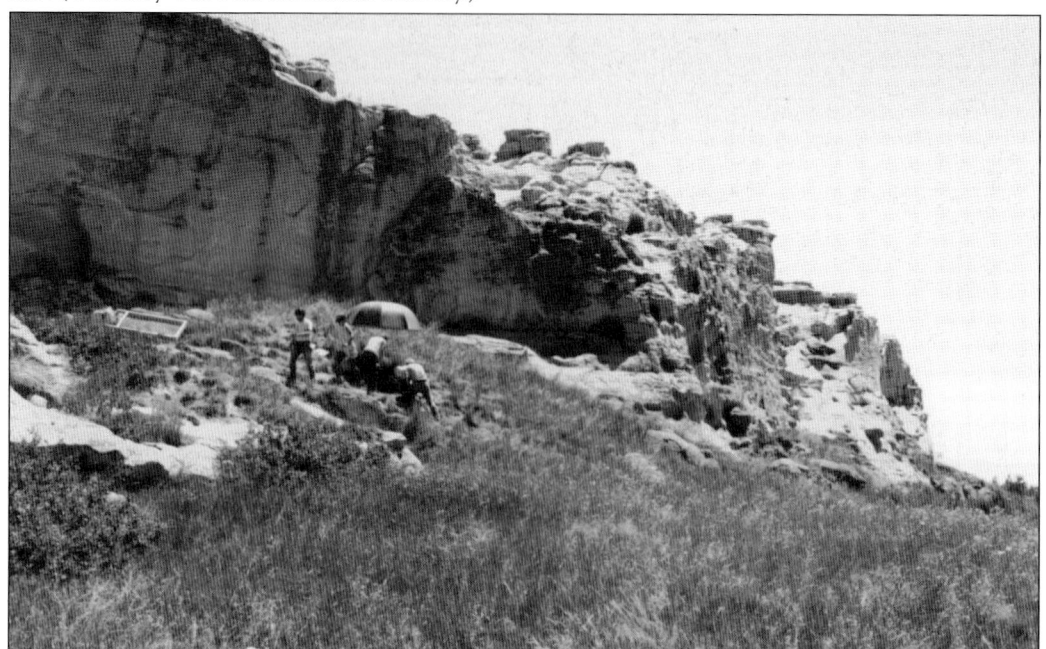

Archaeologists examine evidence from a mid-Archaic (about 6000 BCE) to late-Ceramic (about 1700 CE) bison jump at Crows Roost, east of Colorado Springs. Early people drove herds of buffalo over this steep cliff, leaving behind the stone and bone tools used to process the meat. (Courtesy University of Colorado at Colorado Springs.)

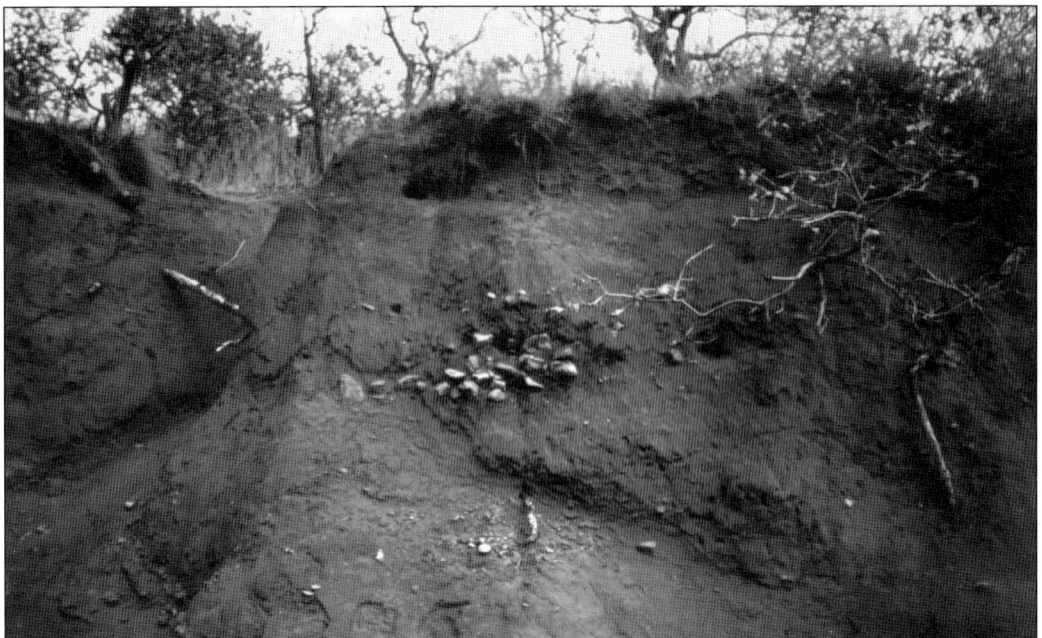

Rain, dust, and erosion buried this prehistoric hearth for more than 8,000 years at Garden of the Gods. Stones from the hearth are clustered in the center of the photograph. Rain has eroded the hillside, giving a nice profile of a fire pit that once warmed an ancient hunter and his family. (Courtesy University of Colorado at Colorado Springs.)

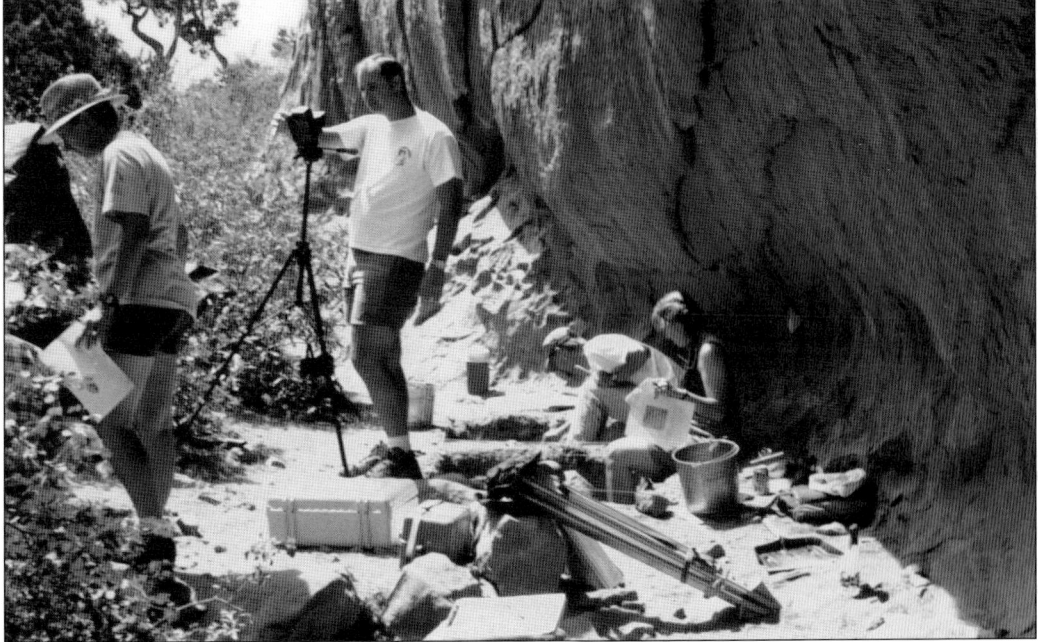

Prehistoric people probably related to the numinous landscape at Garden of the Gods much as American Indians do. This rock shelter, which would have provided a convenient place to camp for the night, was used from about 6000 BCE to around 1800 CE. (Courtesy University of Colorado at Colorado Springs.)

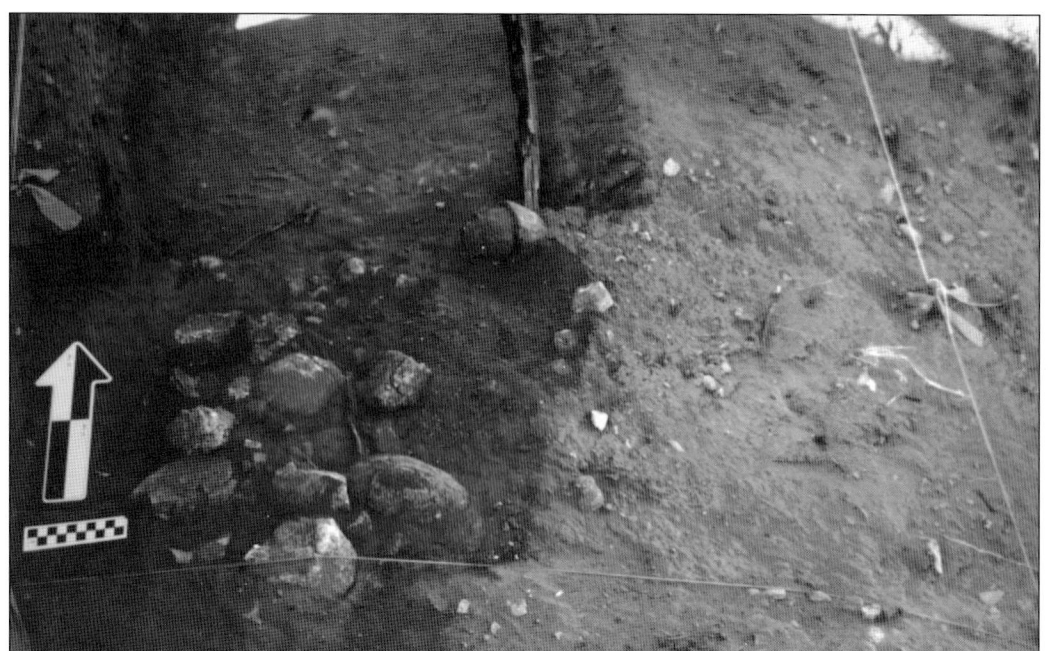

Ute Indians likely cooked their game in this fire pit at Garden of the Gods. Archaeologists date it to approximately 500 CE. Utes referred to the rock features at Red Rock Open Space and Garden of the Gods as the "bones of Mother Earth." (Courtesy University of Colorado at Colorado Springs.)

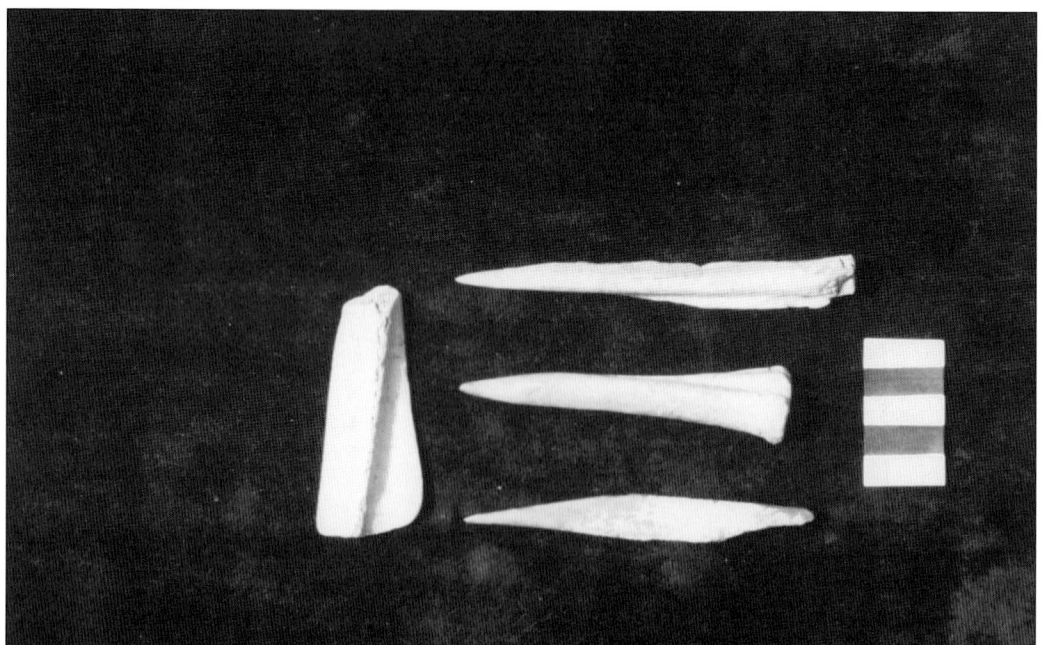

These bone tools, dated to about 790 CE, were found in a burial near the heart of Colorado Springs. Scientists associate them with the Plains Woodland culture. These people generally left few clues to their identity, as their structures were highly perishable. (Courtesy University of Colorado at Colorado Springs.)

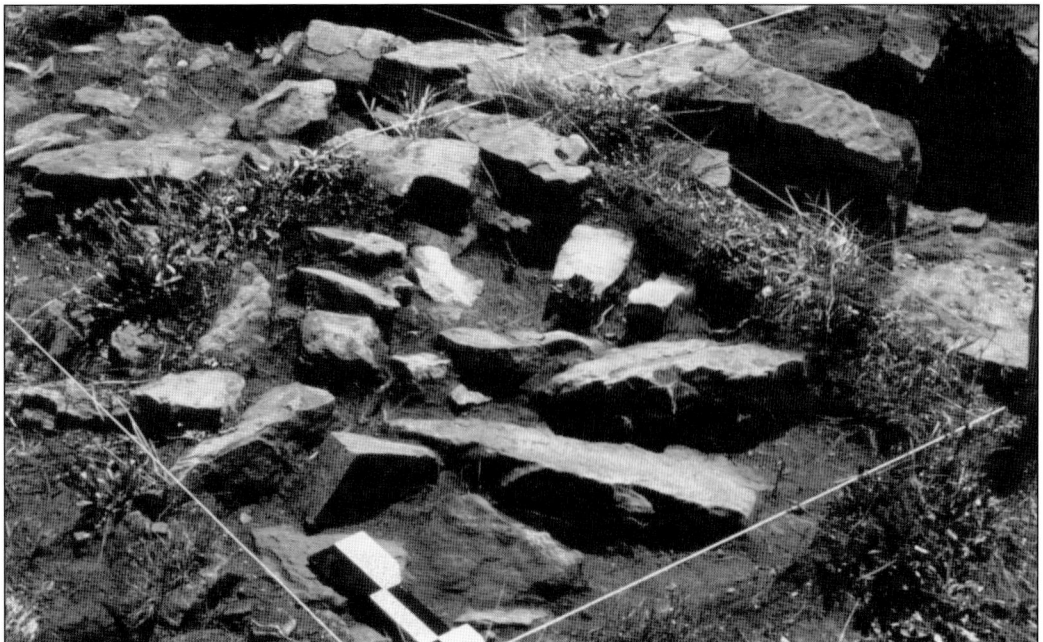

Stones from an Apishapa structure litter the ground on this site at Fort Carson in Colorado Springs. They have been dated from the mid-Ceramic period (around 1300 CE). Some scientists feel that the Apishapa were influenced or connected to the Anasazi because both lived in clustered dwellings and cultivated corn. (Courtesy Centennial Archaeology.)

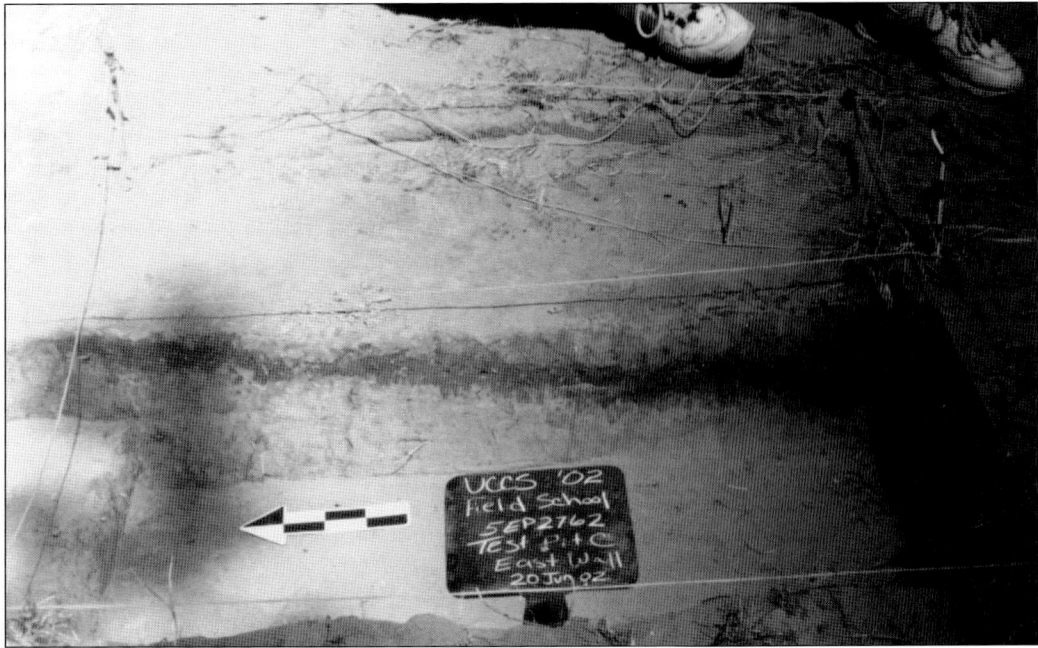

Jimmy Camp, located east of Colorado Springs near the intersection of Highway 24 and Constitution Avenue, holds numerous archaeological treasures. This fire pit dates from approximately 1650 CE, while others date from 665 CE. In addition to fire pits, the area abounds with stone tools, arrowheads, and pottery. (Courtesy University of Colorado at Colorado Springs.)

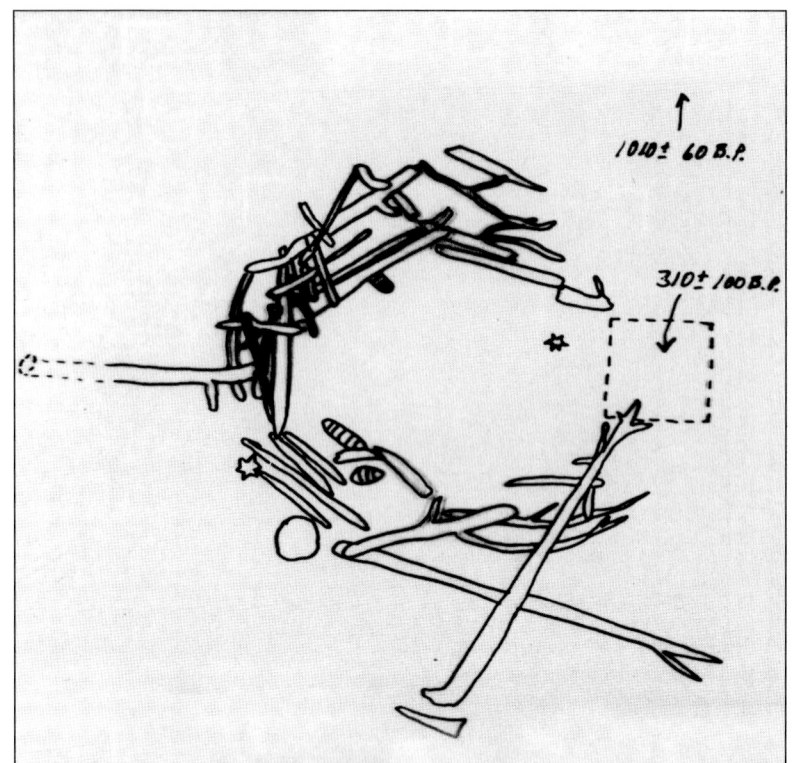

This drawing comes from an archaeological study at a site on the Air Force Academy in Colorado Springs. The structure, possibly Apachean or Athapascan, appears to have been made of brush. A long, dry-laid stone wall (typical of Ute fortifications) is also located at the academy. (Courtesy University of Colorado at Colorado Springs.)

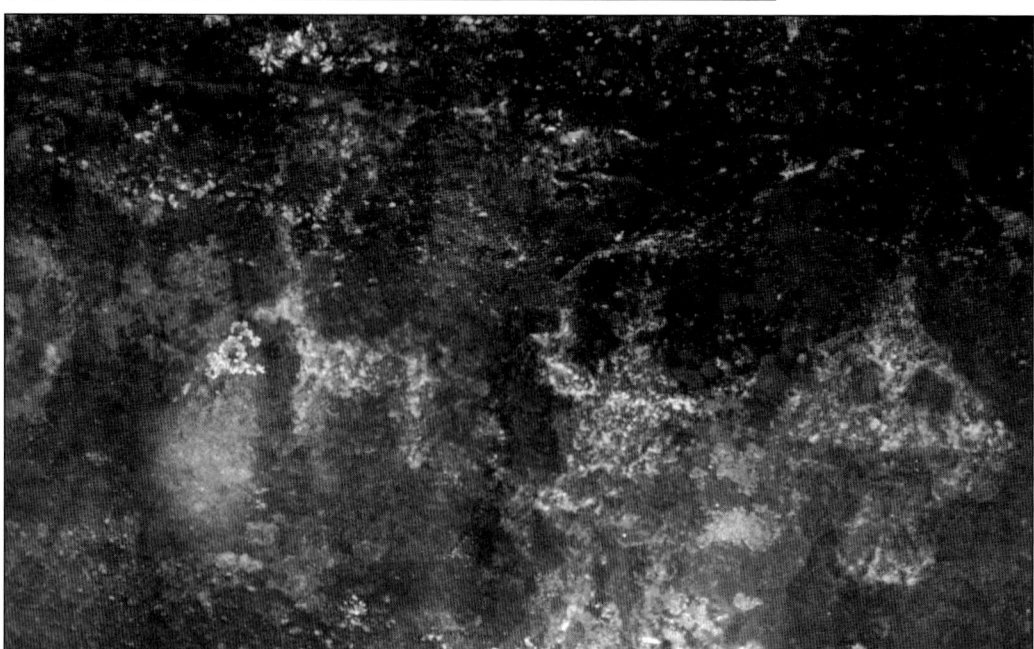

A circle with a dot in the middle, a deer, an anthropomorph (human form), and what looks to be a thunderbird parade across this petroglyph at Garden of the Gods. Archaeologists attribute this artwork to the Ute Nation, but no date has been assigned. (Courtesy City of Colorado Springs.)

Two

NUCHE, THE UTE NATION

John Wesley Powell first identified this nation as *Numa*, "the People." Individual Numas refer to themselves as *nuu-ci*, or Nuche. Frances Densmore writes that their common name, Ute, is a derivative of the Shoshone word *Tsiyuta*, which means "rabbit hunters."

The Nuche are an anomaly among American Indians, as they have no migration legend. As recounted in the introduction, they believe that they were created at Pikes Peak—that they have always been here. Scientists, however, say that the Numic language did not appear in North America until about 500 CE. Hopis, Comanches, Shoshones, and Nahuatls are all part of their Uto-Aztecan language group. In turn, they are part of the larger, Aztec-Tanoan family, which includes the Pueblo Indians as well as the Kiowas. This diverse language family is one of history's mysteries.

Prior to European invasion, Nuche lands included all of Colorado, most of Utah, and northern New Mexico. As you might guess, the state of Utah is named for the Ute people. Prior to European contact, there may have been as many as one million Nuche. However, exposure to foreign diseases decimated the population to about 10,000, according to Spanish records. The nation was loosely organized into about 10 different bands. *Tava* (Sun)—Pikes Peak—was at the heart of the lands inhabited by the *Tabeguache* (People of Sun Mountain) band. To the south of their traditional lands were the Moache and Capote bands.

In an 1868 treaty, the Tabeguache were moved to a reservation on the west slope, where they became known as the Uncompahgre. Under the terms of the Ute Agreement of 1880, the Tabeguache were again relocated, this time to a reservation in Utah. The Capotes and Moaches retained a part of the ancestral lands at the Southern Ute Reservation, south of Durango.

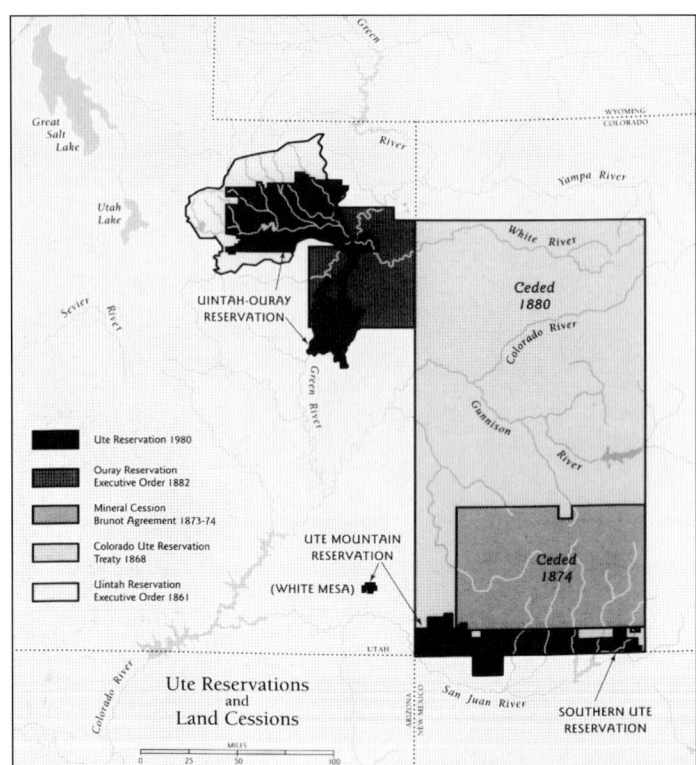

When looking at this map, it is important to remember that the white area represents only a portion of ancestral Ute lands. This First Nation originally occupied almost all of Utah and Colorado and portions of northern New Mexico. The dark areas were defined after 1861. (Courtesy Colorado Springs Fine Arts Center, Taylor Museum, Ute Reservations and Land Cessions, Fig. Pg. 2: Ute Indian Arts and Culture, 2000.)

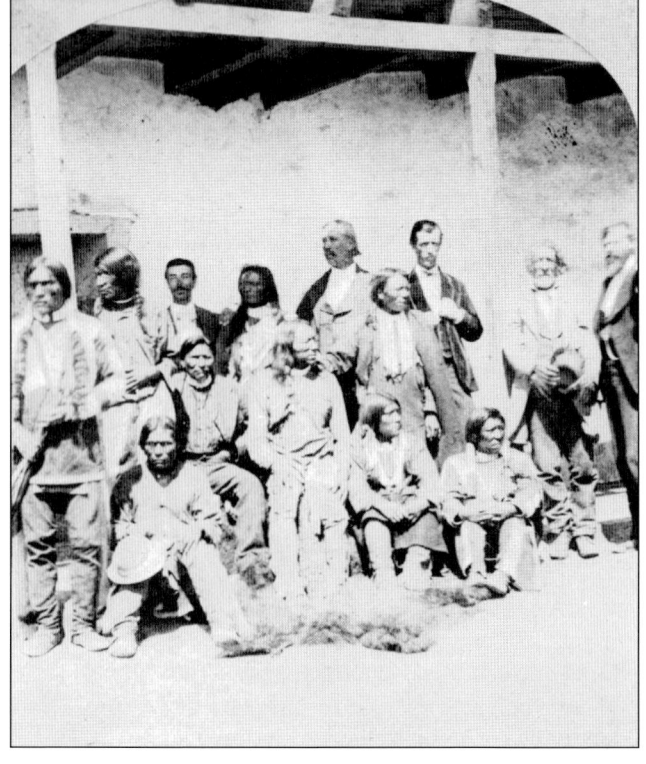

This 1874 photograph from the Wheeler Expedition shows a gathering of Ute men at the Abiquiu Ute Agency in New Mexico. Abiquiu is strategically situated on the Chama River, which provided a natural Ute highway from Colorado into New Mexico. In 1849, it was host to the first treaty between the United States and the Ute Nation. (Courtesy Museum of New Mexico.)

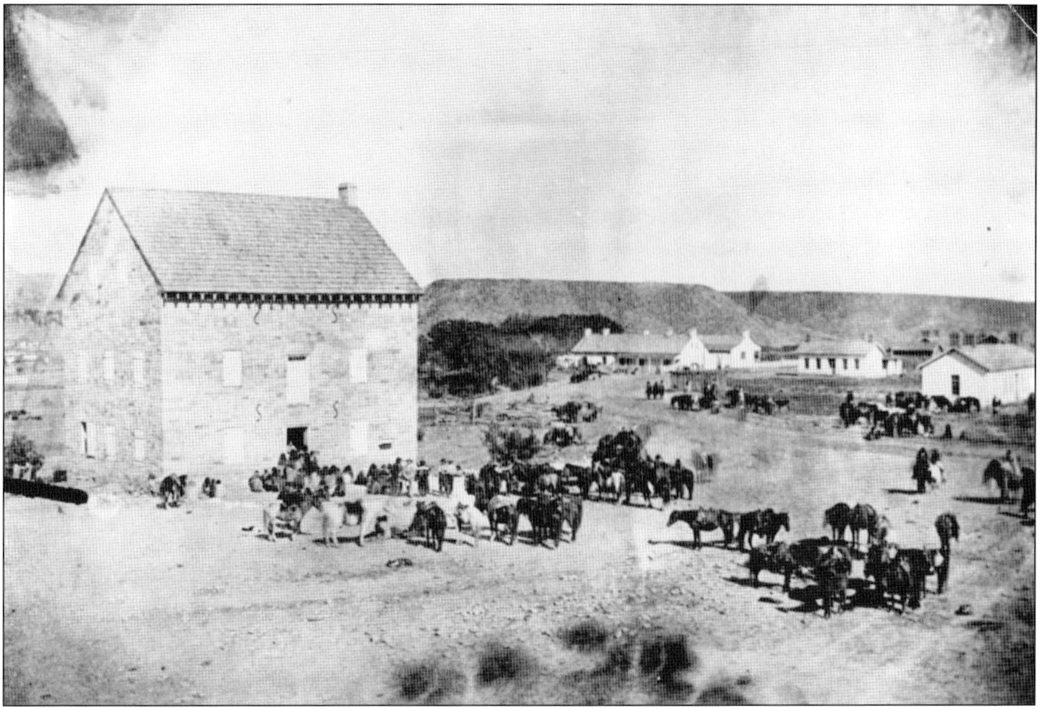

Utes gather at the flour mill in Cimarron, New Mexico, on ration day in the 1860s. The federal government moved the Taos Agency to Cimarron in 1862 to prevent Ute and Apache access to whiskey. (Courtesy Museum of New Mexico.)

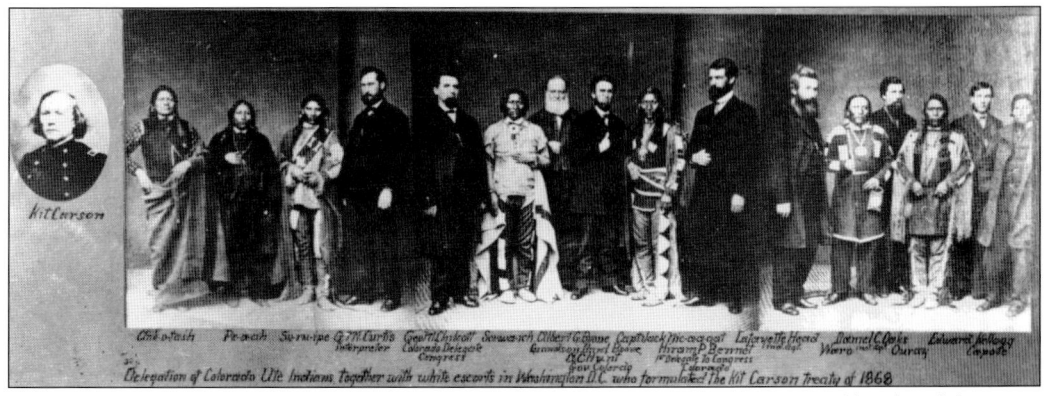

In Washington in 1868, a document dubbed the Kit Carson Treaty was signed by this delegation from the Moache, Capote, Weeminuche, Grand River, and Uintah bands. The agreement shrank Ute territory by more than 50 percent and established agencies at White River (near Meeker) and Los Pinos (near Saguache, later moved near Montrose). Its purpose was to make the "Indians adopt habits of civilized life." (Courtesy DPL.)

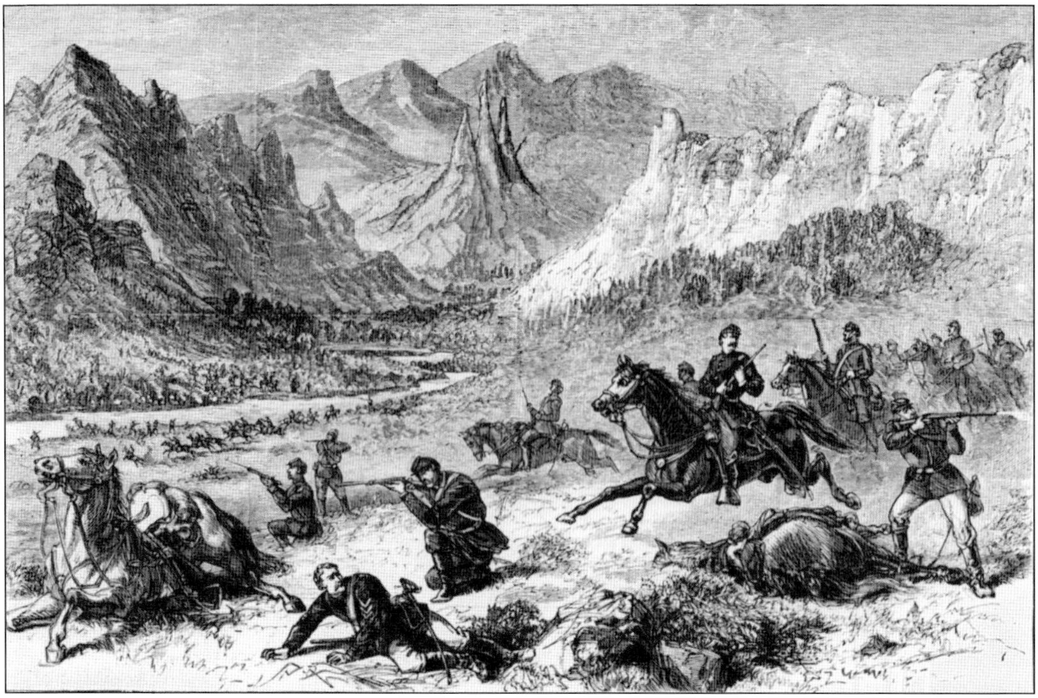

In violation of the 1873 treaty, Maj. T. T. Thornburgh entered sovereign Ute territory on September 29, 1879, with four companies of cavalry and a supply train. In response to this act of war, the troops were attacked by 50 Ute warriors led by Colorow, Antelope, and Nicaagat (Captain Jack). Other warriors at the White River Agency killed agent Nathan Meeker and nine of his men. (Courtesy Museum of New Mexico.)

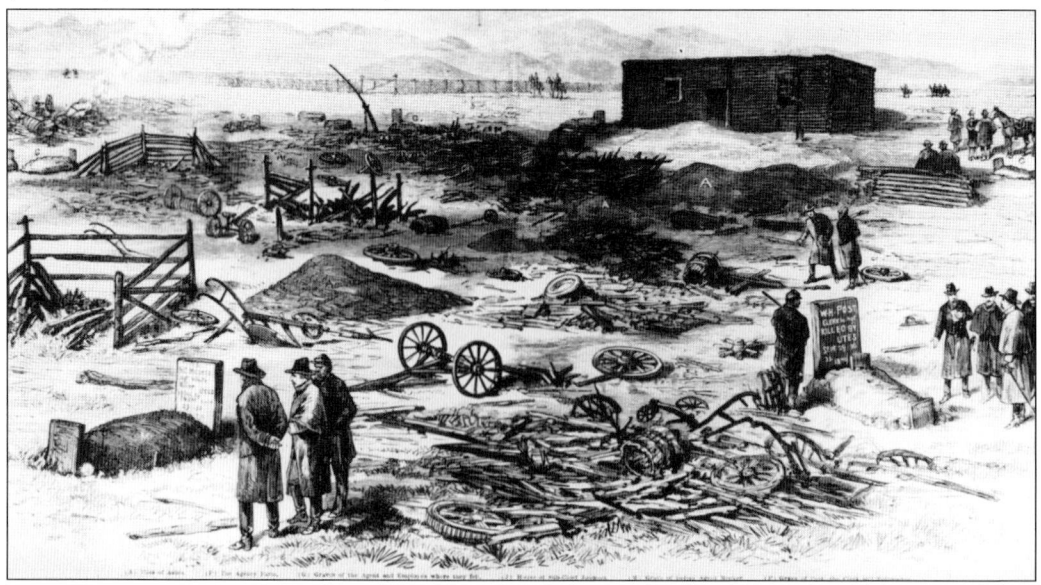

The fate of the Ute people was sealed with the destruction, killings, and abductions at the White River Agency. According to the treaty of 1868, only "bad men among the Indians" would be "tried and punished according to its laws." However, with the Ute Agreement of 1880, all Utes were punished and most of their ancestral lands taken. (Courtesy DPL.)

Chief Ouray (left) appears uncomfortable with Otto Mears in this 1868 photograph. Mears paid $2 to every Ute who signed the 1880 treaty. He told a congressional committee that "two dollars in cash was worth more to them than the government's promise of fifty thousand dollars per year, which they would probably never get." (Courtesy DPL.)

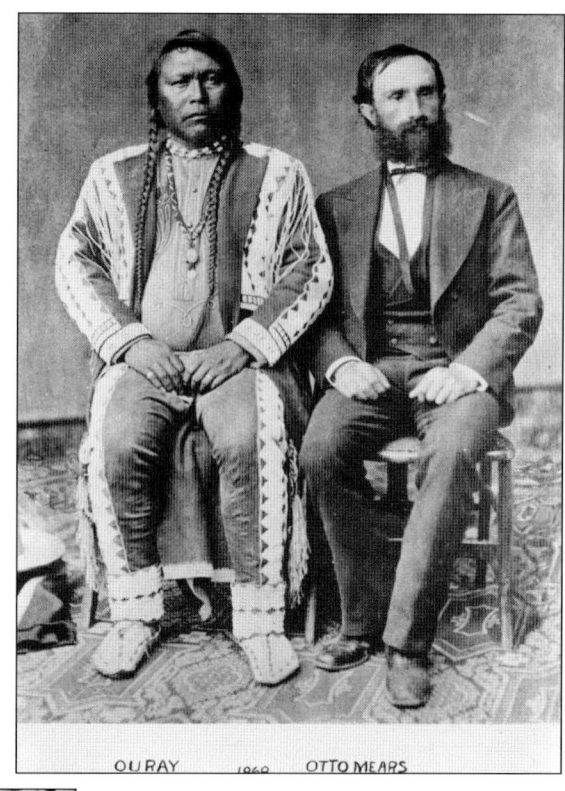

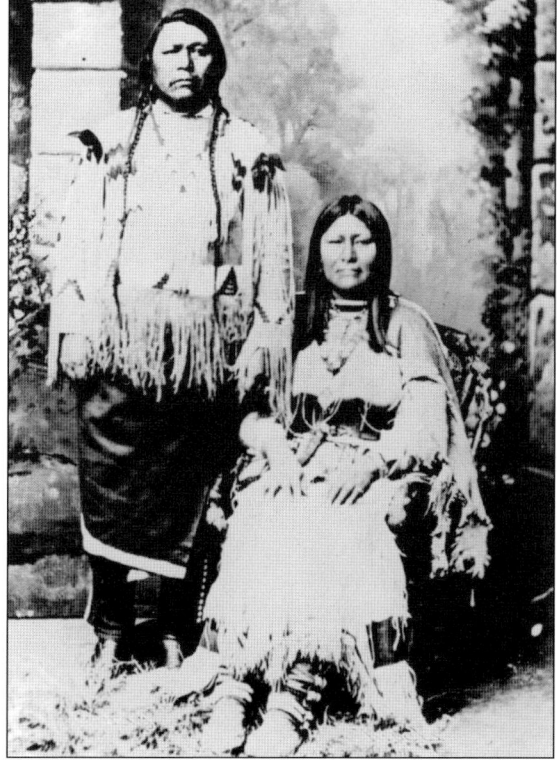

Ouray, chief of the Tabeguache/Uncompahgre, is perhaps the most famous of the Ute chiefs. At 3,000 members, his was the largest of all 10 Ute bands, and for this reason, the federal government unilaterally decided to name him the chief of all the Utes. Chipeta, Ouray's shy and gracious wife, sits quietly beside him. (Courtesy DPL.)

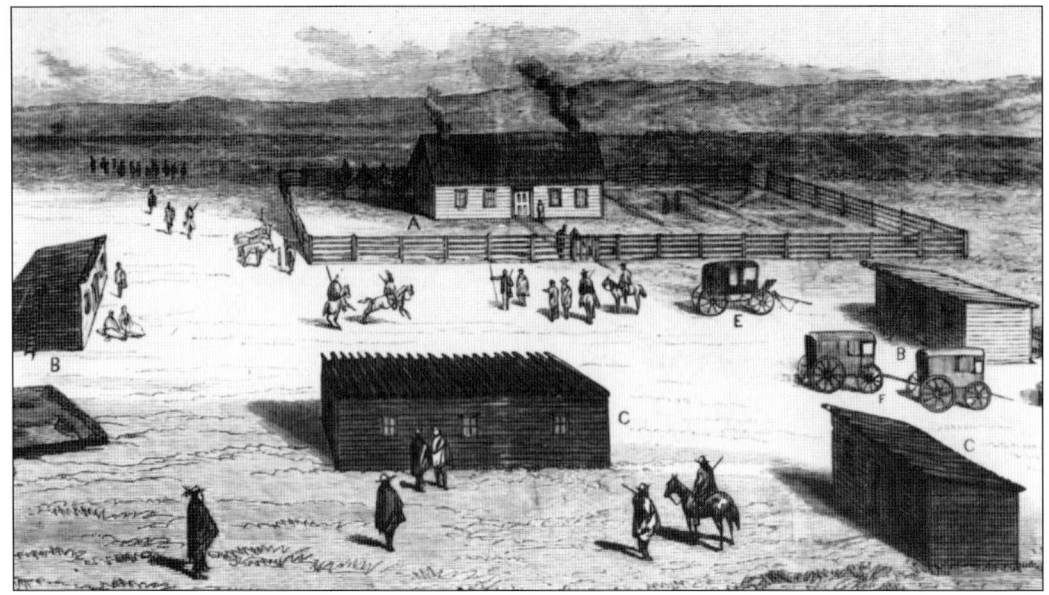

Ouray did his best to adapt to the white man's world. Sen. Nathaniel Hill of Colorado reported, "Ouray lives in a house on a farm [near Montrose] with eighty acres under cultivation. He has as good an eye for farming land as any man I know." This drawing also shows Ouray's carriage as figure E. (Courtesy DPL.)

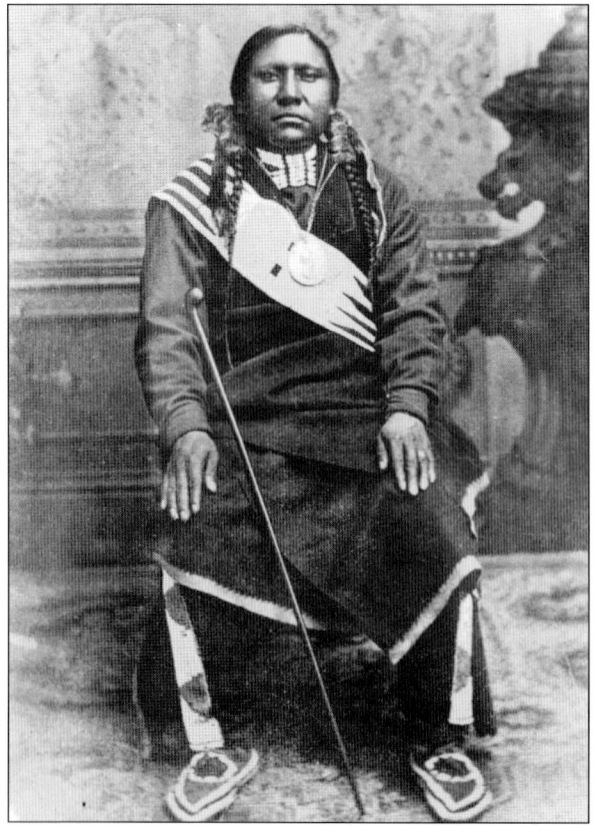

Around 1865, a young Ouray proudly wears what is likely an Abraham Lincoln Peace Medal. These medals were often given as rewards for good deeds or good behavior, and sometimes to acknowledge an Indian's service in advancing government programs. (Courtesy DPL.)

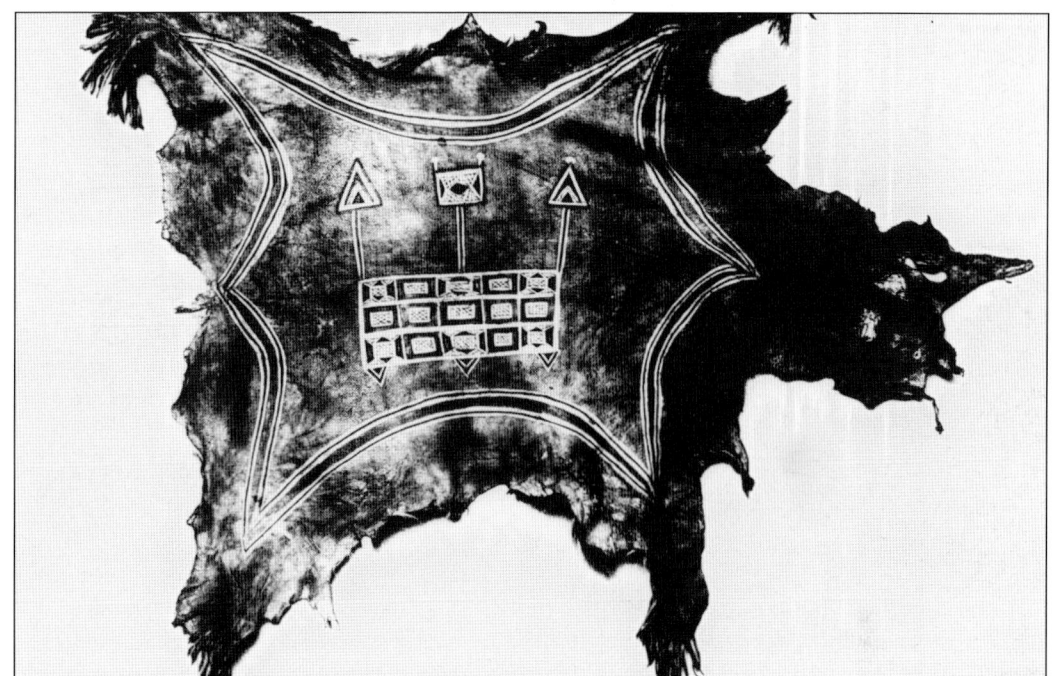

Each rectangle on this painted buffalo robe is a record of a battle fought by Northern Ute chief Colorow. In 1868, as William Buyers (editor of the *Rocky Mountain News*) attempted to lay claim to Hot Sulphur Springs in the middle of Ute territory, Colorow confronted him, warning that Buyers must leave in "three sleeps." (Courtesy DPL.)

Often in warfare, women and children were captured from the enemy. In Ute culture, this was not an act of slavery but of inter-culturation. Just as in nature, new blood was introduced among the people. We see evidence of this cultural mingling among the famous Ute chiefs. Ouray himself was half Apache, and Chief Colorow was Comanche. (Courtesy Ute Pass Historical Society.)

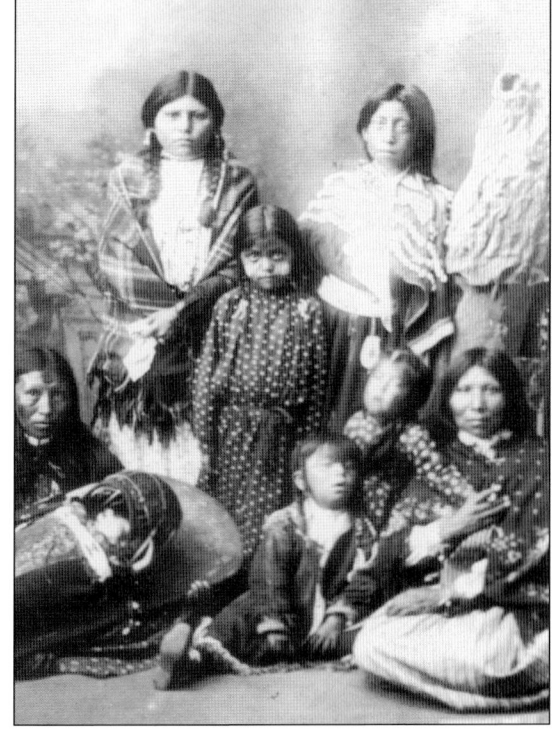

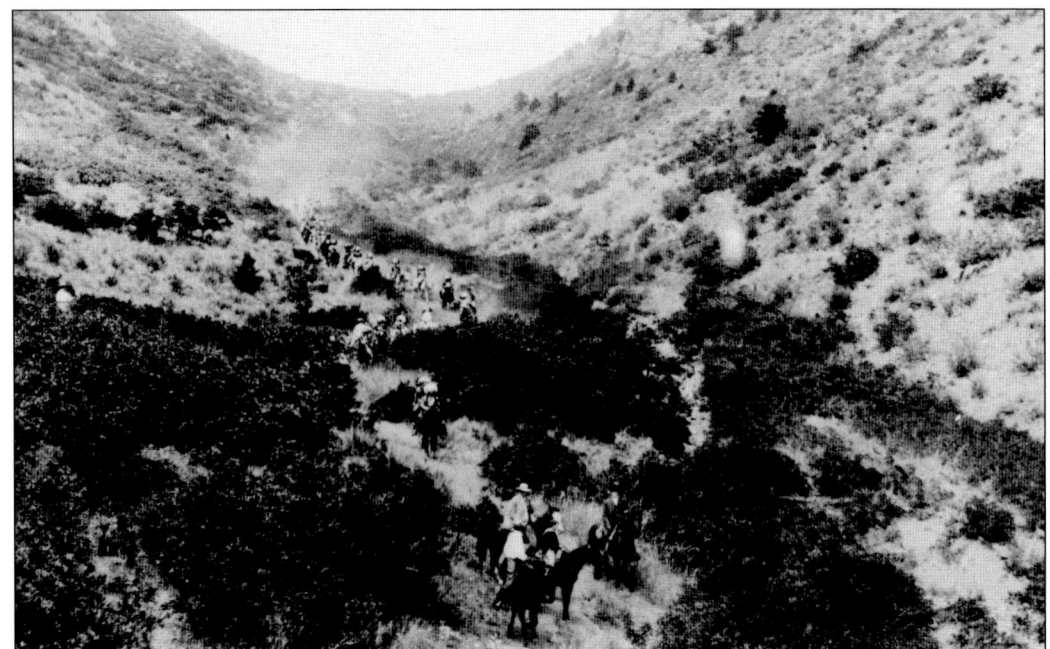

Early pioneer Irving Howbert leads his Ute guests down the trail of their ancestors in 1912. According to Howbert, in the winter of 1866–1867, "a thousand or more Utes camped for several months below Manitou, between the Balanced Rock and the Fountain. . . . Chaveno [Shavano] and Colorow were the principal chiefs of this band." (Courtesy Ute Pass Historical Society.)

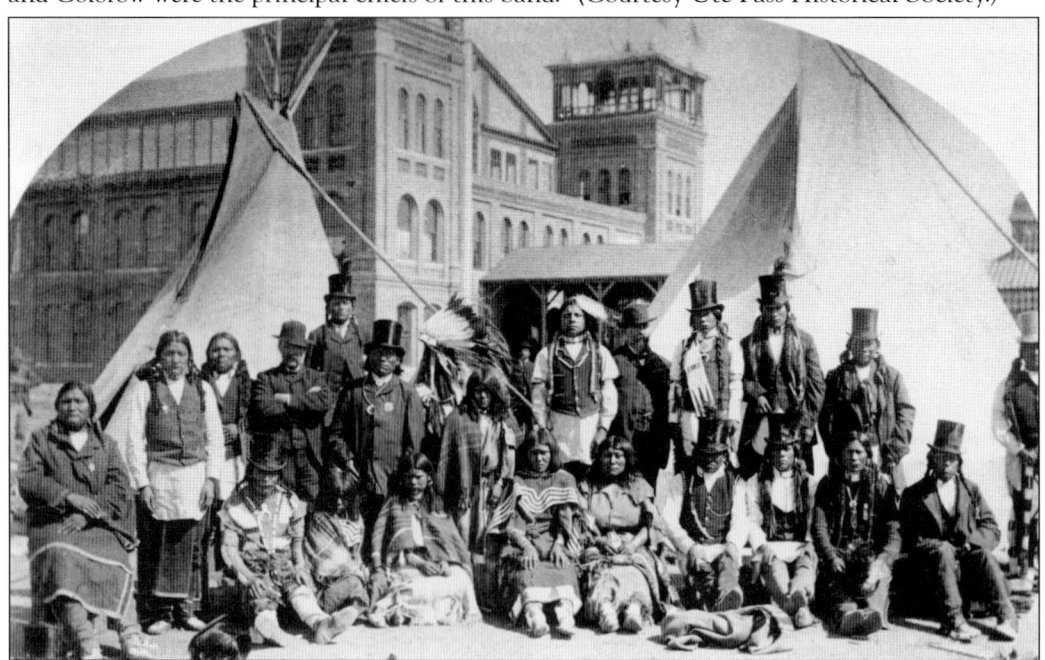

Tabeguache chief Piah (second row, sixth from left) and his band were frequent visitors to Denver. They were called the Denver Utes because of their preference for receiving rations in Colorado's capital after a Ute agency was established there in 1871. In 1875, the Denver Agency was closed after Piah held a traditional Ute scalp dance. (Courtesy DPL.)

Chipeta's brother *Piah* (Black-tail Deer) was the darling of Denver society and a frequent guest at Gov. Edward McCook's mansion. When the Utes were forced to assume Christian names, Piah honored his old friend by adopting the name John McCook. (Courtesy DPL.)

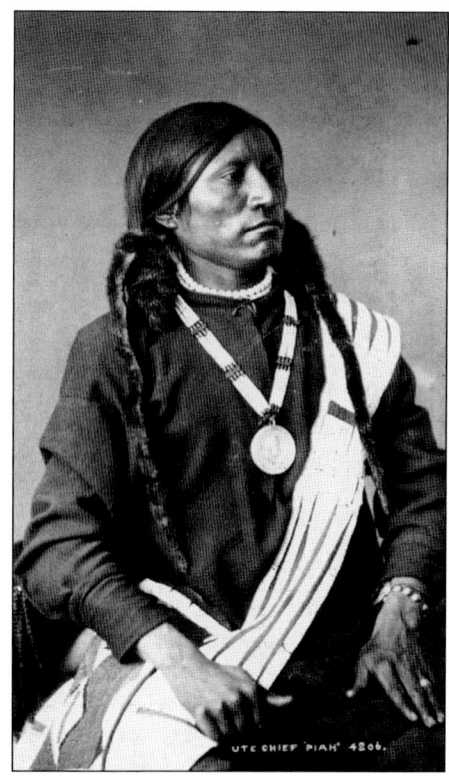

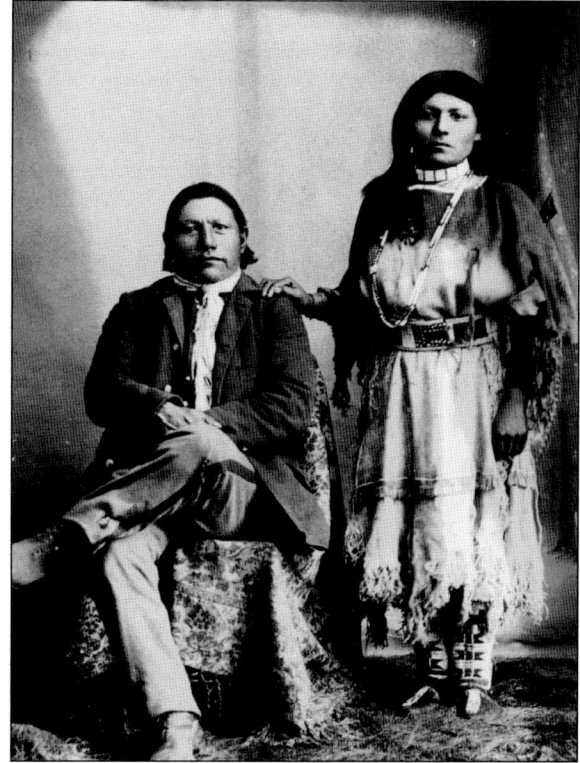

Ignacio's Weeminuche band was originally settled at the Navajo Springs Subagency in 1896. The band later moved to Towaoc in 1917 and was given its own Ute Mountain Reservation. The town of Ignacio, Colorado, was named for this chief. (Courtesy DPL.)

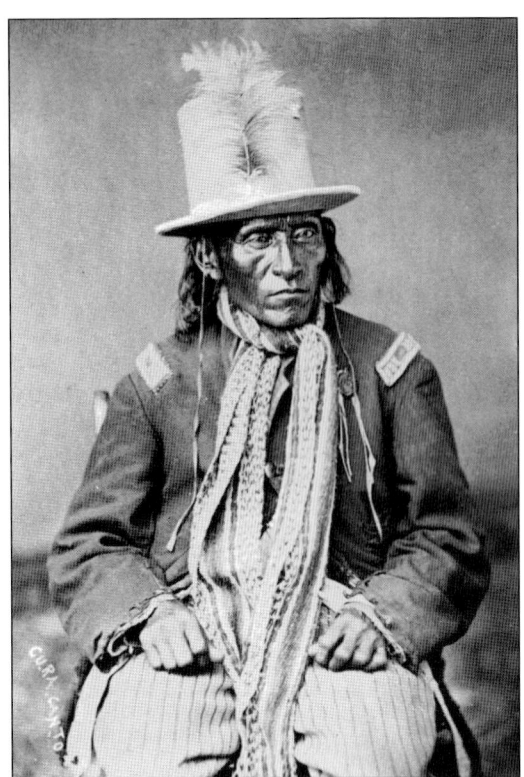

Moache chief Curecanto was the twin brother of another famous Ute chief, Kaniache. When Kaniache's son-in-law was killed near Cimarron in 1866, the chief offered himself as hostage to the Americans to prevent further hostilities. Several months later, a Santa Fe judge awarded $400 to the dead man's family, satisfying demands for revenge. (Courtesy DPL.)

Chief Severo's son Capitancito shows the same warrior spirit as his famous father. This photograph was probably taken in 1894, when Severo took part in a staged battle at the Broadmoor Casino in Colorado Springs. (Courtesy DPL.)

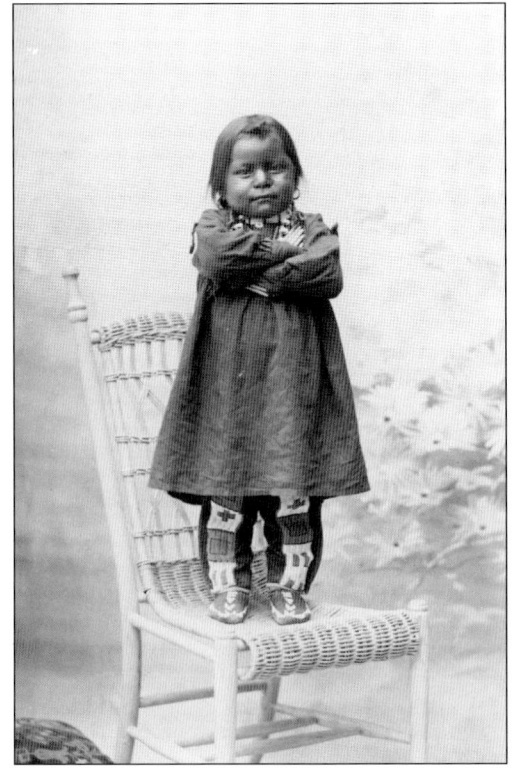

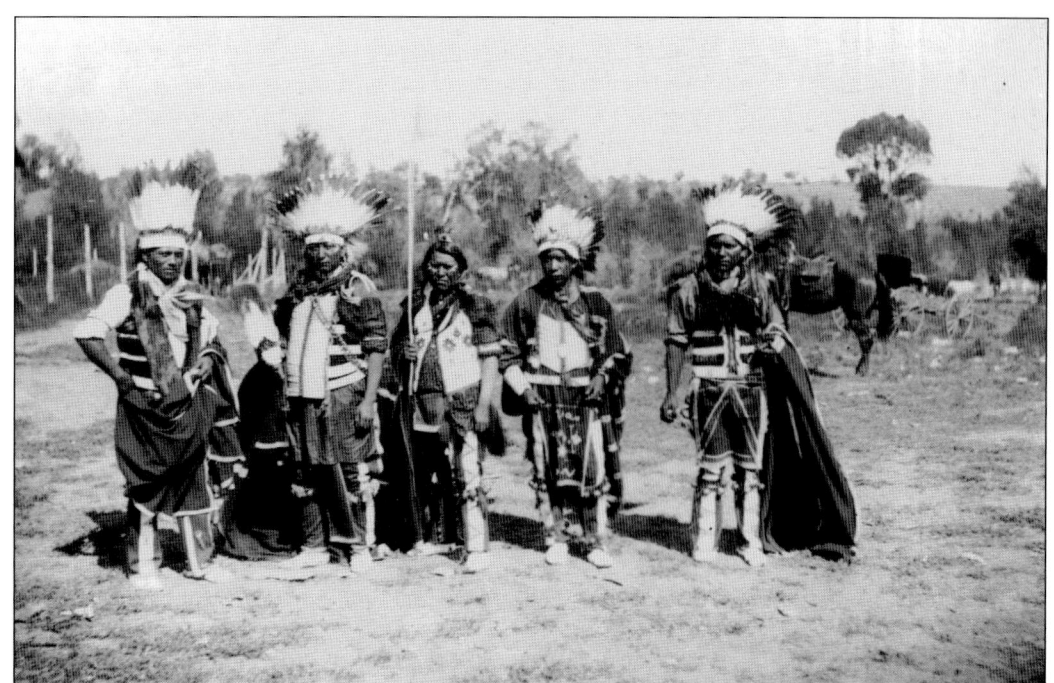

Seen from left to right are Southern Ute leaders Isaac Cloud, Edward Cloud, Antonio Buck Sr., and two unidentified warriors. Antonio Buck Sr., a Capote, became the last traditional chief of the Southern Utes. When he died in 1961, the nation was without a chief. (Courtesy DPL.)

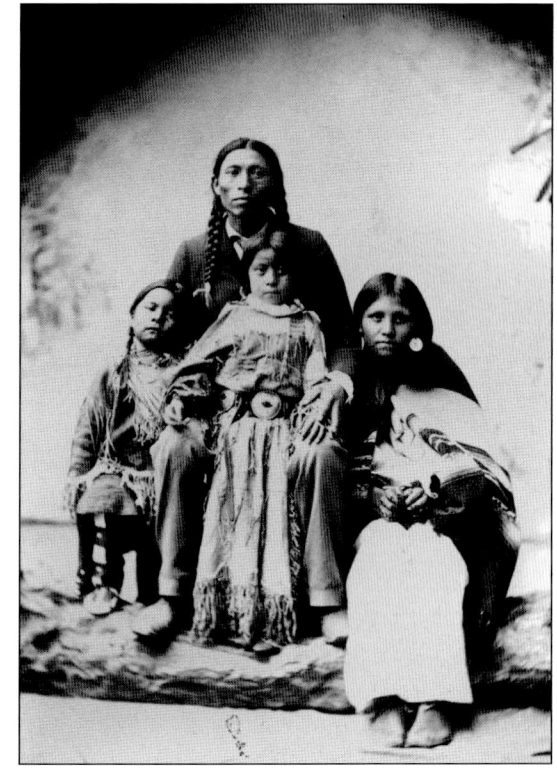

Charles Stobie wrote, "One evening Julian Buck—Pah-quan, Grog—son of Chief 'Buckskin Charlie,' rode into our camps on the San Juan River. He had for years been a pupil at Indian Schools, had become a member of the Presbyterian church and had an ambition to preach." Buck is pictured here. (Courtesy DPL.)

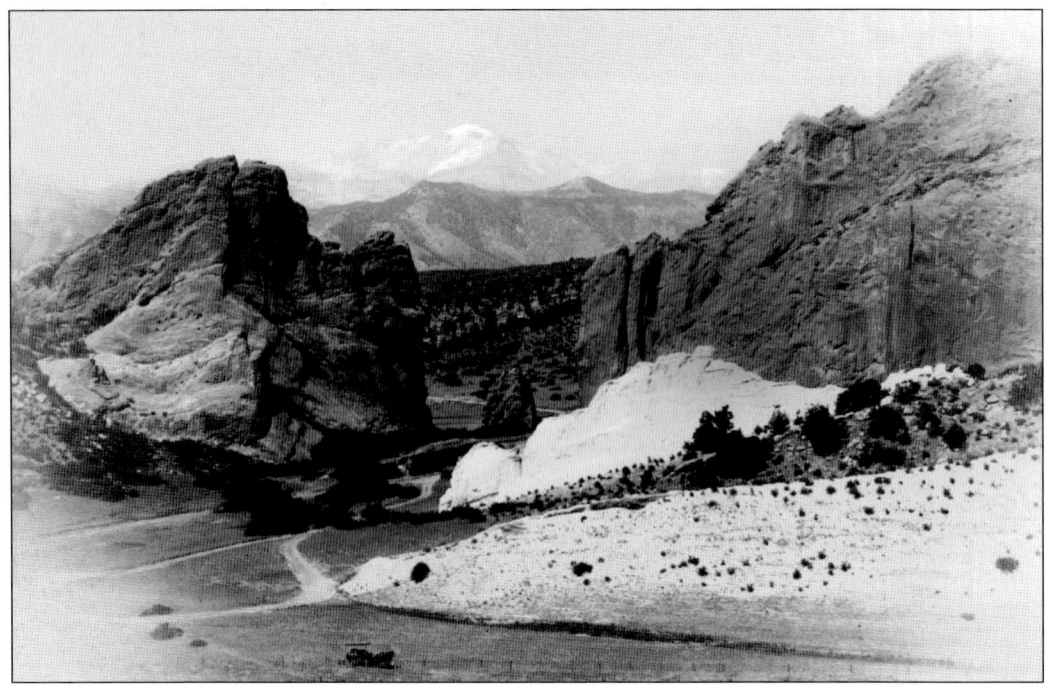
Rising majestically above the front range of Colorado's Rocky Mountains is *Tava*, the Ute name for Pikes Peak, which means "sun." The ancestral Utes who frequented the Pikes Peak region called themselves the *Tabeguache* (Tab-ee-watch), meaning "People of Sun Mountain." (Courtesy DPL.)

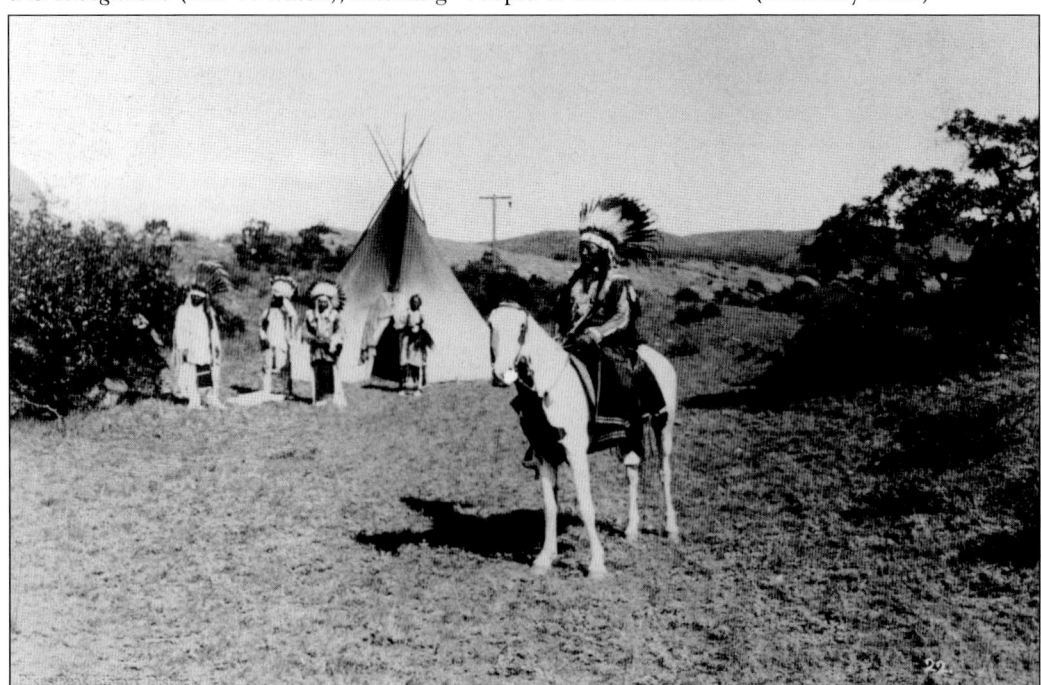
This group is part of the Tabeguache band that was forced onto the Uncompahgre Plateau by the treaty of 1864. They now called themselves Uncompahgre, because the Ute people always greeted one another by asking, "What land do you belong to?" (Courtesy Pikes Peak Library District.)

An aging Chipeta is shown here in 1902. After Ouray's death in 1880, Chipeta married Accumooquats, an Uncompahgre. Her people had been relocated to Utah, where their agent noted that they "constantly talk of their old home in the direction of the rising sun." (Courtesy DPL.)

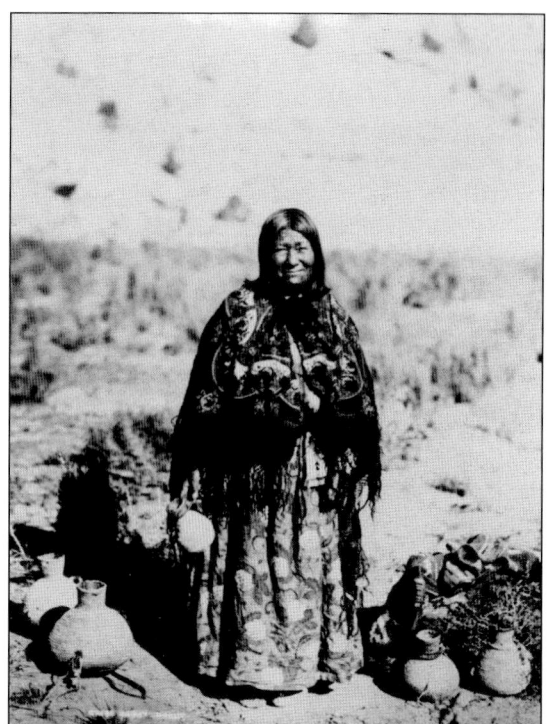

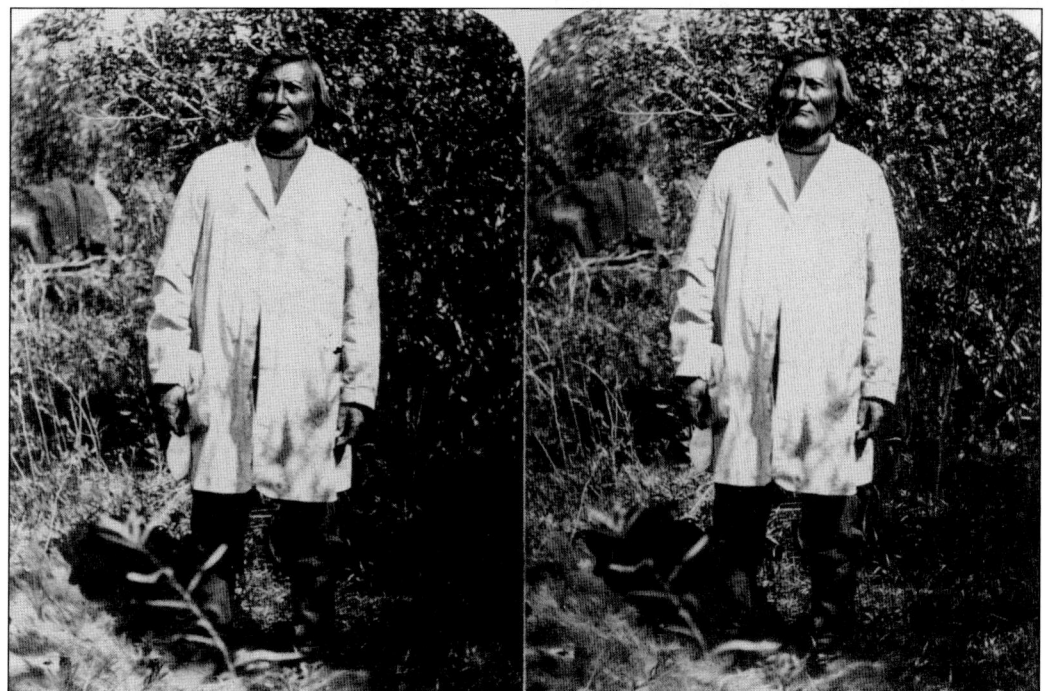

Tavaputs, "Shield," was photographed by J. K. Hiller during John Wesley Powell's 1868 sojourn in Colorado. He appears to have been given a white man's coat and pants by his guests. Tavaputs was undoubtedly of the Tabuats (Tabeguache) band under Douglas and Antero, who were also wintering at White River near Powell's camp. (Courtesy DPL.)

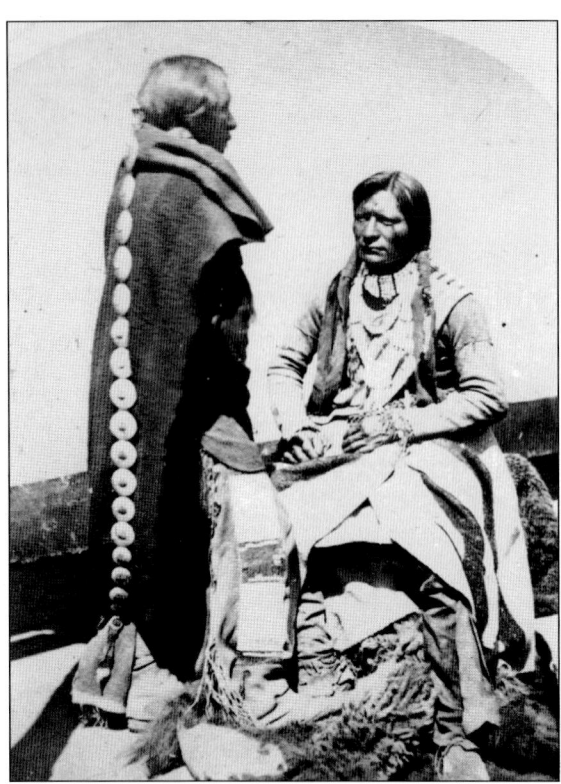

Capote warriors are pictured at Abiquiu in 1874. Their band name was borrowed from the Spanish *capote*, meaning "cloak." The blanket cloak ornamented with Spanish silver conchos (worn by man on left) bears testimony to the source of the Capote name. The band's traditional territory included the area northwest of Taos and in southwestern Colorado. (Courtesy Museum of New Mexico.)

Chief Ignacio, shown here with his family, refused to allow the federal government to divide ownership of ancestral lands among his people. He insisted on retaining collective ownership and tribal identity. As stated earlier, he was instrumental in establishing the Ute Mountain Reservation. (Courtesy Pikes Peak Library District.)

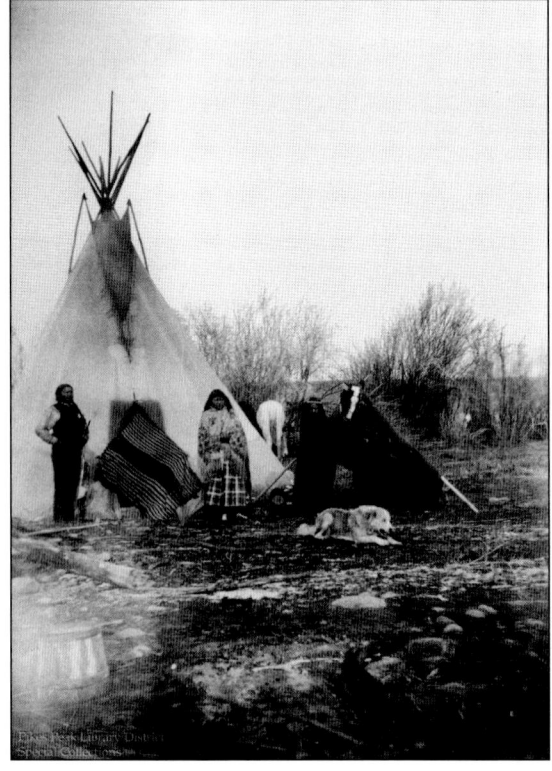

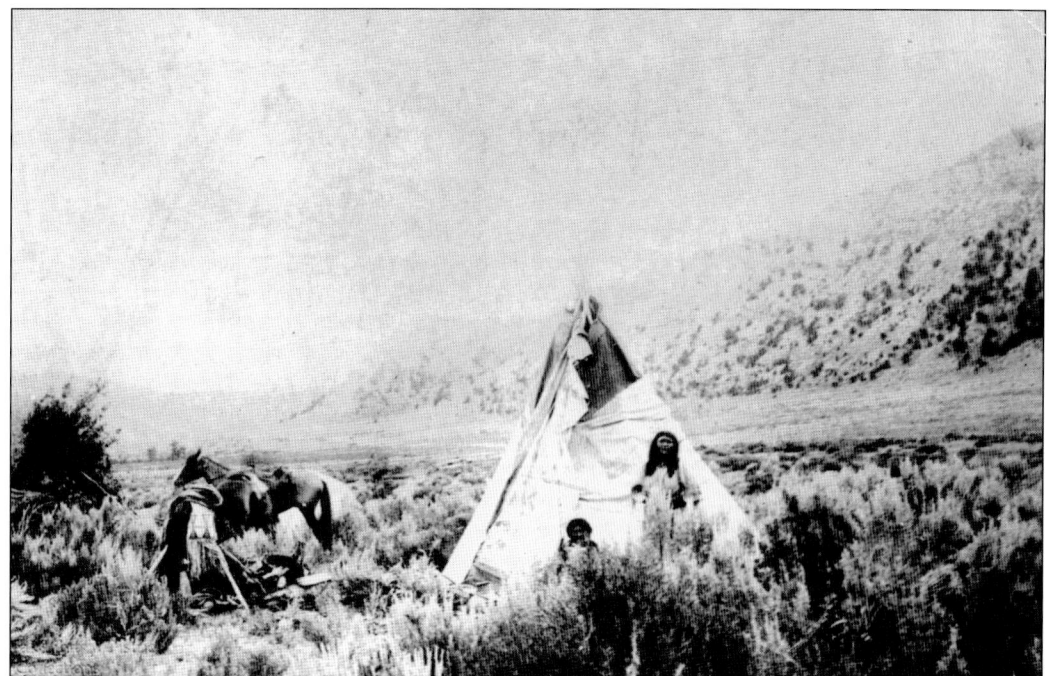

This Ute family, photographed on Powell's 1874 expedition, is probably on its way to visit relatives in one of the southern bands. Today the northern and southern bands come together each year in September for a powwow at Delta, Colorado. (Courtesy Pikes Peak Library District.)

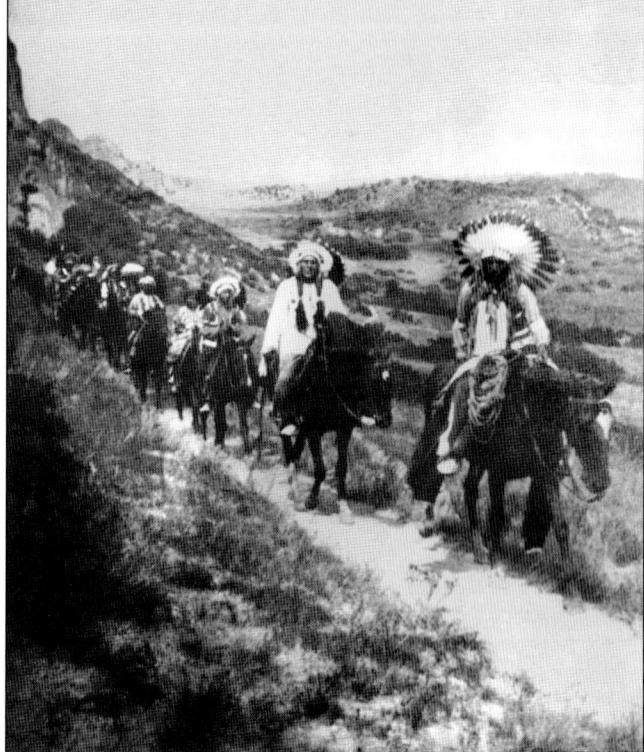

Southern Ute leaders Edward Cloud (far right) and George Norris (second from right) lead their warriors into Garden of the Gods. Beginning in 1911, General Palmer's Denver and Rio Grande train made a special run to Ignacio, returning with Southern Utes for the Shan Kive celebration. Unfortunately, the Denver and Rio Grande did not run to the Unitah/Ouray Reservation in Utah; if it had, the Tabeguache Utes would have been able to return to their ancestral lands. (Courtesy DPL.)

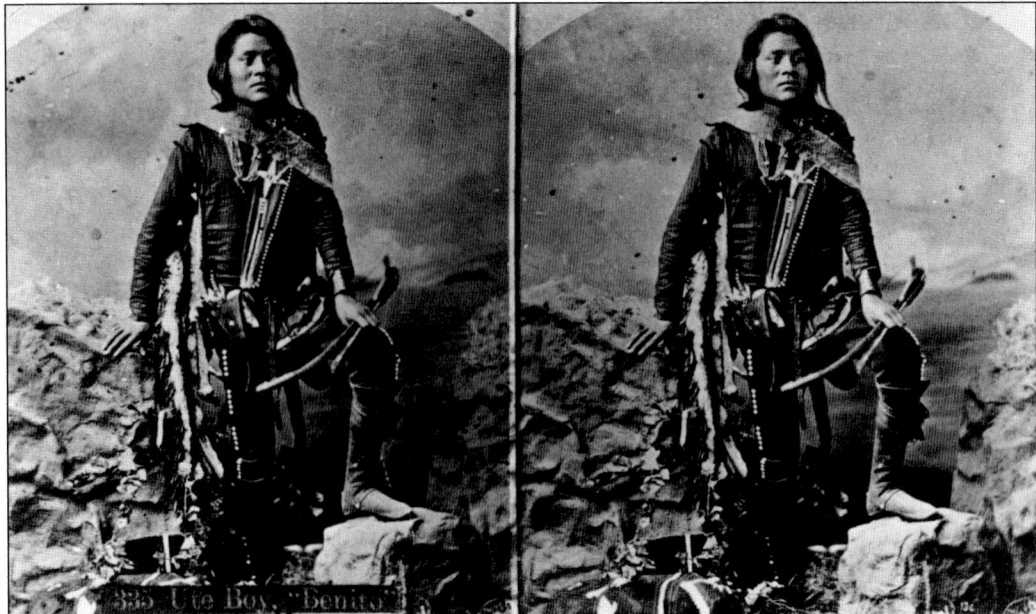

The teenage Benito epitomizes the fierce warrior spirit of the Utes, whose war cry was the deep, guttural "Waugh!" of the grizzly bear. Plains Indians constantly challenged the Utes for possession of their mountain strongholds. In 1860, for example, C. H. Alden wrote that 400 Cheyennes, 500 Comanches and Kiowas, and 112 Arapahos gathered near Fort Garland to launch a joint attack against the Ute Nation. (Courtesy DPL.)

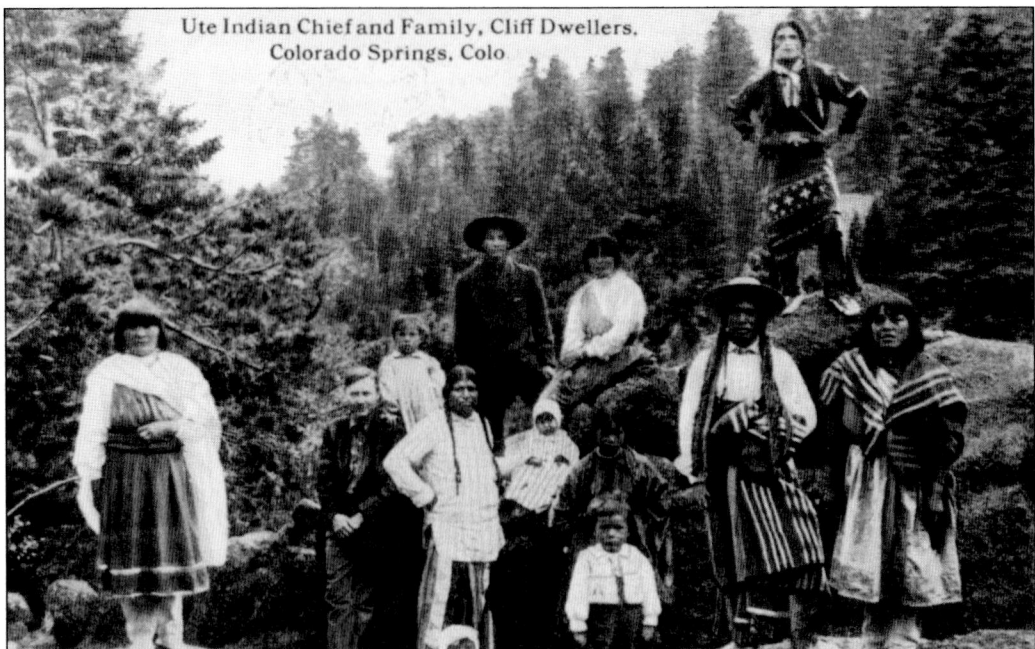

In this 1915 photograph at the cliff dwellings, Plains and Pueblo Indians have been hired to present their culture to tourists. This mixture of nations is a legacy of the sacred springs at Manitou and the sacred grounds at Red Rocks and Garden of the Gods, where enemies paid homage to the spirits and warfare was forbidden. (Courtesy Ute Pass Historical Society.)

These two unidentified warriors embody the spirit of the Ute people. In 1862, agent William F. M. Arny reported that 400 Plains Indians attacked a band of 12 Utes. Nine of these warriors were killed or wounded, and the remaining three continued to fight until the invaders grew tired and retreated. Arny wrote that such "bravery is scarcely to be found either in civilized or in savage history." (Courtesy DPL.)

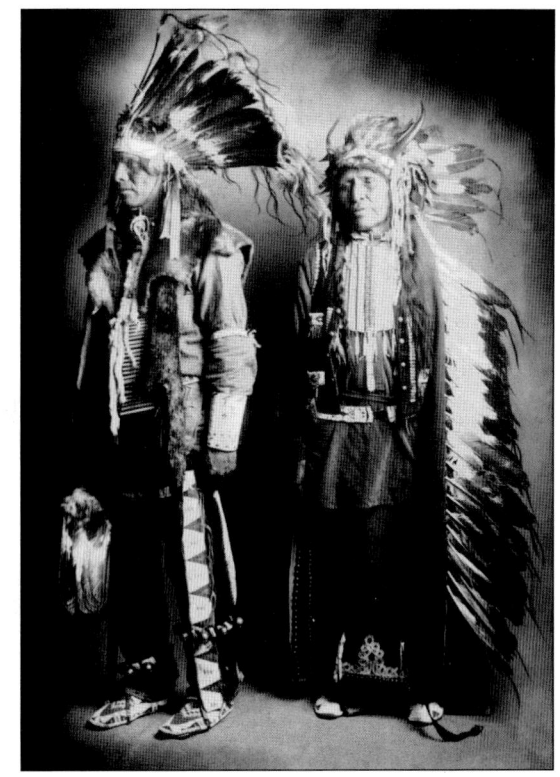

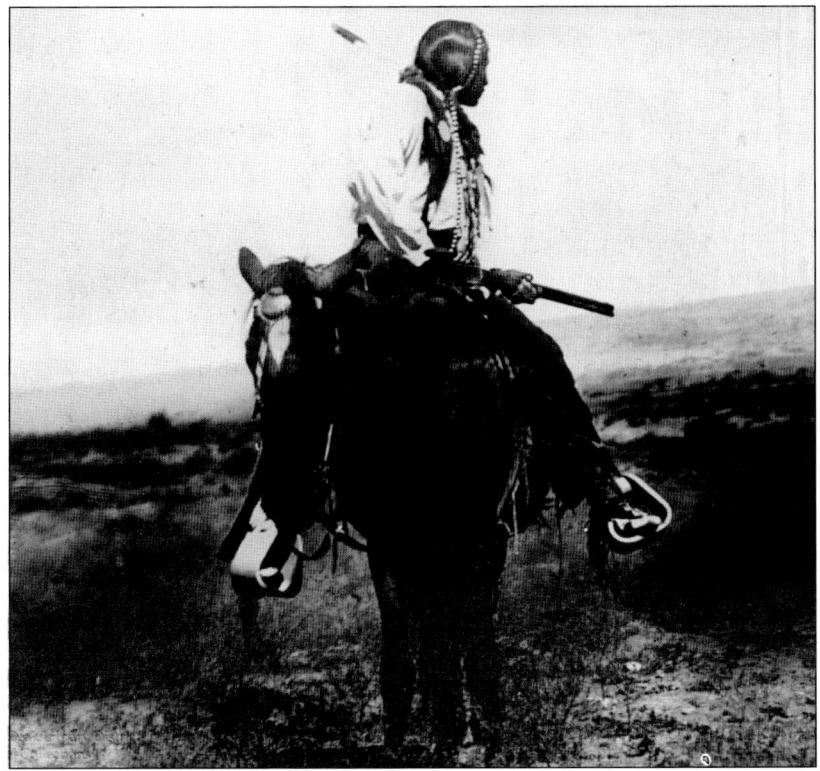

Ute scouts, such as this warrior, were vital to Juan Bautista de Anza's success against the Comanches. He sent these spies ahead of his main army because they knew their homeland so well. His 1779 Comanche campaign succeeded where others had failed, because he was able to approach the enemy, unseen, through Ute Pass. (Courtesy Pikes Peak Library District, Poley.)

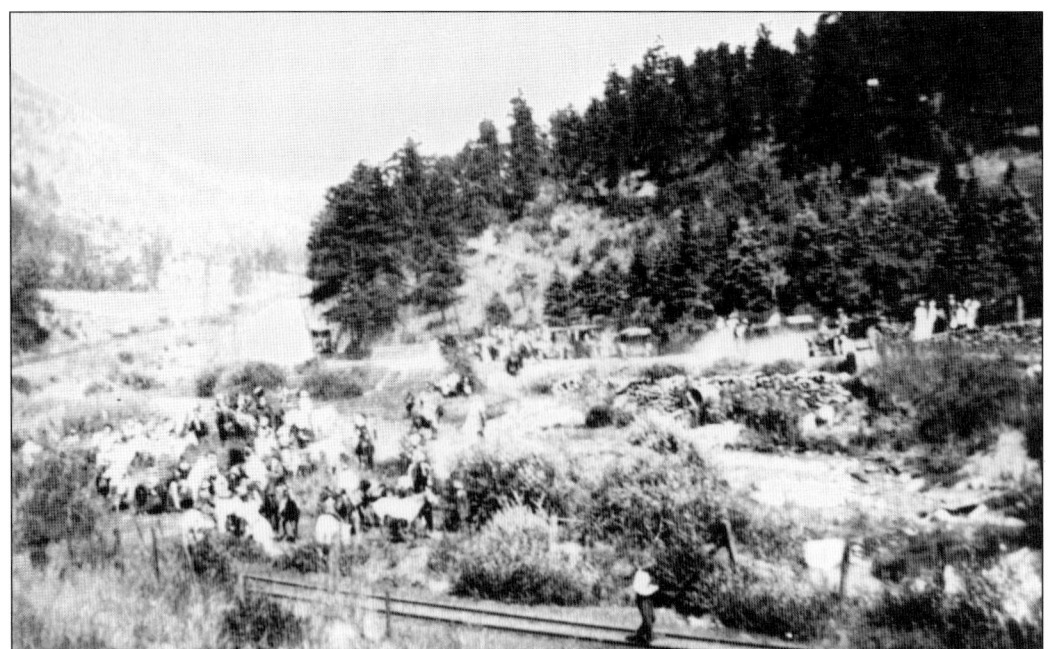

This melee of Ute horsemen at Cascade evokes the image of Anza's army of 800 men (including 200 Utes and Apaches) and 2,400 horses. They camped near this same site on August 30, 1779, before their crippling attack on the Comanche village the next afternoon. (Courtesy Ute Pass Historical Society.)

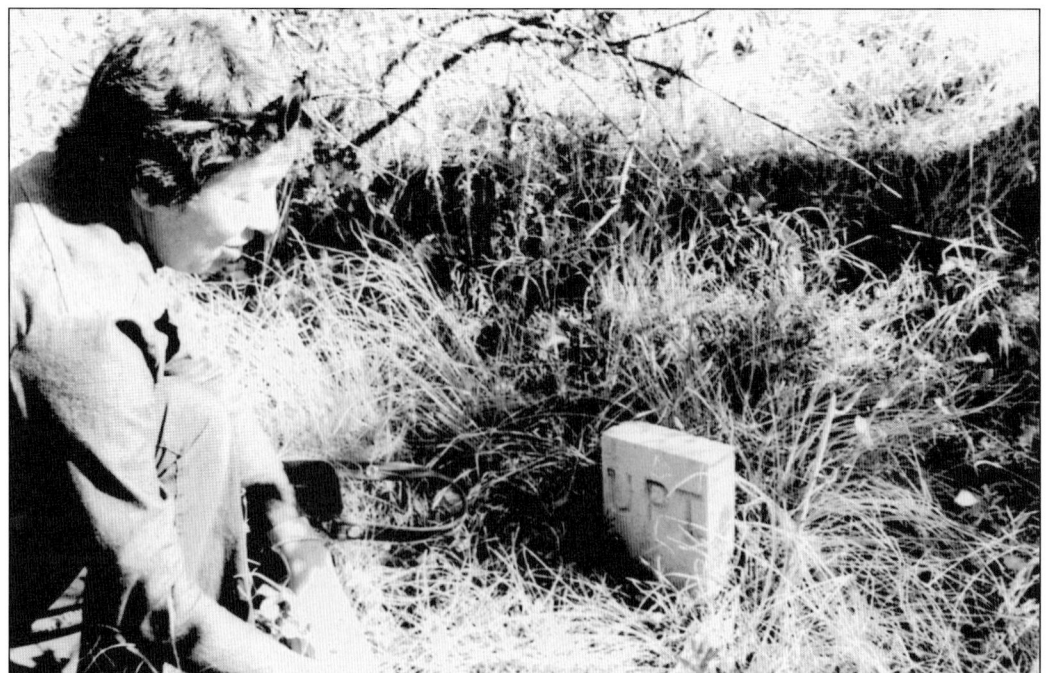

Only a few of these trail markers still remain along the Ute Pass Trail from Cascade to Manitou Springs. This is likely the same route taken by Anza and his army in 1779. (Courtesy Ute Pass Historical Society.)

Ute warriors Moon Face (left) and Eagle Eye stand on a mesa near Garden of the Gods at the approximate location where six of their ancestors were captured by Irving Howbert and his companions in 1864. Unfortunately, there were no translators present, and when the mounted Utes made a break for it, their panicked captors fired, killing them all. (Courtesy Ute Pass Historical Society.)

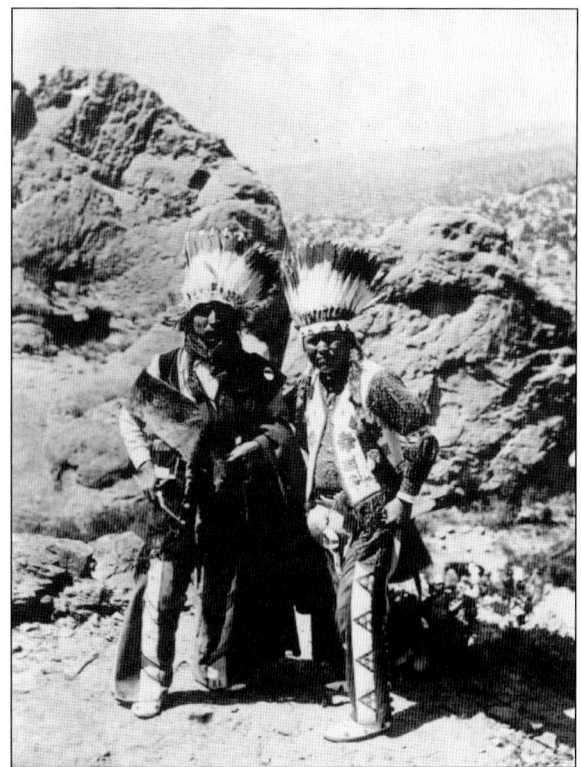

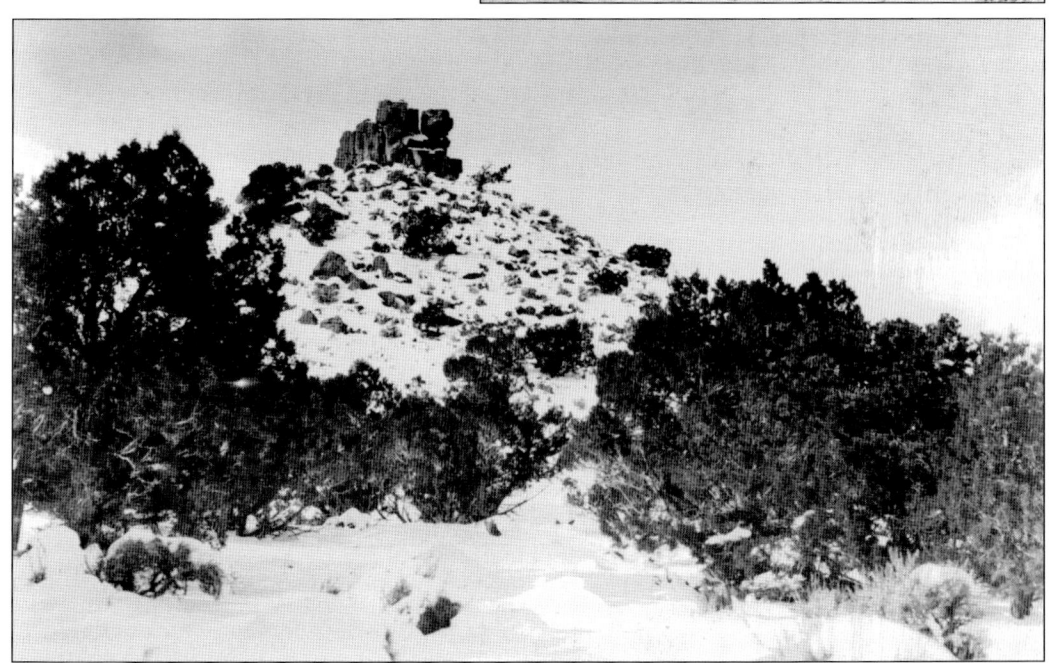

Historians write that the Ute Indians are one of the few tribes known to have constructed stone fortifications, or forts, such as this one near Montrose. These were usually built on a promontory commanding the junction of several trails. In addition to strategic defense, they may also have been used for ceremony. (Courtesy DPL.)

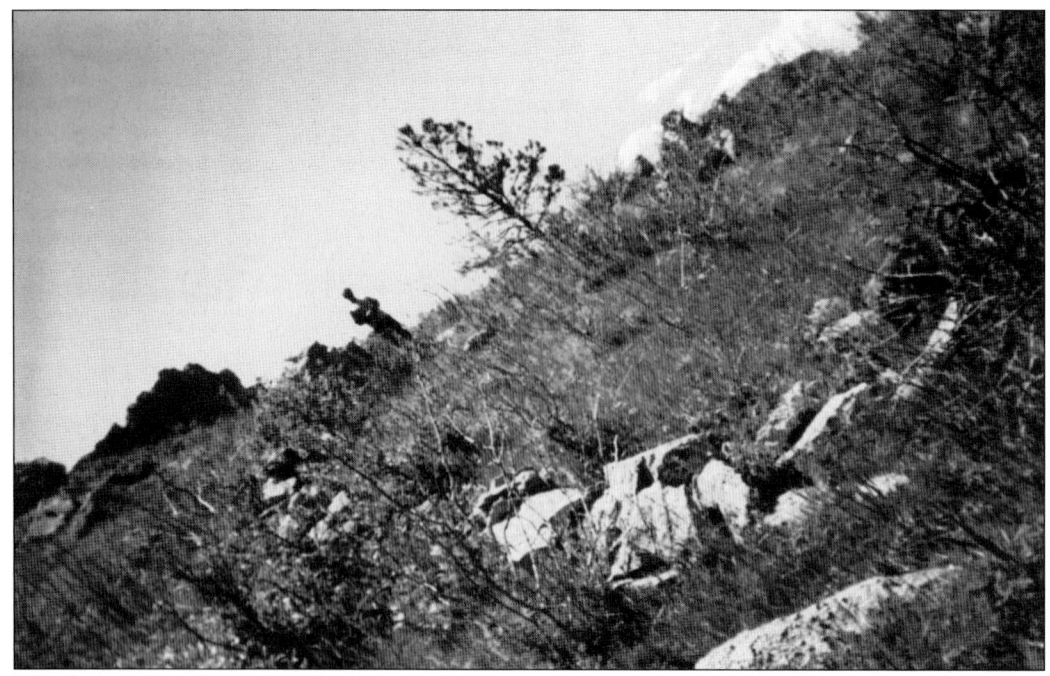

This low rock wall at a Ute fort near Colorado Springs is typical of this kind of structure. These fortifications include stone circles, or rifle pits, large enough for two or three warriors. Always on a high promontory with water close by, they provide a defensive position overlooking well-traveled trails.

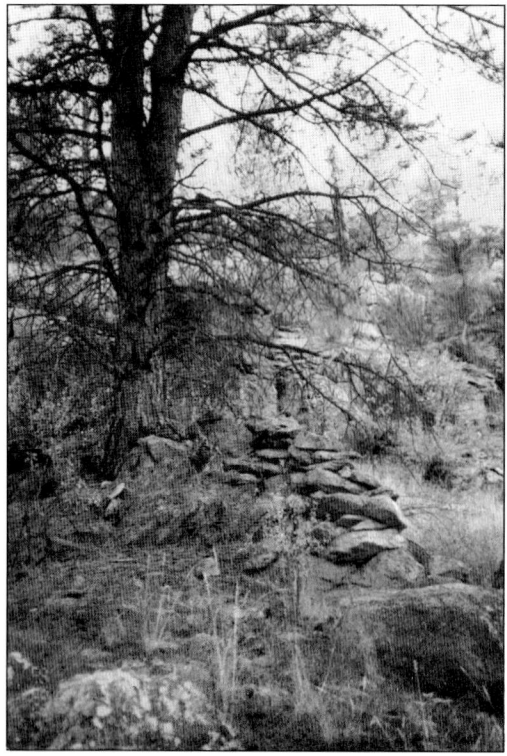

A signature rock wall indicates a Ute fort on the west slope of Pikes Peak. Ute scouts were stationed at these fortifications to watch for incursions by Plains Indians. When they spotted intruders, they used smoke signals to summon their main body of warriors.

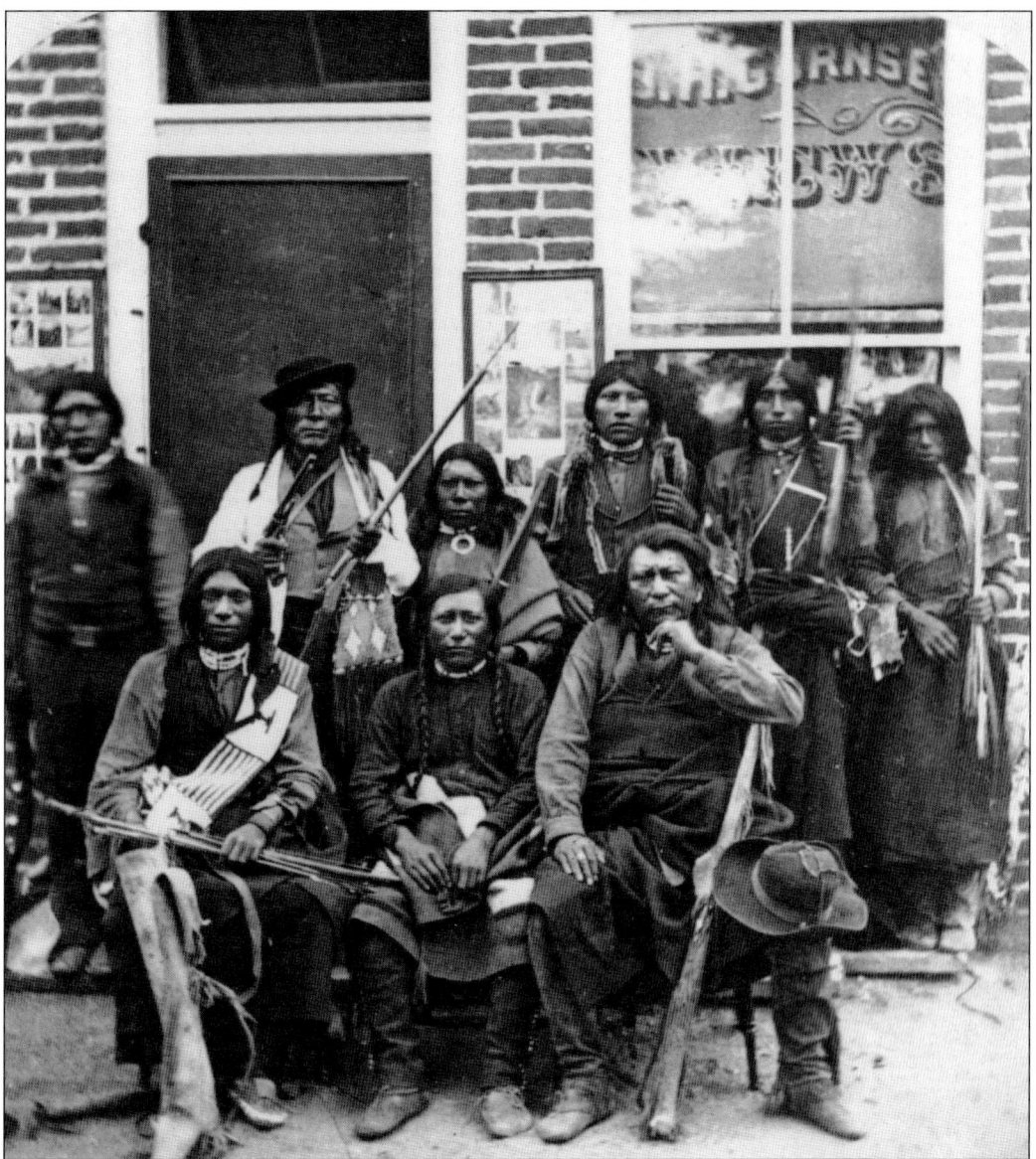

Wanzits, Chief Antelope (first row, center), is shown here with Chief Colorow (first row, far right) and his band in Old Colorado City. This group of warriors played a key role in the Meeker Incident of 1879, when the U.S. cavalry invaded the White River Ute Reservation. After warning the troops four times not to enter their sovereign lands, warriors attacked them near the Milk River. Approximately 50 Utes pinned down Major Thornburgh and four companies of cavalry for six days while other warriors at the agency killed Meeker and nine of his men. (Wanzits is generally credited with killing Meeker.) This "Meeker Massacre" resulted in the loss of ancestral Ute lands, and the Tabeguache band was forcibly relocated to the Unitah/Ouray Reservation in Utah. (Courtesy Colorado Historical Society.)

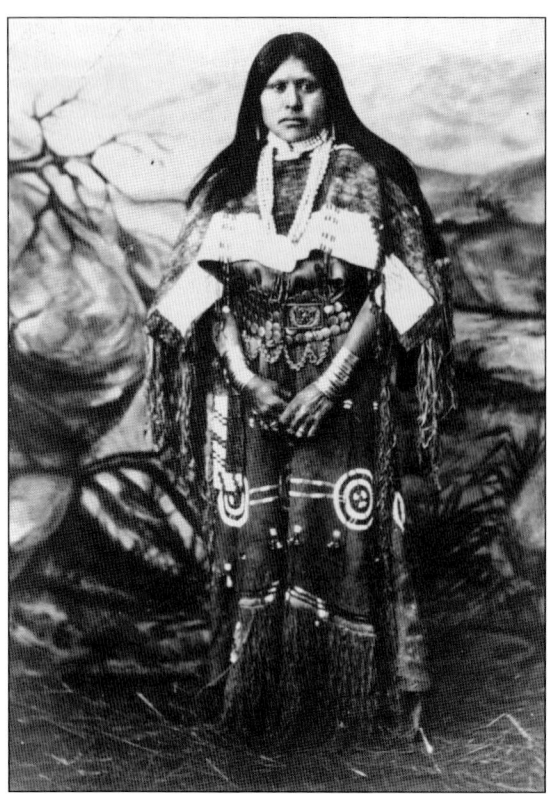

Tsashin (Susan), Ouray's sister, is actually the woman in this photograph. She played a key role when the Meeker women were abducted following the battle at Milk Creek. Flora Price told officials that Tsashin treated her "just like a mother" and made moccasins for her little girl. Later Tsashin boldly interrupted the council with Gen. Charles Adams, insisting that the women captives be released unharmed. (Courtesy DPL.)

Ute chiefs used criers such as this mounted warrior to keep their bands informed of crucial events. On October 2, 1879, Ouray used his brother-in-law Sapavanero in this capacity. "You are hereby commanded to cease hostilities against the whites." With these words, Ouray prevented a full-scale Ute war. (Courtesy DPL.)

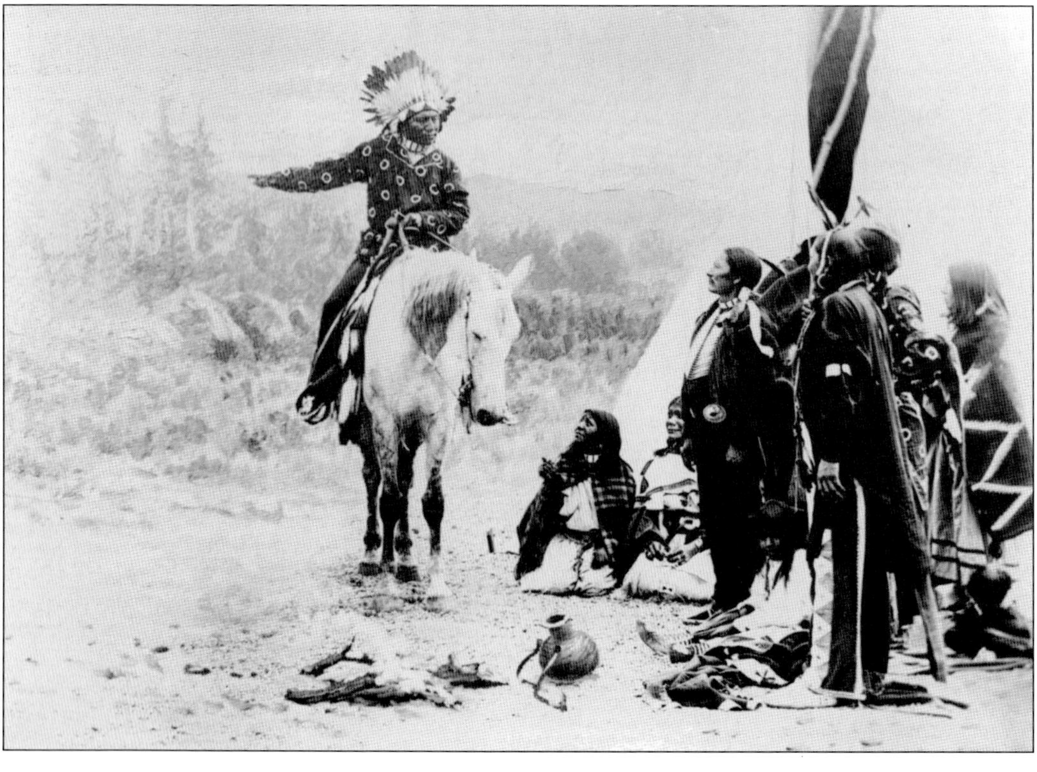

Before the Utes acquired horses from the Spanish, they harnessed dogs to their travois. This connection to dogs also had a deeper significance, as it was thought that the Creator often manifested in physical form as Wolf, *Sunawiv*. (Courtesy DPL.)

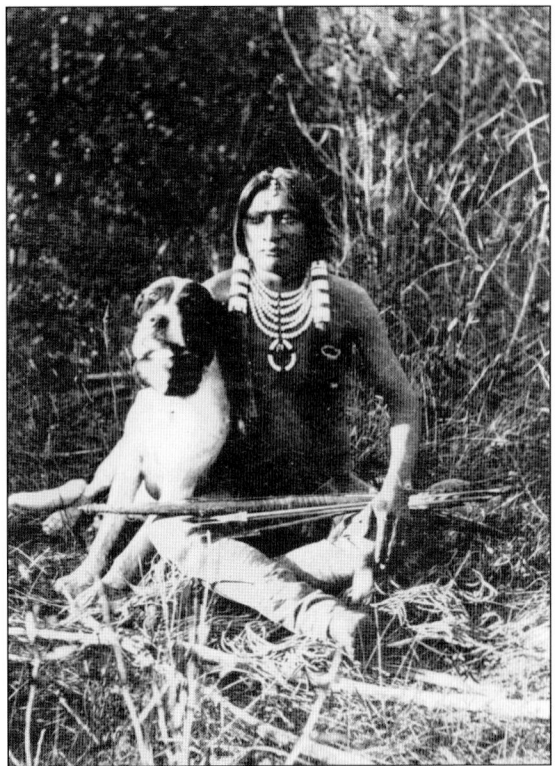

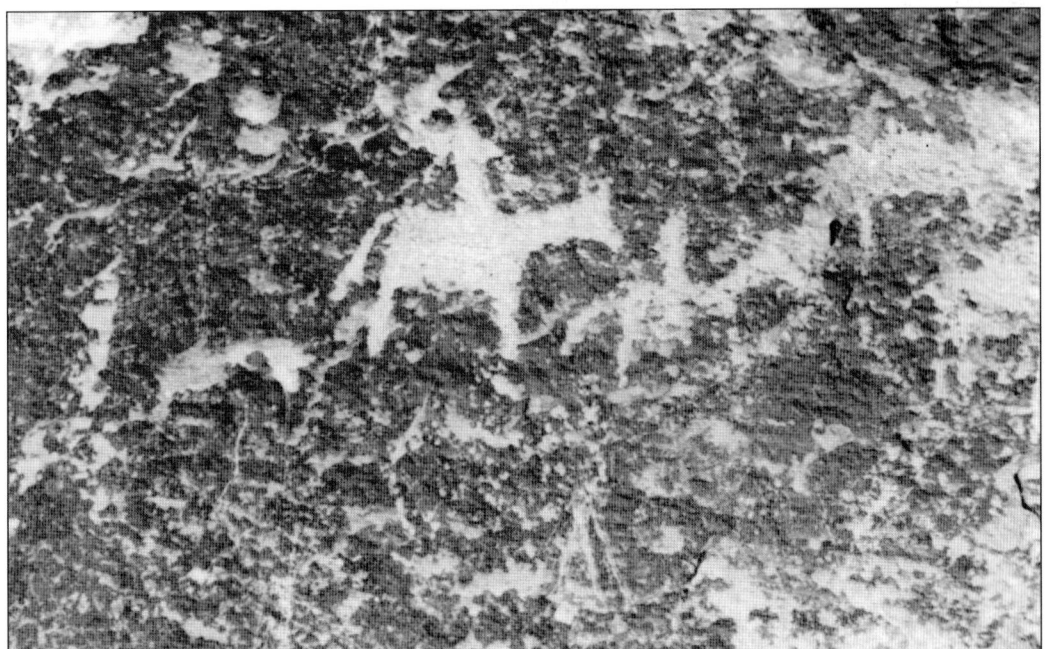

This ancient Ute petroglyph near Olathe, Colorado, provides a written record of the nation's early acquisition of the horse. In a 1637 document, Gov. Luis de Rosas of Santa Fe reported a mounted battle between his troops and a band of Utes. This is the first documentation we have of American Indians having acquired horses from the Spanish. (Courtesy Ute Pass Historical Society.)

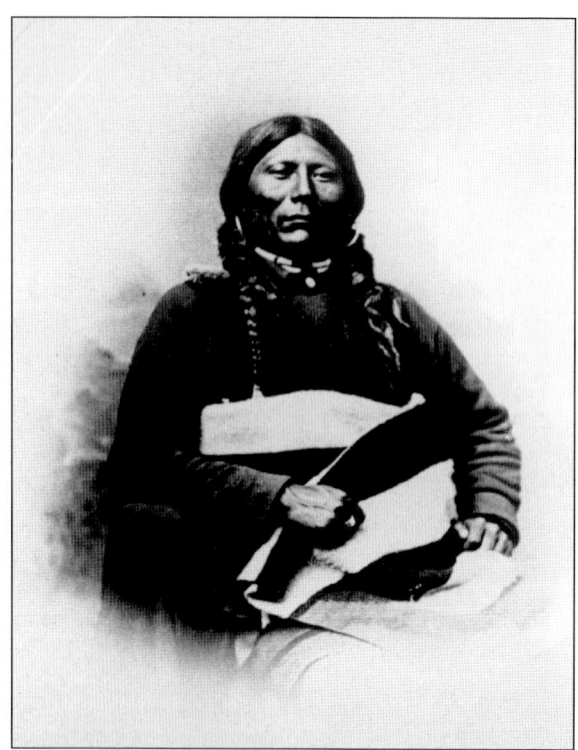

Antelope, or *Wanzits*, seemed to attract notoriety. In an altercation near Florissant in 1875, a miner who had stolen his horse was killed. Indian agents reported that this frequently happened, as gold seekers arriving by wagon with their supplies soon needed a mount. The thousands of Ute horses near the mining camps proved tempting for these foot-sore miners. (Courtesy DPL.)

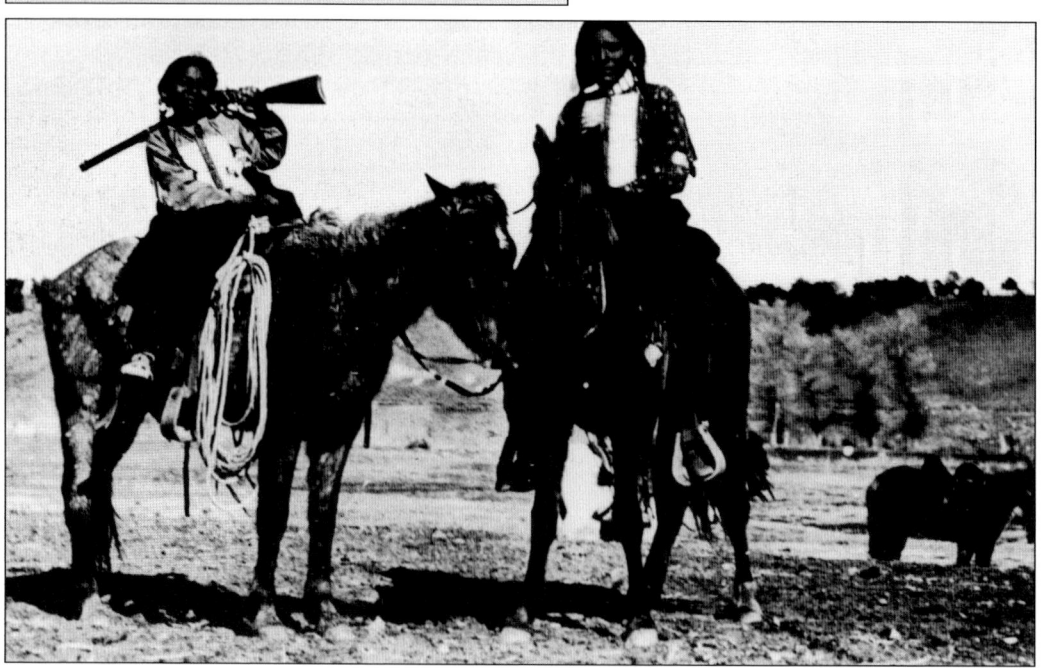

Ute warriors rode as soon as they walked. Richard Townshend wrote, "I beheld . . . warriors riding towards us at a gallop. . . . Then as if by magic [Shavano] sent [them] flying this way and that, forwards and backwards, weaving a maze of figures like a dance, and every man of the eight hundred as he raced along seemed to be a part of his pony." (Courtesy Pikes Peak Library District, Poley.)

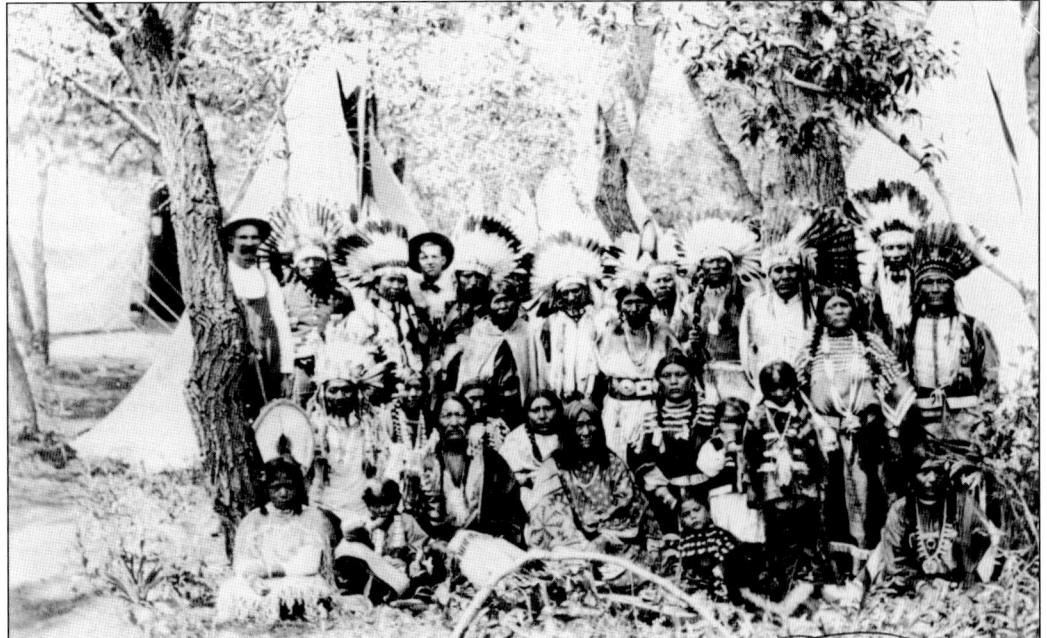

Chipeta (first row, fourth from left) and her Ute people are camped in Cheyenne Canyon. When their ancestors stole horses from the Plains Indians, Irving Howbert said, they drove them up "over the northern point of Cheyenne Mountain and on to the west along a trail that ran not very far distant from the route now followed by the Cripple Creek Short Line." (Courtesy Ute Pass Historical Society.)

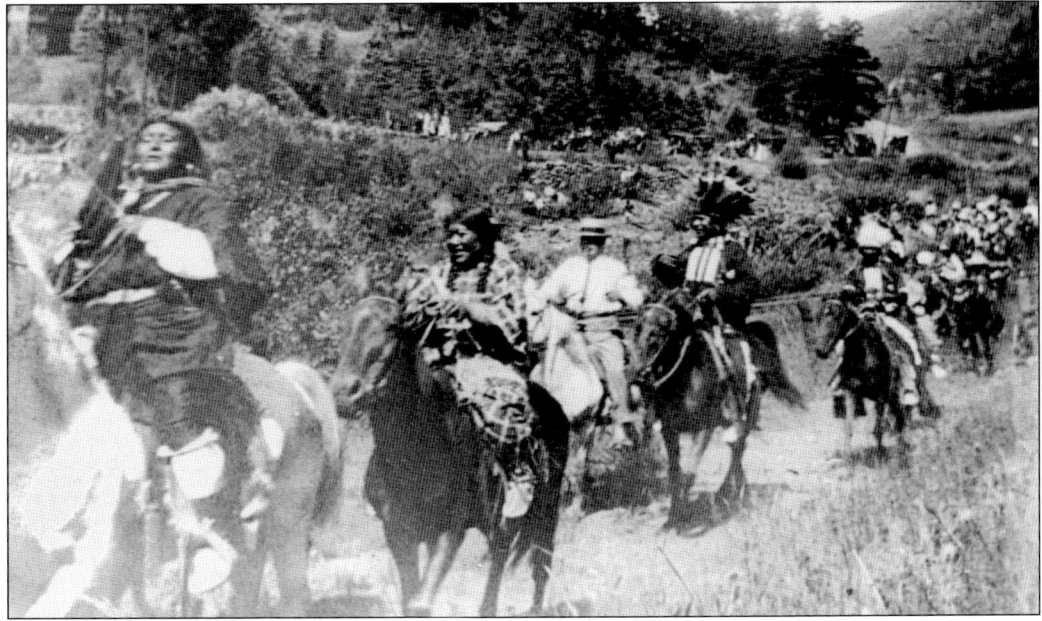

These Ute people are obviously reveling in their relationship with horses. Frances Densmore wrote, "In former times if the Utes were gathered in a large camp a 'parade' took place every morning. Both men and women were on horseback . . . [and] all the company sang the Parade songs." (Courtesy Ute Pass Historical Society.)

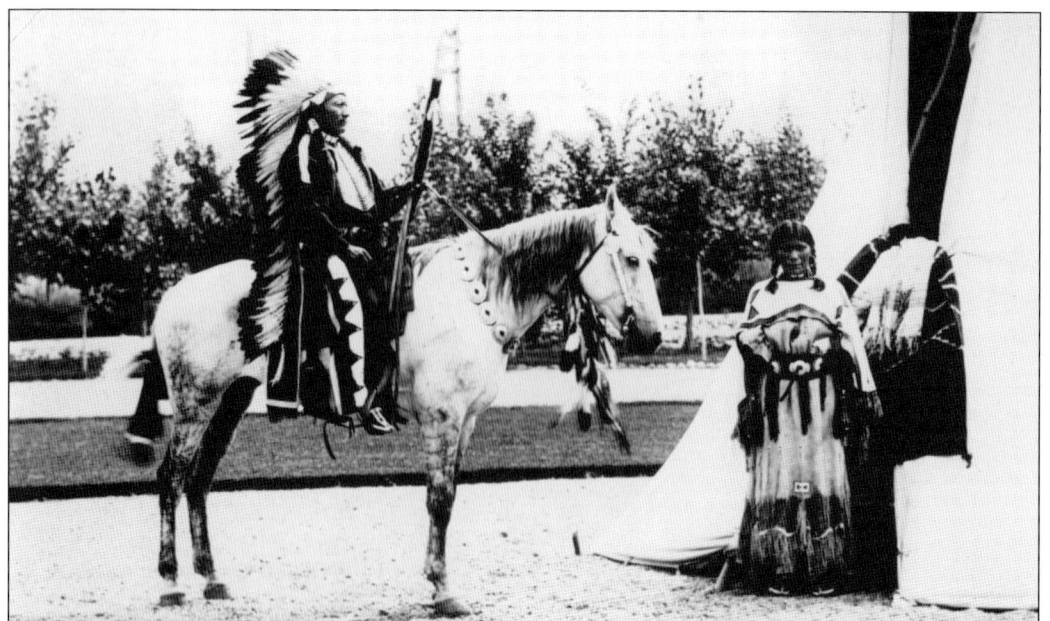

Chief Buckskin Charlie and his wife, Towee, pose in their finest regalia. His horse, however, steals the show. An abundance of eagle feathers cascades from his silver bridle, indicating honors won for speed and valor. Coup stripes on his forelegs bear further evidence of battles well fought. Silver conchos encircling his neck indicate the great value his owner has placed in this warhorse. (Courtesy DPL.)

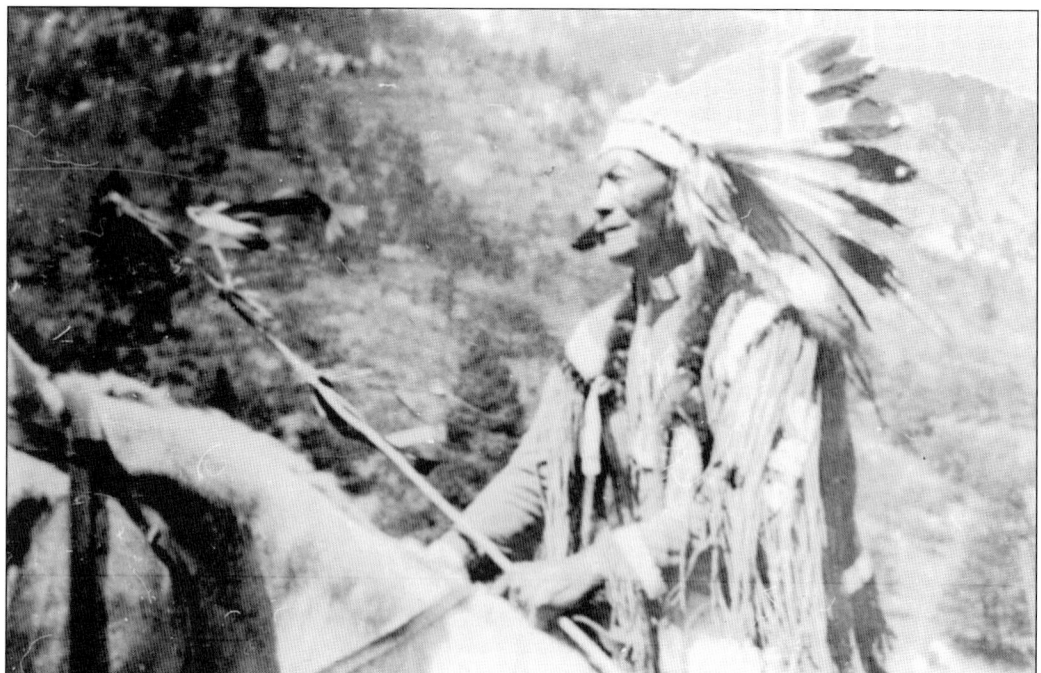

NaNace, a spiritual leader of the Southern Utes, presides at the Ute Pass Trail ride reenactment in 1912. Ute horsemen sang as they rode and offered special songs for mountain passes. (Courtesy Ute Pass Historical Society.)

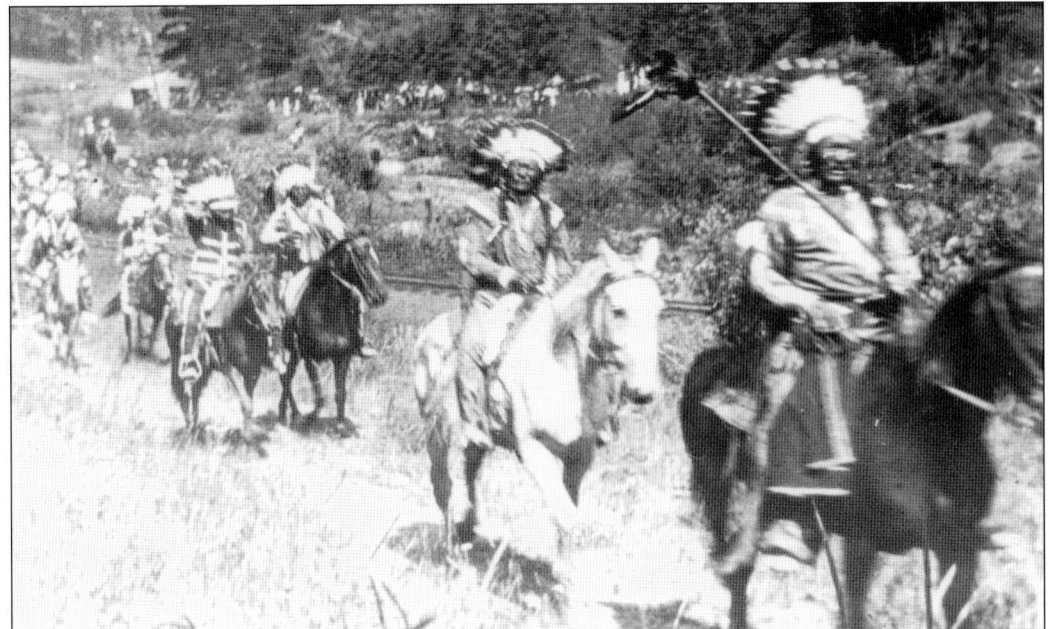

NaNace leads this Ute horse parade along French Creek in Cascade. When Powell studied the spirituality of the Utes in 1868, he concluded that the people were "zootheistic" and therefore "savages." He failed to understand the Ute cosmology of a Creator "everywhere and within everything," including animals. Ute people are actually monotheistic. (Courtesy Ute Pass Historical Society.)

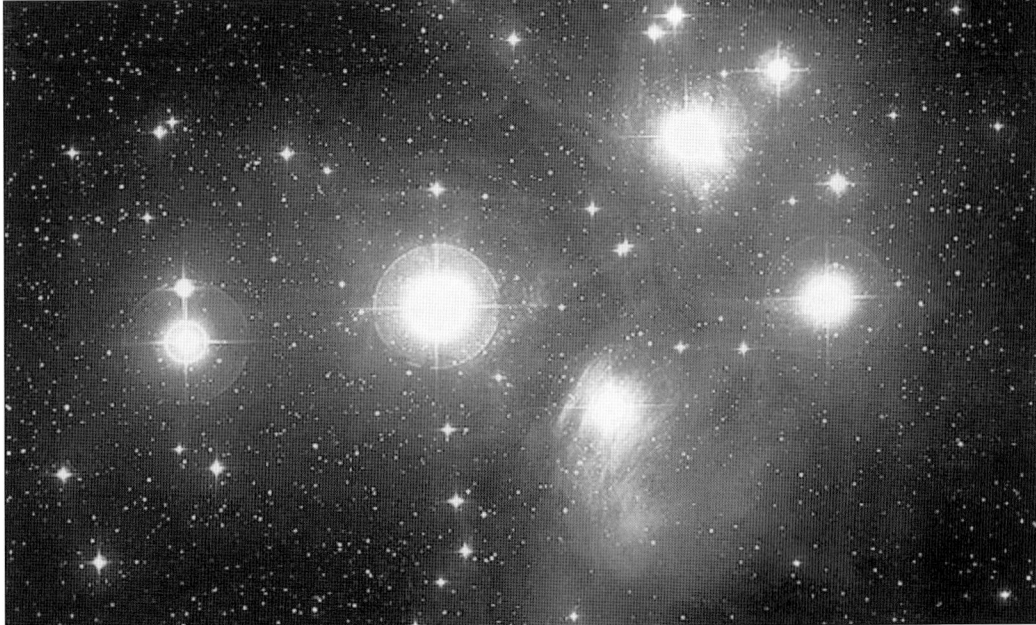

Ute Indians are unique among Native Americans in that they do not have a migration legend. In addition to the stories of their creation on Pikes Peak, they say that they come from the distant star cluster we call the Pleiades. This deep understanding of their relationship to the rest of the universe impacts every aspect of daily life. (Courtesy Royal Observatory Edinburgh.)

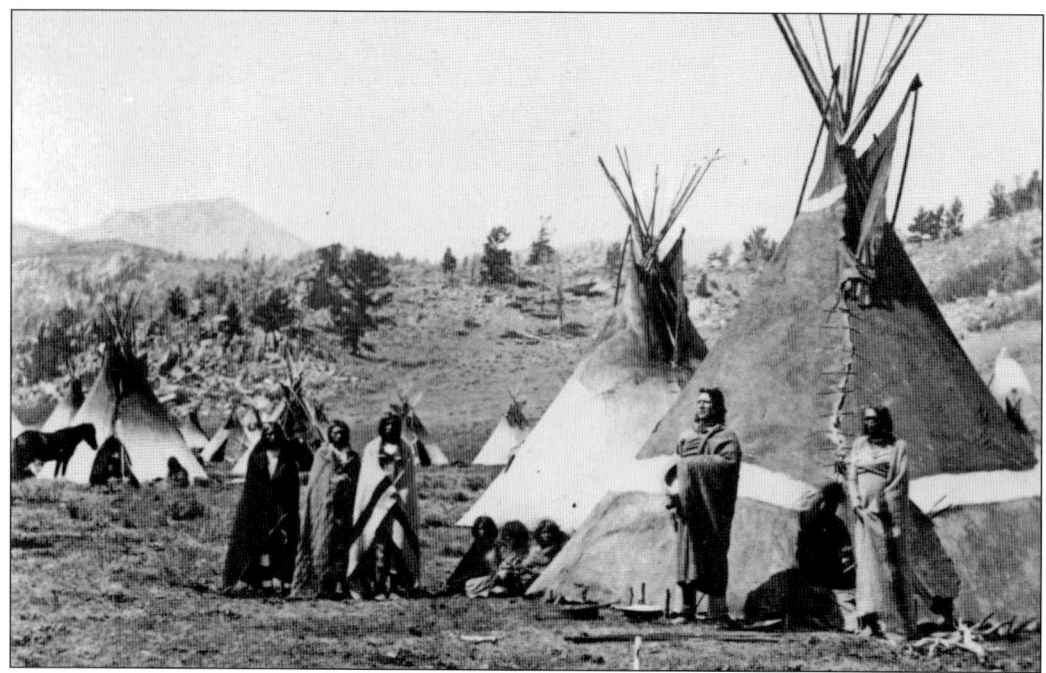

"As above, so below." In accordance with this teaching, the Ute people set up their encampments in the shape of the Pleiades star group. The crescent shape of *soniawi* can be seen in this encampment in Florissant. The three brightest stars in the group are represented here by the medicine man's tipi (painted, far right), the chief's tipi (second from right), and the medicine wheel (not shown). (Courtesy Colorado College, Tutt Collection.)

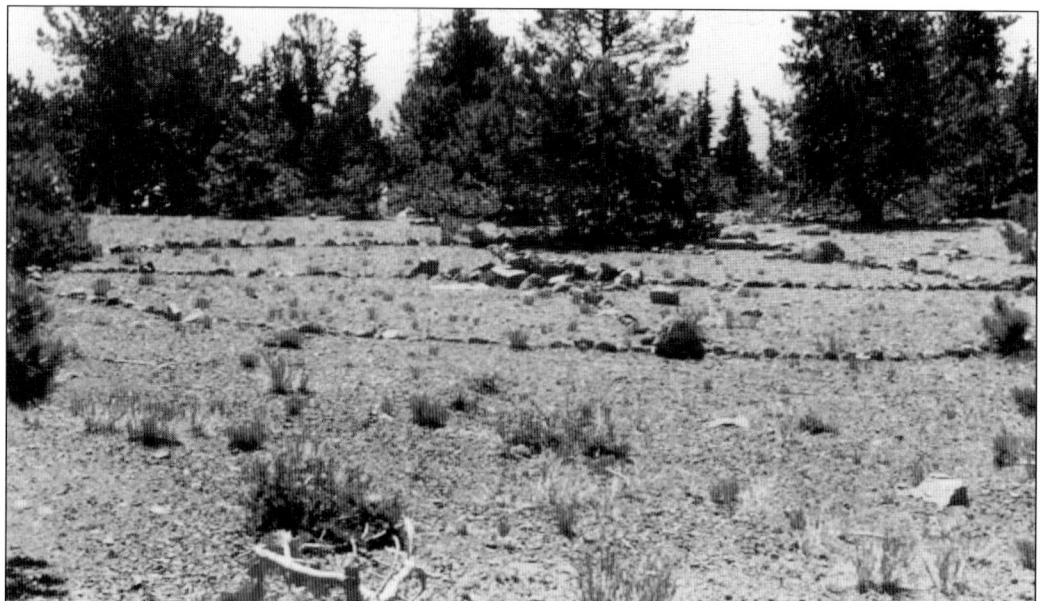

According to Clifford Duncan, "At each encampment, the medicine man or woman would first build a Medicine Wheel . . . at the center of all the tipis. Then, as the people harvested, . . . the very best parts of the harvest were offered to Mother Earth at [this wheel]. They gave back to Mother Earth. This was like an umbilical cord connecting them to their Mother."

After a long, hard winter, the Ute story goes, the starving Dog People gathered in a large tipi. The ground was muddy, so the dogs left their leggings, with tails attached, on a post near the door. Lightning struck, the lodge caught fire, and they raced out the door, grabbing the wrong leggings. This is why dogs sniff under each other's tails. (Courtesy DPL.)

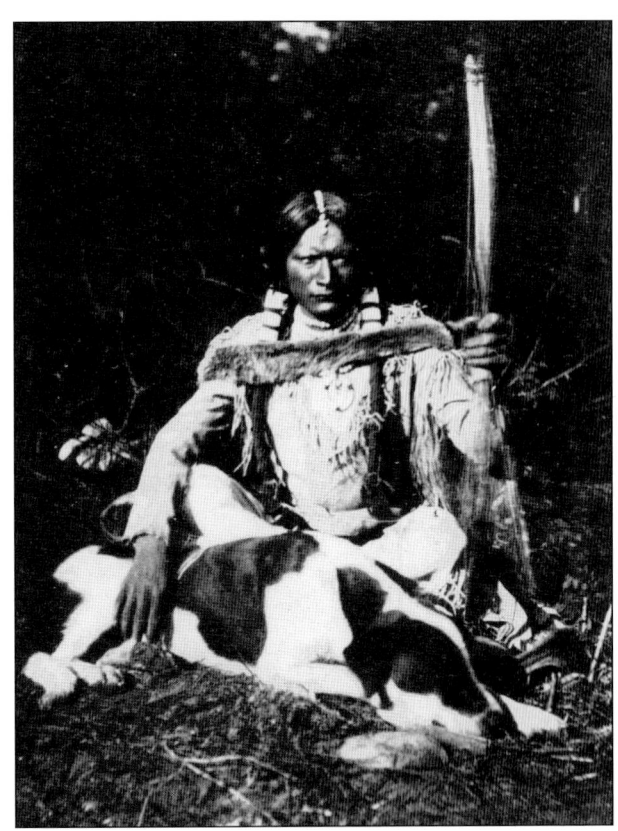

Quiagat, or bears, are sacred to the Ute people. Legend tells of the Creator's daughter being seduced by Bear on Pikes Peak and the Ute Nation issuing from this union. It is therefore taboo for a Ute to kill a bear. Medicine men or women who have special healing powers are called M'*sut t'Quiagat*, or "Power of the Bear." (Courtesy Ute Pass Historical Society.)

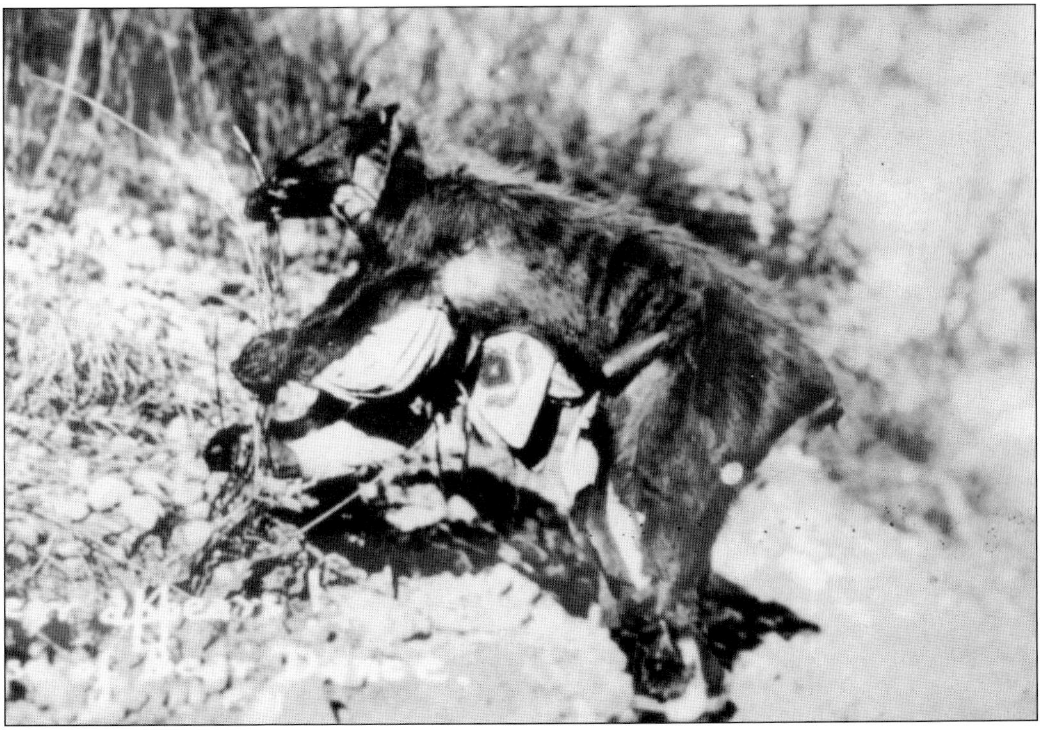

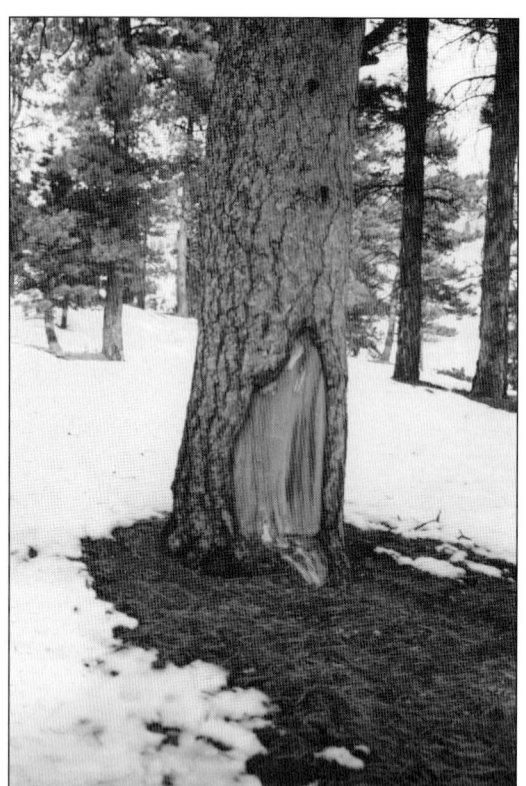

Ute medicine men and women would cut a straight line on the pine tree with a stone or metal ax, then pry a sharp stick into the cut, lifting and peeling bark from the tree. Strips of inner bark were then ingested in a healing ceremony. Hundreds of these medicine trees were left by the Utes as living artifacts in the Pikes Peak region.

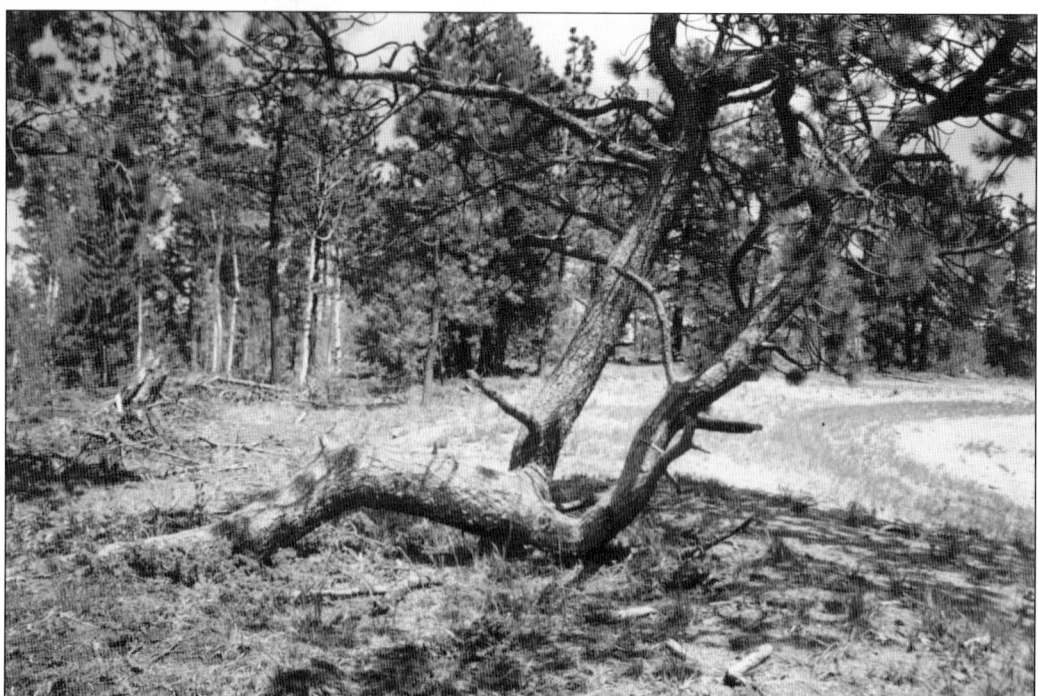

Prayer trees are bent and tied parallel to the ground with yucca rope when they are saplings. Ceremonies are still held at these trees to send the prayers of the people to the Creator.

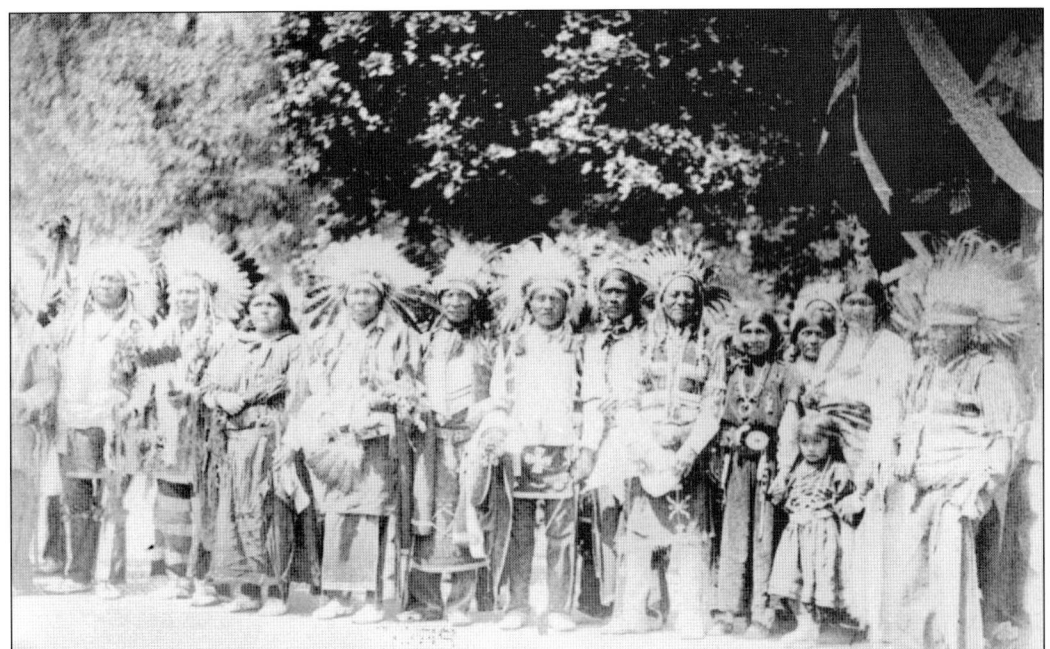

Dressed in ceremonial regalia, this Ute delegation is gathered at Manitou Springs. When George Ruxton encountered these sacred springs in 1848, he wrote that "the basin of the spring was filled with beads and wampum, and pieces of red cloth and knives," while the trees nearby were "hung with strips of deerskin, cloth, and moccasins." (Courtesy Ute Pass Historical Society.)

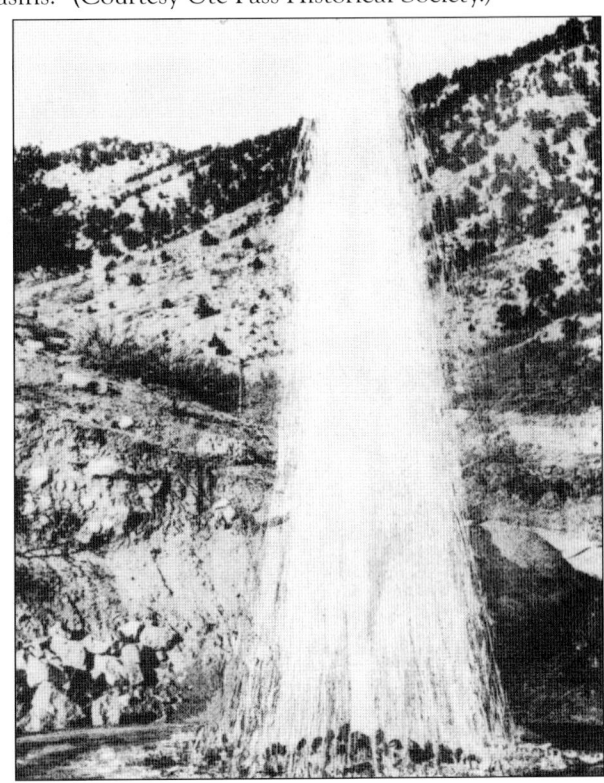

The Ute Chief Manitou Gusher, in Manitou Springs, was incorrectly named by white men who came to the region. *Manitou* is an Algonquin word for Great Spirit. In the Ute language, the word is *Sunawiv*. Utes also felt that water spirits, *pong-a'-pits*, dwelt in these springs. (Courtesy Ute Pass Historical Society.)

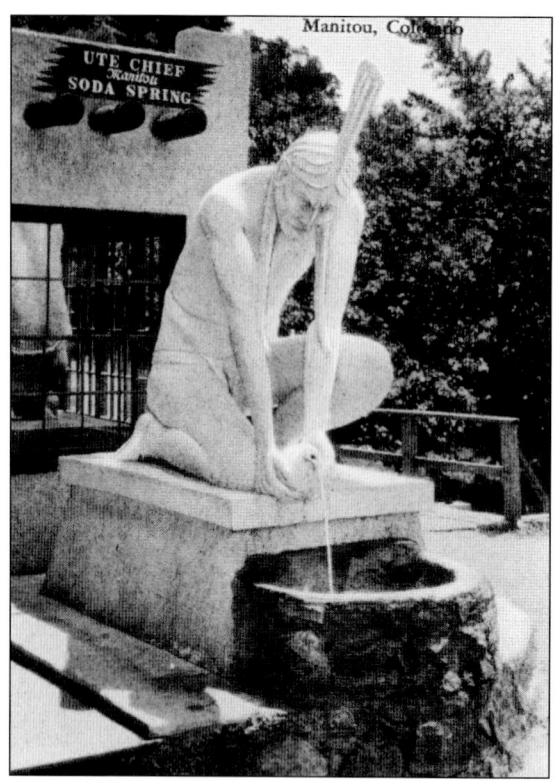

In 1848, Ruxton noted that this spring, now the Ute Chief Soda Spring, was "equal to the very best soda-water, but possesses that fresh, natural flavour, which manufactured water cannot impart." He was half-dead with thirst when he dipped his cup into the bubbling water, which "almost [blew] up the roof of [his] mouth with its effervescence." (Courtesy Ute Pass Historical Society.)

Brush wickiups such as these are generally associated with Ute culture. These temporary structures are made from limbs and poles interlaced in tipi fashion. Even now, dozens of wickiups can be found in the pine forests on Pikes Peak, where the Northern Ute people perform their Sundance ceremony each summer. (Courtesy DPL.)

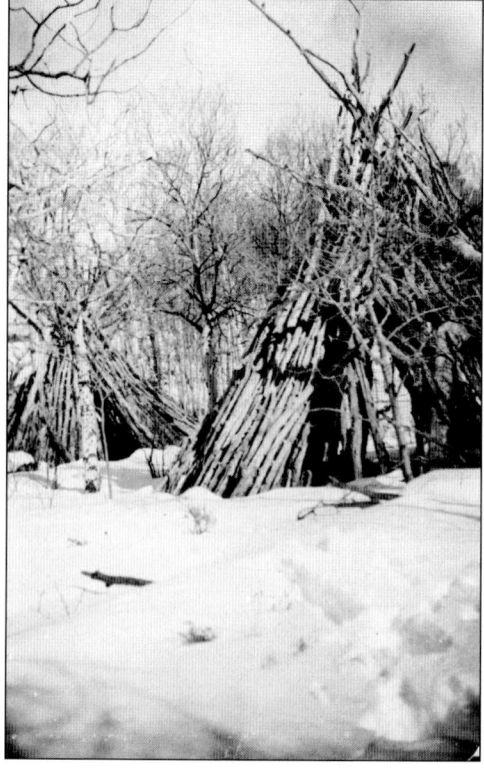

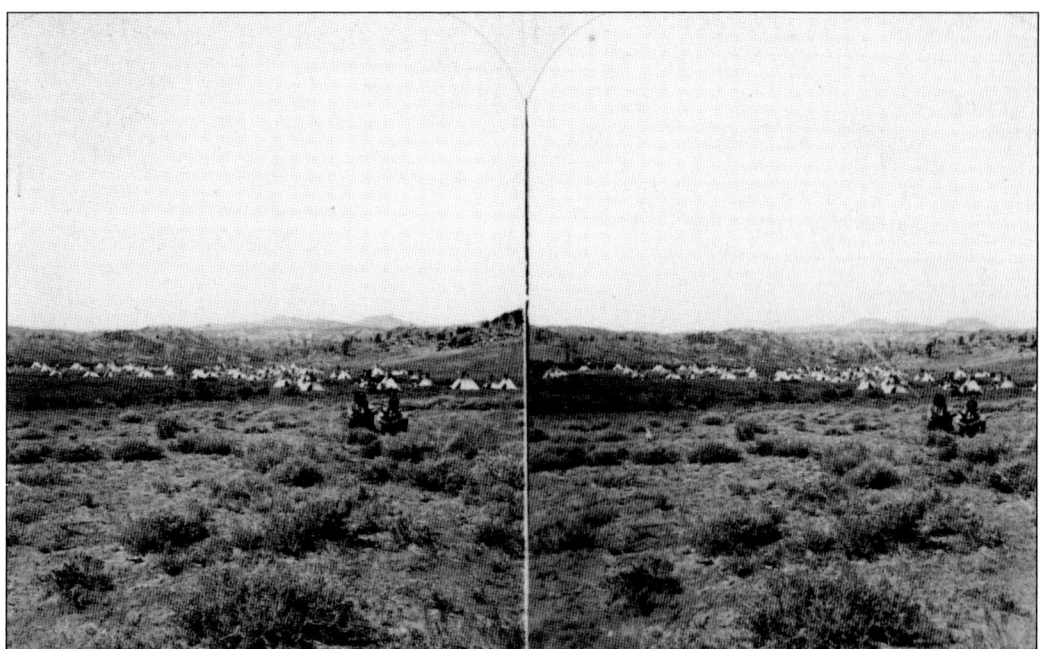

Approximately 50 tipis are visible in this 1800s Ute encampment. However, in the 1870s, Atlanta Thompson wrote that Ute encampments in the Florissant valley numbered about 500 lodges. She was struck by the camps because "every tepee had a figure of a warrior or horse painted on one or both sides of it with . . . bright red, green, and yellow paint." (Courtesy Pikes Peak Library District.)

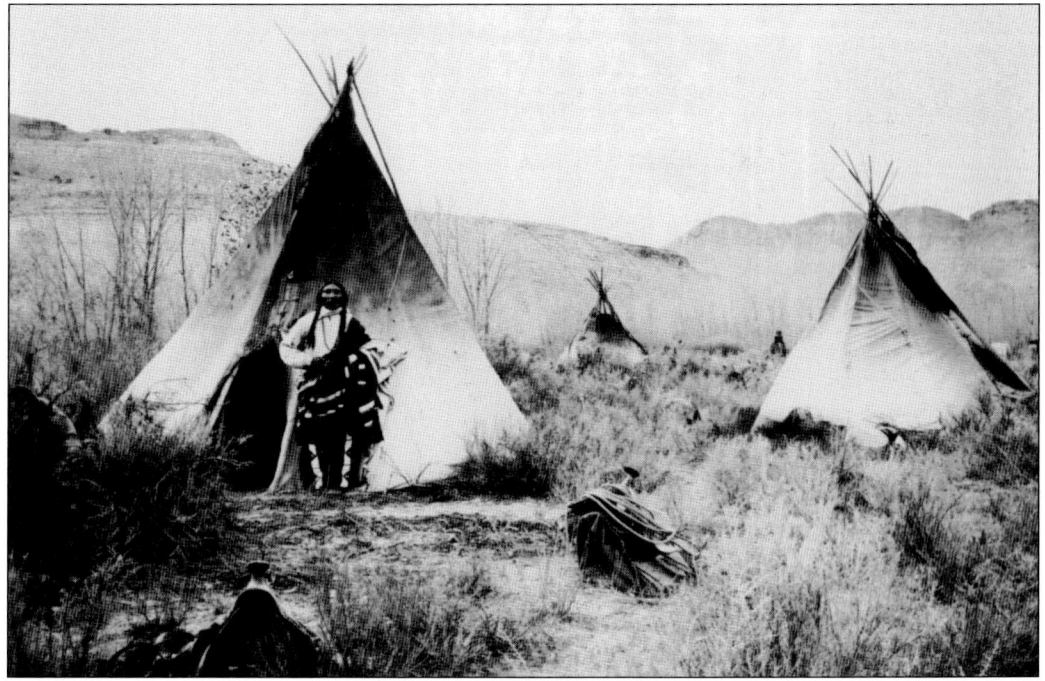

Utes harvested the abundant pine from Pikes Peak for their lodge fires. Heavy pine resins create a thick, black residue that coats the smoke holes of tipis with its signature color. This distinguishes Ute lodges from the yellow-brown of Plains lodges. (Courtesy DPL.)

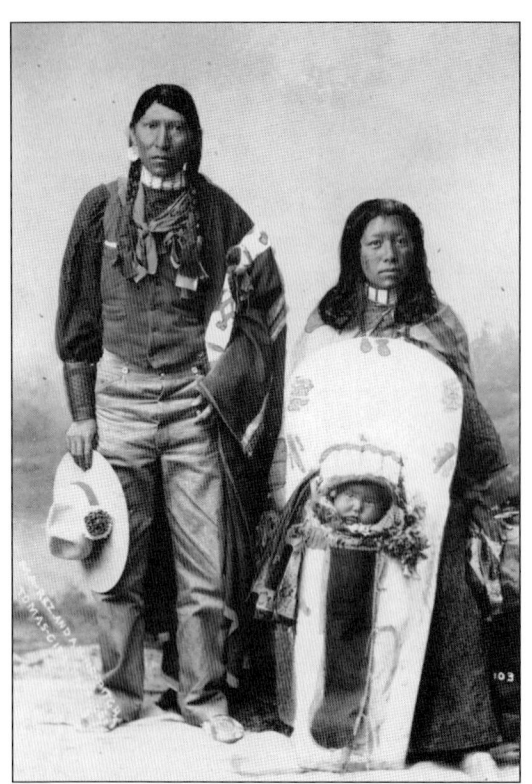

Ma-rez, a warrior and dashing cowboy, wears the black silk neck scarf preferred by Utes. When Antoine Robidoux established Fort Uncompahgre near Delta, Colorado, in 1828, these silk scarves were one of his hottest trade items. Often too poor to afford a blanket for burial, many Utes went to their grave with only a silk scarf covering their face. (Courtesy Museum of New Mexico.)

Donning their finest regalia, these Utes epitomize the beauty and elegance of American Indian culture. Hour upon hour of backbreaking labor is required to harvest animals and tan their hides, trap eagles and harvest their feathers, and carefully stitch beadwork. (Courtesy Pikes Peak Library District.)

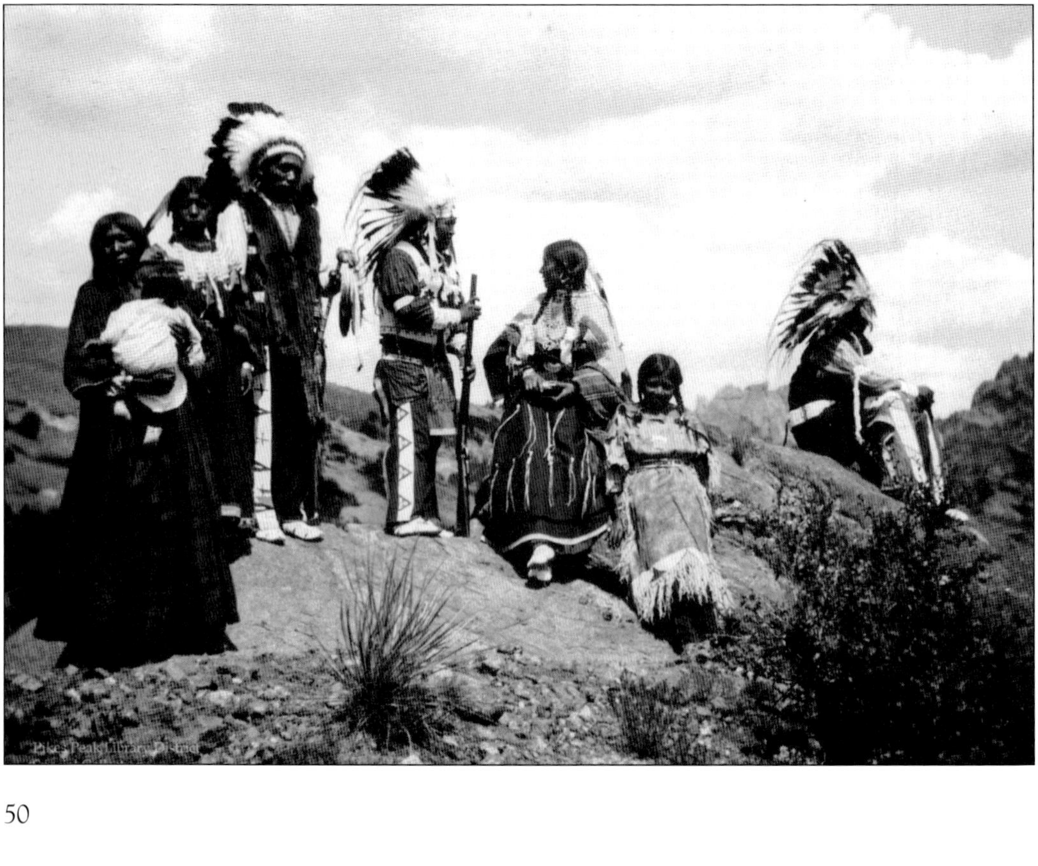

Native crosses dance across the cape and the skirt of this Ute dress. It probably dates from the 1870s, indicated by the heavily beaded yoke and the fringed border along the bottom. This soft, white, brain-tanned hide was highly prized as a trade item. When it became soiled, women simply pounded the stain with powdered chalk from Mount Princeton. (Courtesy DPL.)

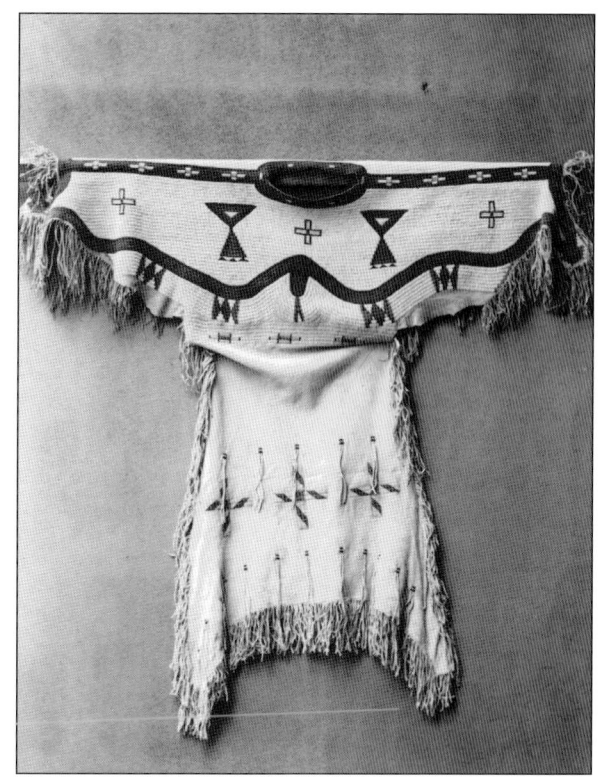

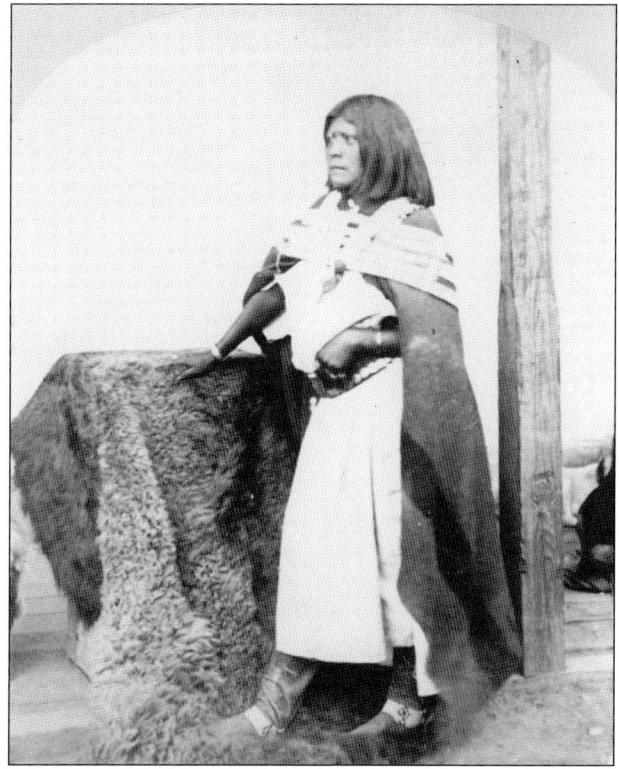

Pah-ge, of the Capote band of Utes, poses for the camera in this 1874 photograph from the Wheeler Expedition. In sad irony, she stands on a buffalo robe. Her woolen cape (*capote* in Spanish) provides a replacement for the buffalo robes her people used prior to the European invasion. (Courtesy Museum of New Mexico.)

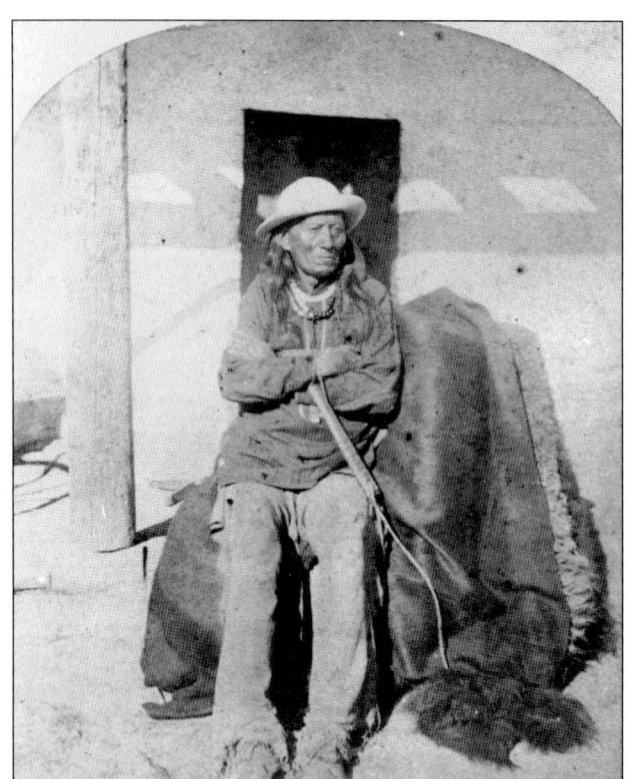

An unknown Ute elder, probably a Capote chief, is pictured at Abiquiu in 1874. His threadbare calico shirt and white man's hat give evidence of the European inter-culturation experienced by the Southern Utes because of their proximity to Spanish territory. (Courtesy Museum of New Mexico.)

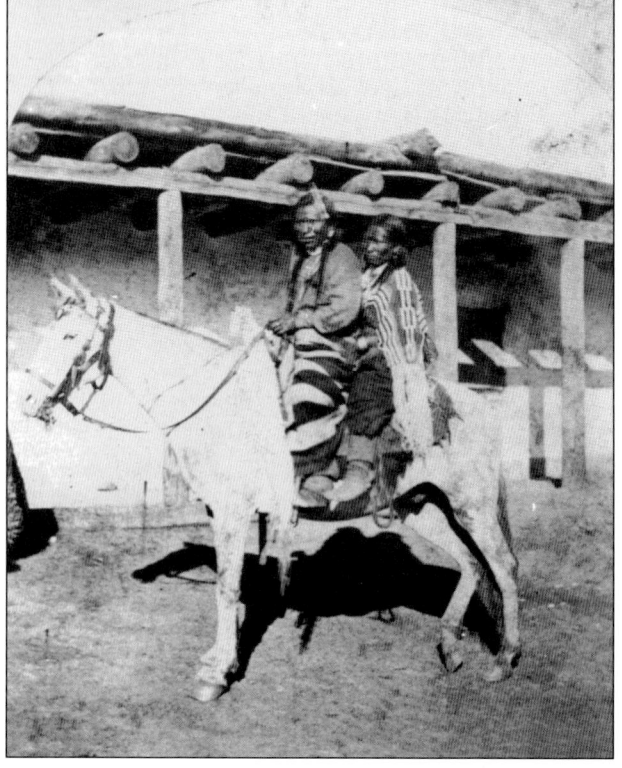

This Ute husband and wife are probably visiting Abiquiu for ration day. Her heavily beaded yoke is undoubtedly what caught the photographer's eye. These fully beaded yokes, popular among Ute women, could weigh as much as 30 pounds. They were detachable from the everyday hide dress and easily transferable to a new garment. (Courtesy Museum of New Mexico.)

Eagle feathers are earned, not simply taken. This chief's bonnet flows all the way to the ground, indicating his prowess as a warrior. Unfortunately, the photographer did not record his name for posterity when he took this photograph in 1885. We can surmise from his European cotton tunic and lack of blanket cape that he is probably a Moache Ute. (Courtesy Museum of New Mexico.)

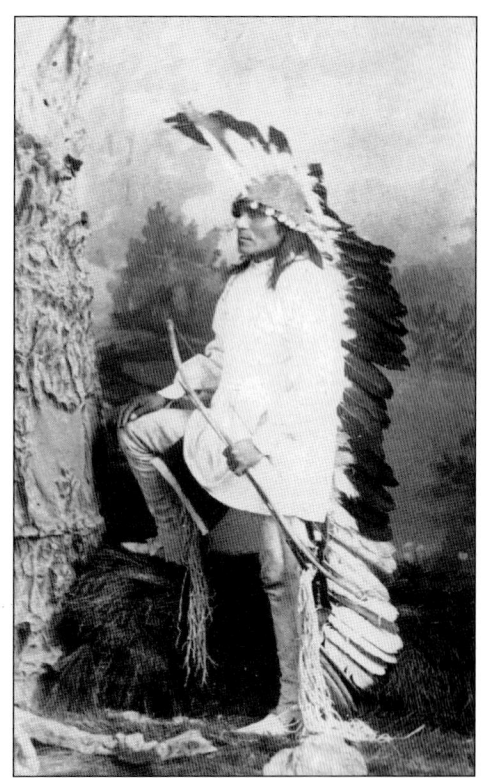

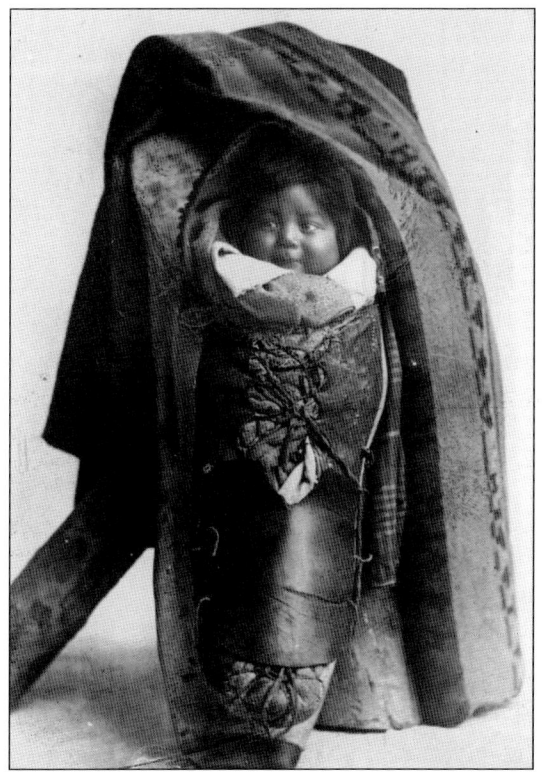

Twinkling eyes and a mischievous smile clearly indicate this little girl's pleasure at being snugly wrapped in her cradleboard. Ute cradleboards were originally made of a framework of willow. After the reservation period, however, there was a trend toward using boards inserted into a buckskin sack. (Courtesy DPL.)

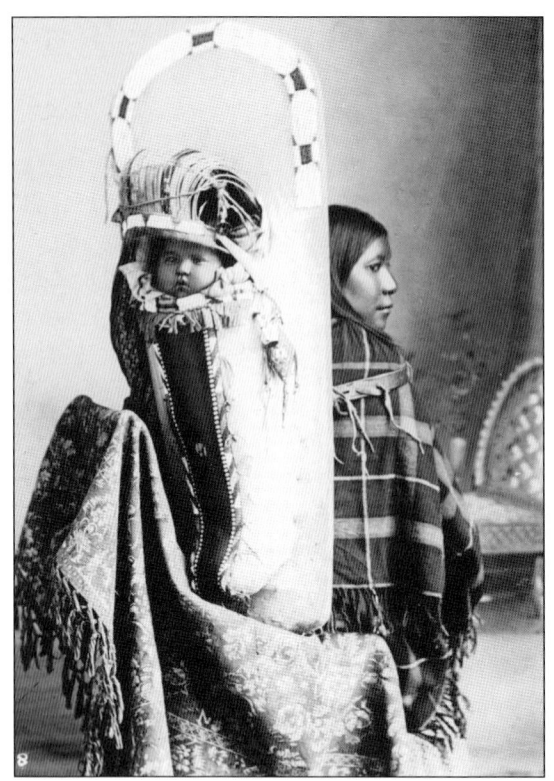

This Ute woman proudly shows off her baby in the traditional willow cradleboard. The medicine bundle attached to the board near the baby's left shoulder probably contains his umbilical cord. Next to it is a beaded amulet of a turtle, assuring him of a long life. A small hole in the front accommodates the child's penis, so he can urinate outside the cradle. (Courtesy DPL.)

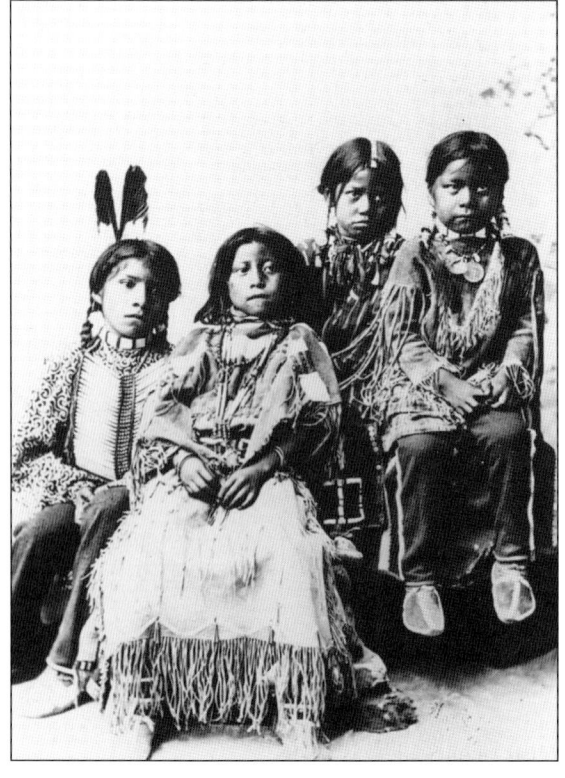

The sad eyes of Severo's children mirror the sorrow and confusion of the Ute people during the reservation period. Their traditional spiritual practices were now a federal crime. They could no longer roam their ancestral lands. And soon they would be forced to attend boarding schools, where they would be stripped of traditional clothing and their hair cut in the white man's fashion. (Courtesy Ute Pass Historical Society.)

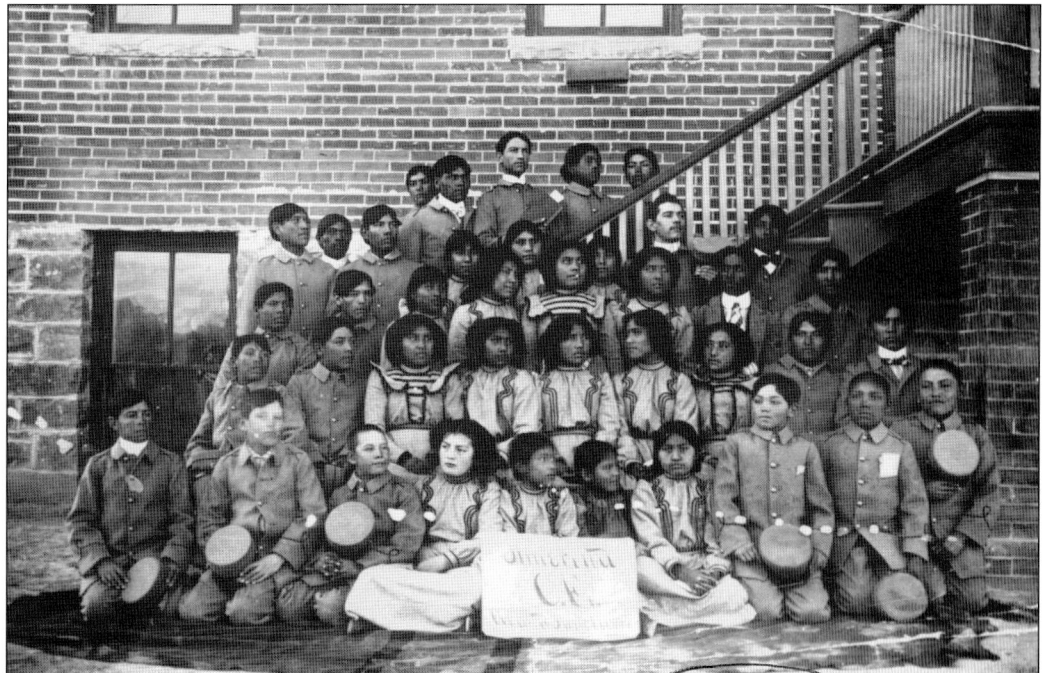

The Teller Institute, an American Indian boarding school in Grand Junction, was established in 1885. According to the treaty of 1868, the education of Ute children was deemed a necessity in order to "insure the civilization of the bands entering into this treaty." The painted white face of the little girl (first row, fourth from left) shows the impact of this indoctrination. (Courtesy DPL.)

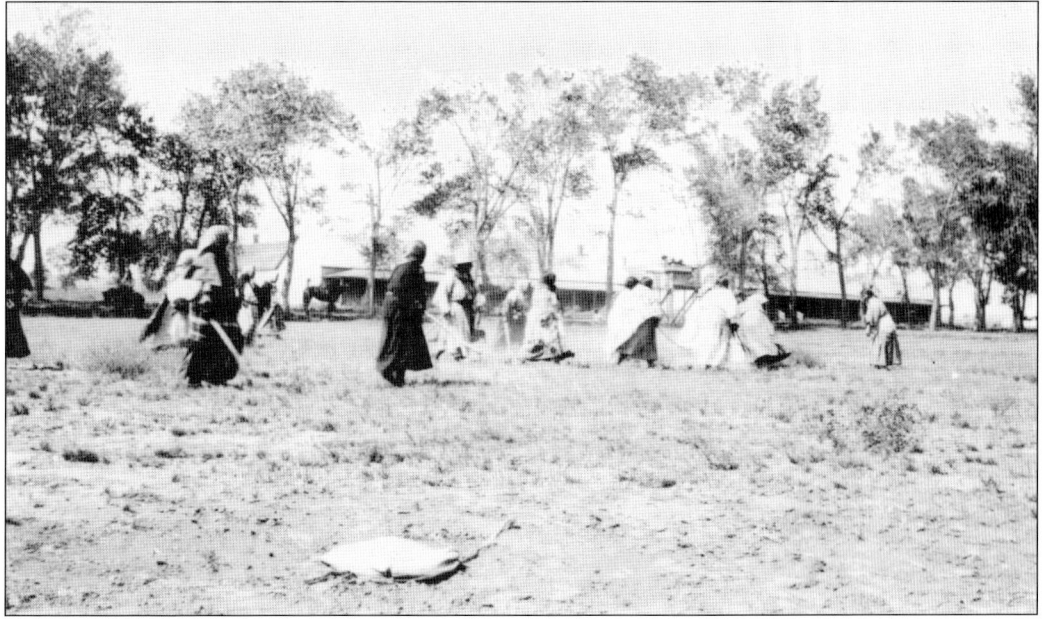

Ute women enjoy a lively game of Shinny. The rules of this game are comparable to modern hockey, and similarly curved sticks are used to hit a small leather ball. In this free-for-all, played only by women, kicking or grabbing another's stick is allowed, as is tripping. (Courtesy Ute Pass Historical Society.)

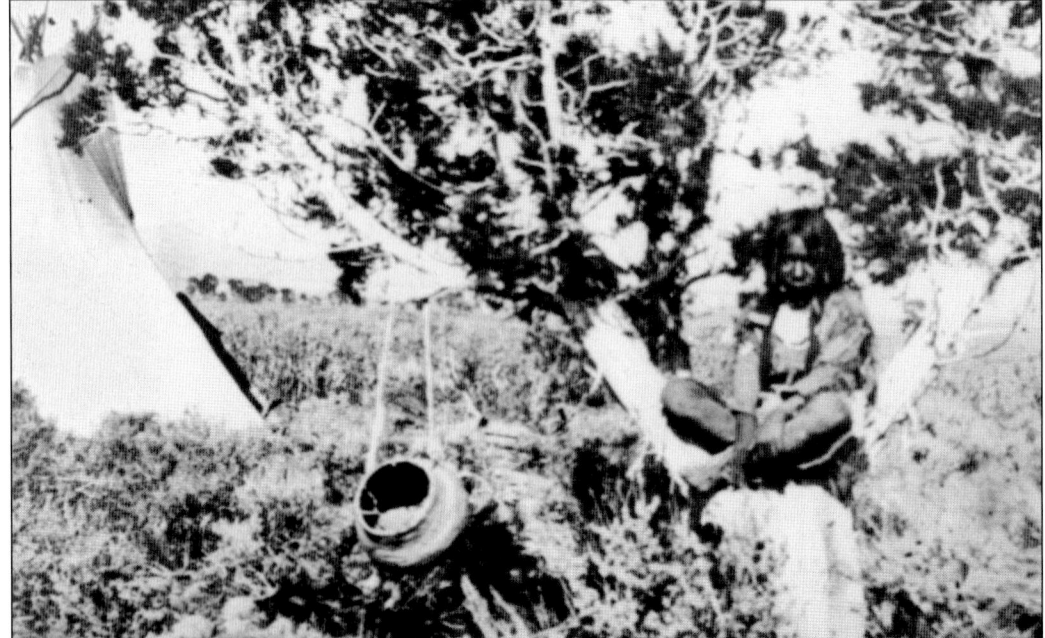

This Northern Ute boy has been posted in a tree, probably to watch over the basket of food hanging on a nearby branch. In the winter, when confined to their tipis, children were regaled with stories, *tu-gwe-nai*, related by the elders. These stories were told over and over, night after night, until the children could repeat them verbatim. (Courtesy Ute Pass Historical Society.)

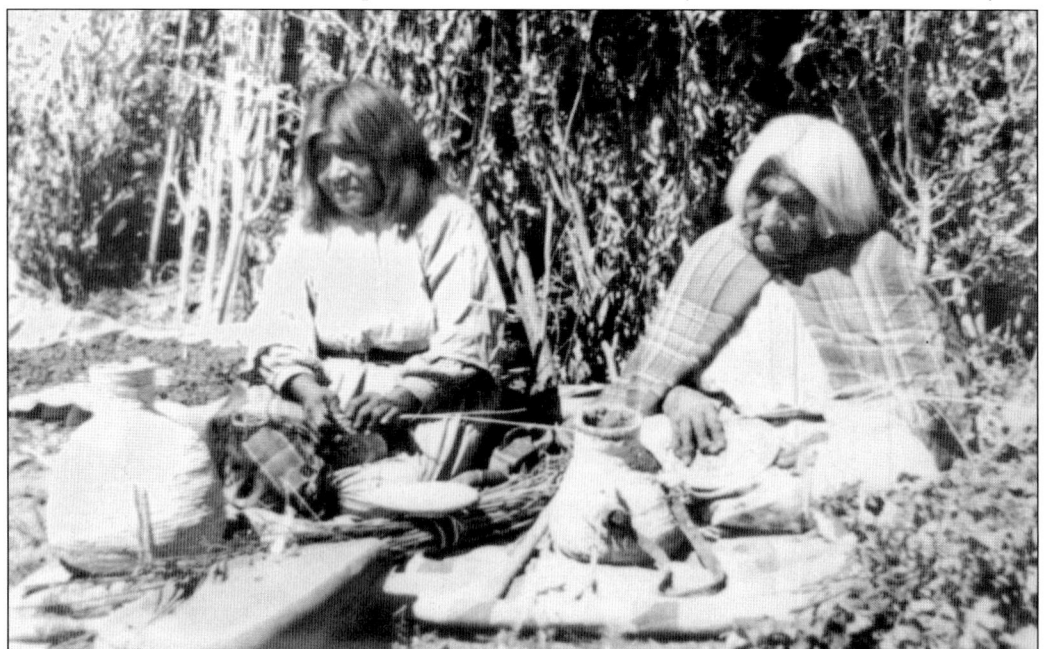

These aged women weave baskets that will soon be coated with pine pitch for storing water and food. When the elderly could no longer be of service and instead became a burden, they went off alone to sing their death chant: "Alas, alas. Here long enough have I walked the earth. Let me die, let me die." (Courtesy Ute Pass Historical Society.)

Archup, a Northern Ute warrior, was photographed during Powell's visit on White River in 1868. He is probably the same Archup that Ann Smith interviewed for her ethnographic work in the early 1900s. In her book *Ute Tales*, Archup relates some fascinating battles between Utes and Comanches and Arapahos, providing an insider's view of these conflicts. (Courtesy Ute Pass Historical Society.)

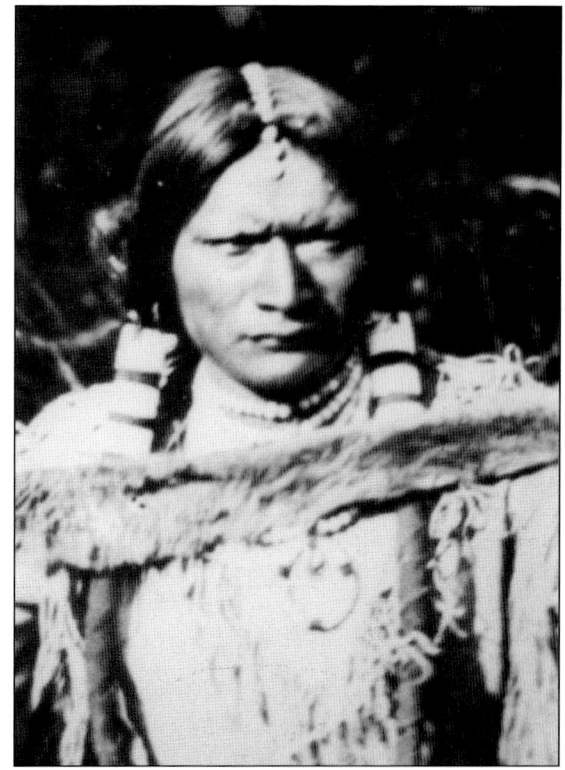

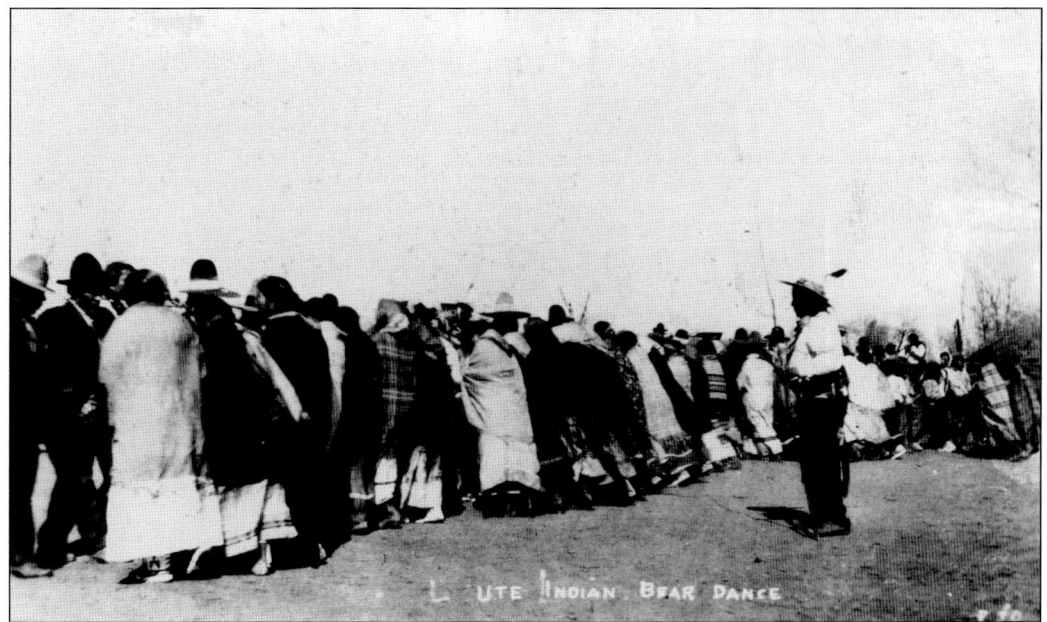

According to Frances Densmore in 1918, "The characteristic dance of the Ute Indians is the Bear dance, which is held every year in the early spring. The intention is to hold the dance at about the time that the bear comes from his hibernation, yet the Indians seem to expect that snow will fall either during or soon after the dance." (Courtesy Pikes Peak Historical Society, Forster Collection.)

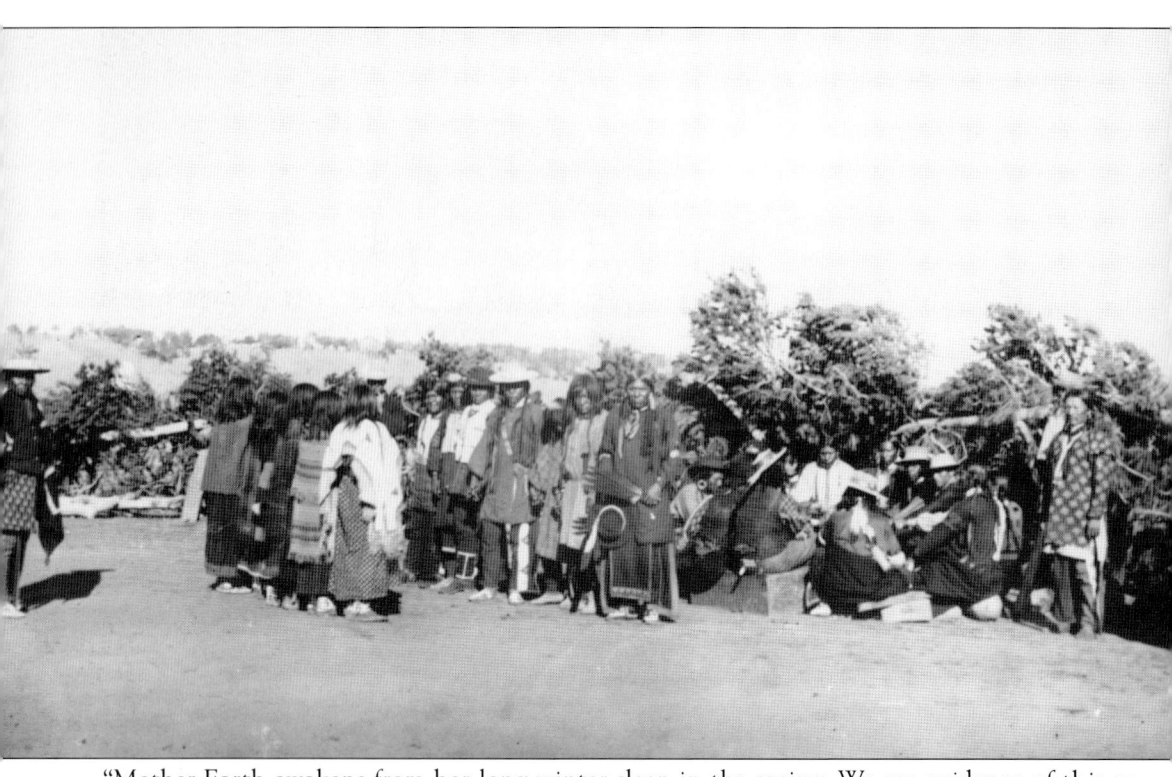

"Mother Earth awakens from her long winter sleep in the spring. We see evidence of this as mountain streams, her blood, thaw and begin to flow again. As She stretches and yawns, She causes the boulders resting on Her knees to slide off the hillsides and Her blanket of snow slowly disappears. *Quiagat*, asleep in his den, is awakened." A Ute elder explains the reason for the springtime Bear Dance. It is an honoring and thanking of Mother Earth, and therefore it is a woman's choice dance. The men seated on the right of this photograph are the musicians. They have placed a rasp, or *morats*, on a hollow log or pit covered with corrugated tin. As they rub a stick along the morats, it creates a deep resonance like the growling of a bear. The Bear Dance is unique to the Ute culture. (Courtesy DPL.)

Pahriats holds the tether of his eaglet in this photograph from Powell's 1874 expedition. These captive birds were fed a diet of rabbit while their feathers were periodically harvested. Eagle flew higher than any other bird and was honored as a special messenger from the Creator. His feather was awarded for one's brave actions or other sacrifices on behalf of the people. (Courtesy DPL.)

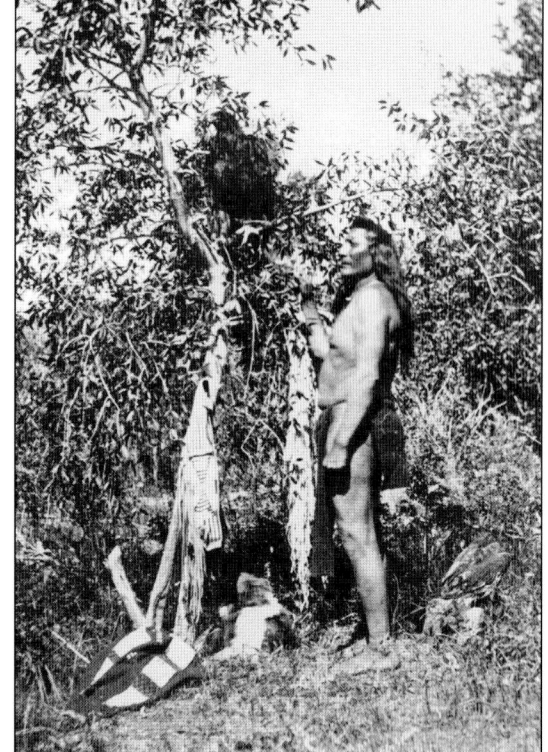

Various authors have identified this photograph as depicting either an Eagle Dance or a Round Dance at Garden of the Gods. Since this is clearly a dance of Ute leaders, as indicated by the eagle headdresses, it is probably an Eagle Dance. (Courtesy DPL.)

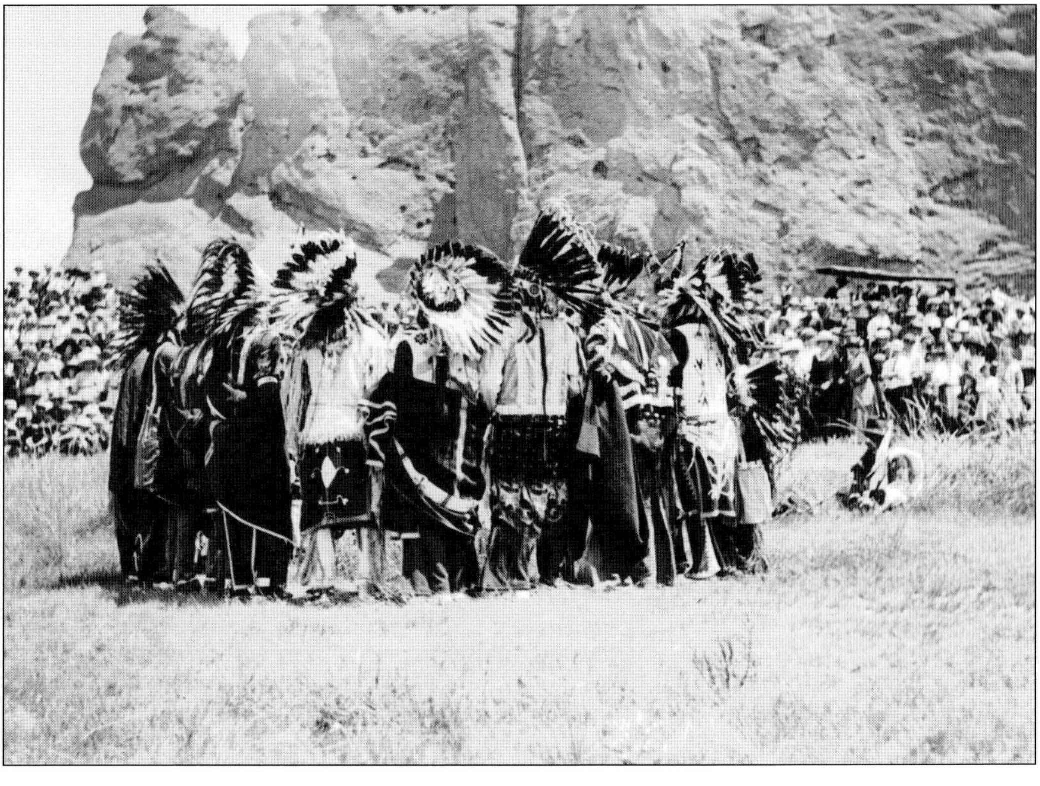

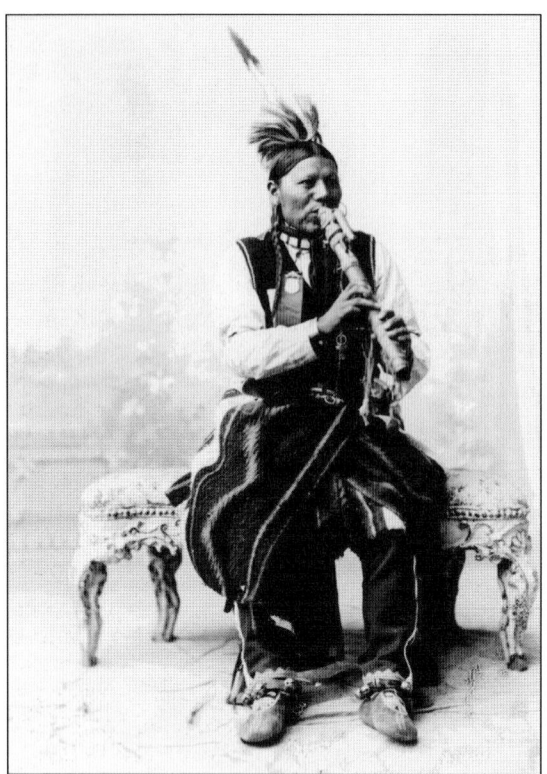

In 1922, Frances Densmore wrote that the Ute flageolet (flute) had "an extended range and a pleasing quality of tone." Her informants also told her that "American song tunes can not be played on it." These six-holed flutes were used primarily for courting. The song from a young man's flute could reportedly touch a maiden's heart and win her hand. (Courtesy DPL.)

A young Ute warrior proudly displays his peace pipe for the photographer. Ethnographic studies reveal that early Ute pipes were of steatite rather than catlinite. Densmore recorded three "smoking songs" by Jim Kolorow of the Uncompahgre/Tabeguache band. (Courtesy Ute Pass Historical Society.)

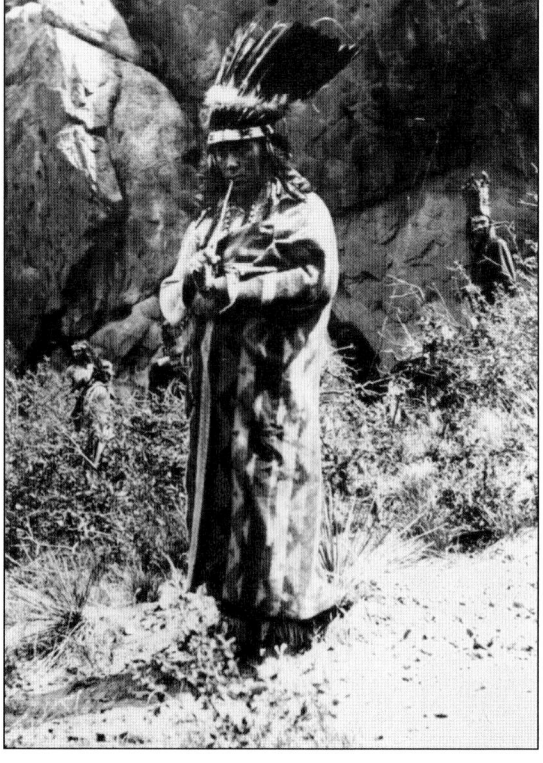

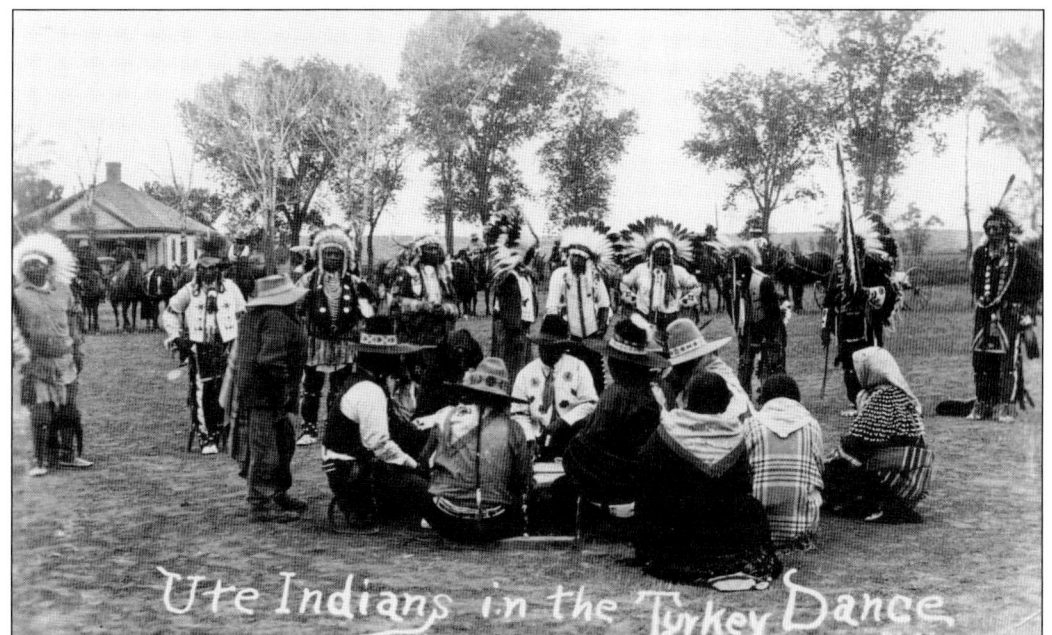

According to Frances Densmore in 1918, "One of the principal dances of the Utes at the present time is known as the Turkey dance.... The accompanying instrument is a large drum placed on the ground at the right of the entrance to the dance circle, the drummers being seated around the drum and singing as they beat upon it." (Courtesy Pikes Peak Historical Society, Forster Collection.)

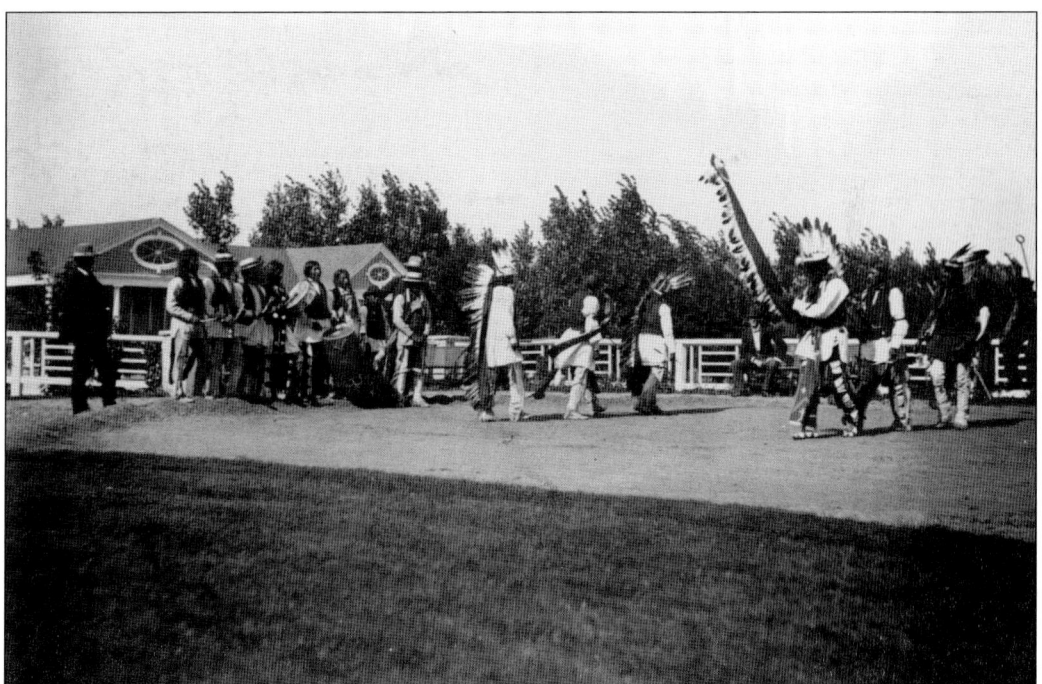

His eagle staff held high, a Ute chief leads the Eagle Dance in this 1896 ceremony at the Broadmoor Hotel in Colorado Springs. Today's Broadmoor bears little resemblance to the modest cabins in the background. It is now an elegant, five-star hotel. (Courtesy DPL.)

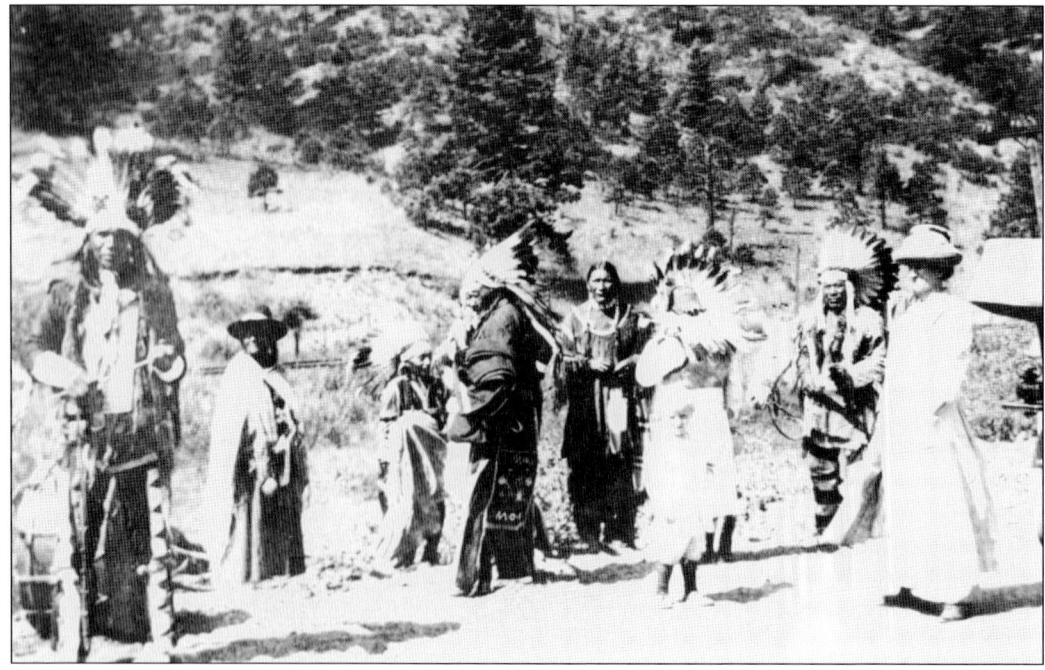

The Ute man on the left stands beside his drum with beater in hand as he and other representatives of the Ute Nation prepare for a ceremony. These Southern Utes from Ignacio have gathered in Ute Pass for the Ute Indian Trail Dedication in August 1912. (Courtesy Ute Pass Historical Society.)

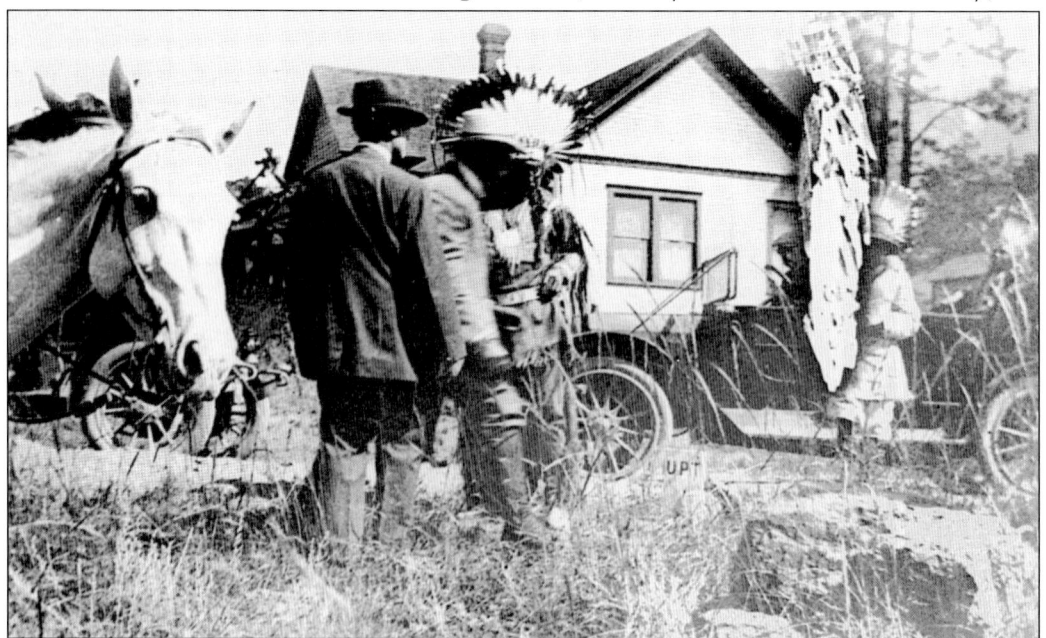

From left to right, former governor Alva Adams, D. N. Heizer, and NaNace officiate in placing the first Ute Pass Trail marker (to the right of the car's front tire). The only representative of the Tabeguache at the event was Chipeta, an old friend of the governor's wife. Today, however, members of the Tabeguache band are able to return to their ancestral lands courtesy of the Pikes Peak Historical Society. (Courtesy Ute Pass Historical Society.)

Three

T IN-NE-AH, THE A PACHE N ATION

As with most other First Nations, Apaches call themselves simply *Tin-ne-ah*, meaning "the People." Their common name is believed to have originated from the Zuni word for enemy, *apachu*.

Linguistically, the Tin-ne-ah belong to the Athapascan family, which includes the Navajos in the south and the Tlingits and the Haidas in the north. Colorado archaeologist Steve Cassells writes, "Plains Apaches are . . . thought to have been a late entrant into the New World," having arrived in the Colorado area "well after the development of the Puebloan societies." As stated earlier, they likely arrived in the Pikes Peak region in the 1400s.

In historical times, the Tin-ne-ah settled into two main divisions: the western and the eastern. The western division includes the Jicarillas, the band most closely associated with Pikes Peak. Their name was undoubtedly proffered on them by the Spanish, for in that language *jicara* refers to a bowl made from a gourd. *Jicarilla* indicates a small bowl, probably in reference to the Tin-ne-ah's unique baskets. The Jicarillas are organized in two bands: Llaneros, or plains people; and Olleros, or mountain-valley people.

In the 1700s, Comanches forced the Tin-ne-ah from their hunting grounds along the Arkansas River and into northwestern New Mexico. However, in 1779, Tin-ne-ah warriors and their Ute allies joined the Spanish army in a decisive battle against the Comanches. As a result, it was the Comanches' turn to be forced from Pikes Peak. In an 1851 treaty with the United States, the Jicarillas were given a reservation near Abiquiu, New Mexico. In 1887, they were assigned their present reservation in Dulce, New Mexico. Today there are approximately 3,300 members of the Jicarilla Apache Nation.

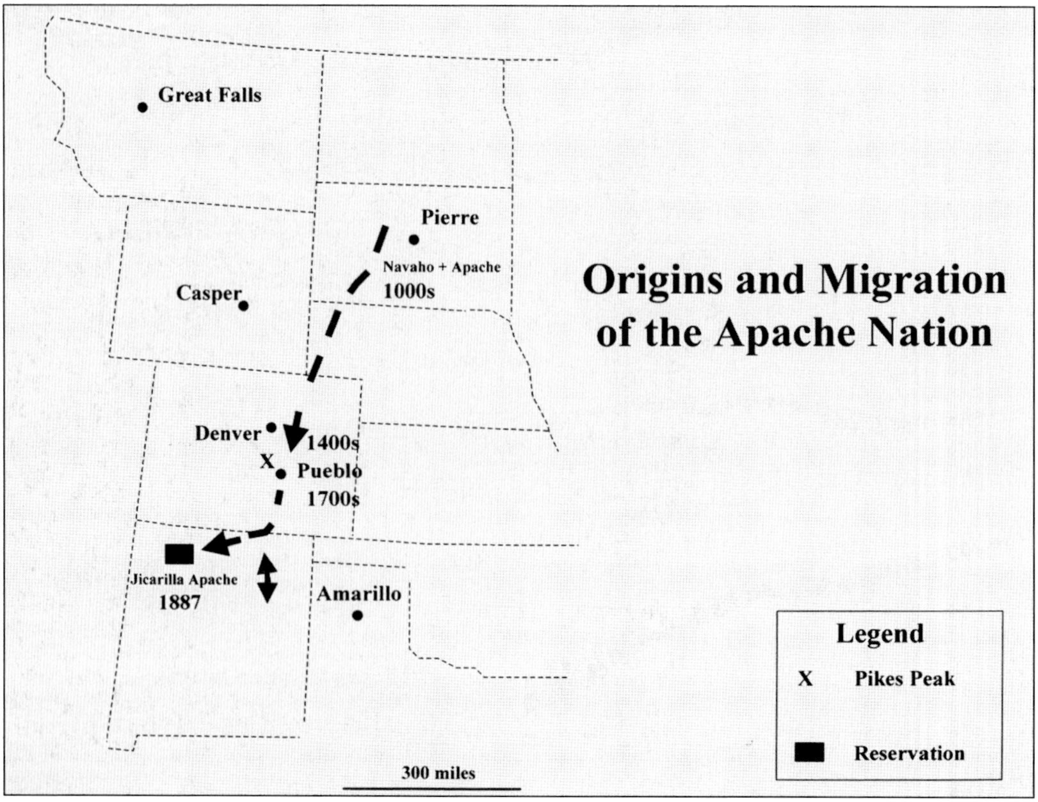

Origins and Migration of the Apache Nation

Map showing migration: Navaho + Apache 1000s (Pierre area), 1400s (Denver), 1700s (Pueblo), Jicarilla Apache 1887 reservation.

Legend:
X — Pikes Peak
■ — Reservation

Scale: 300 miles

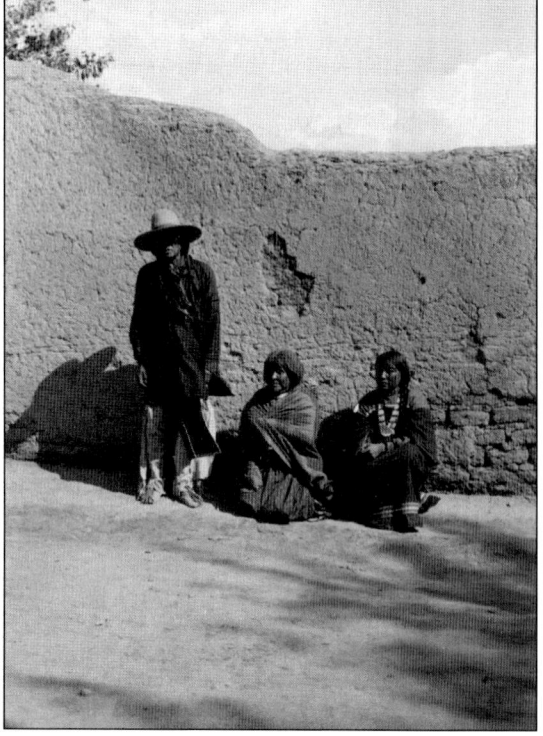

There is no definitive date that can be attached to the Athapascan migrations across the Bering Strait. At some point thousands of years ago, they began moving southward along the Rocky Mountains. Apaches, their descendants, arrived in Colorado and New Mexico around 1400 CE. The Spanish explorer Coronado made first contact with them in 1542 at Pecos Pueblo in New Mexico.

When Don Juan de Onate marched into northern New Mexico in 1598, he claimed the countryside through violence. More than 2,000 American Indians died in resisting the Spanish invasion. Onate was the first European to bequeath the name *apache* (from the Zuni word for enemy) on these "Lords of the Plains" when he described their nation. (Courtesy DPL.)

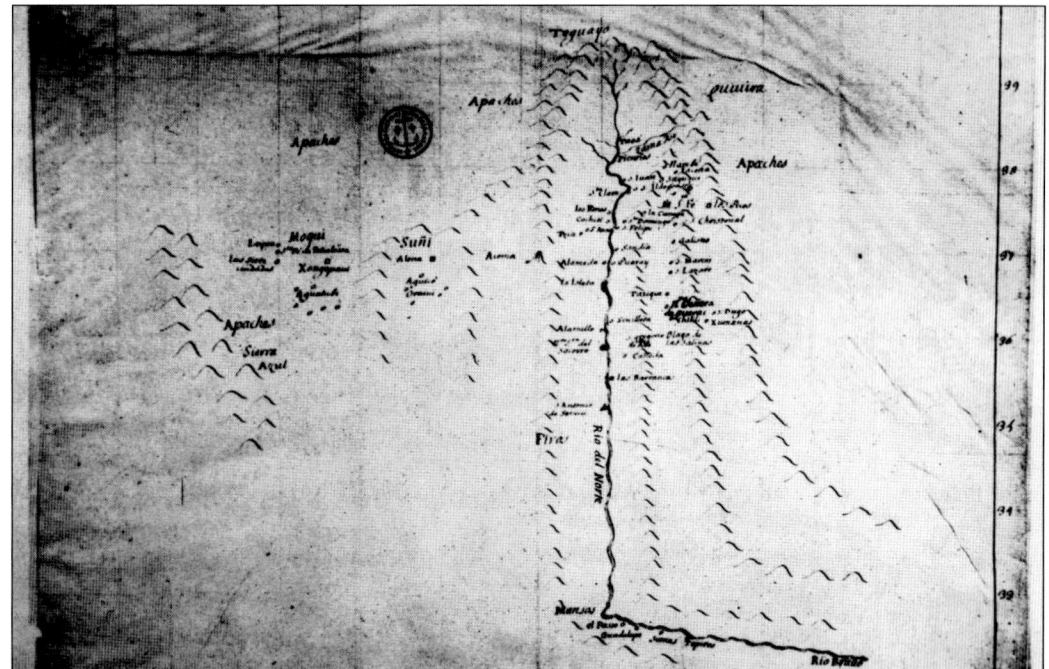

Penalosa carefully noted the locations of all First Nations on this 1680 map after the Pueblo Revolt forced a Spanish retreat into Mexico. The uprising defined Spanish-Indian politics for the next century. (Courtesy Museum of New Mexico.)

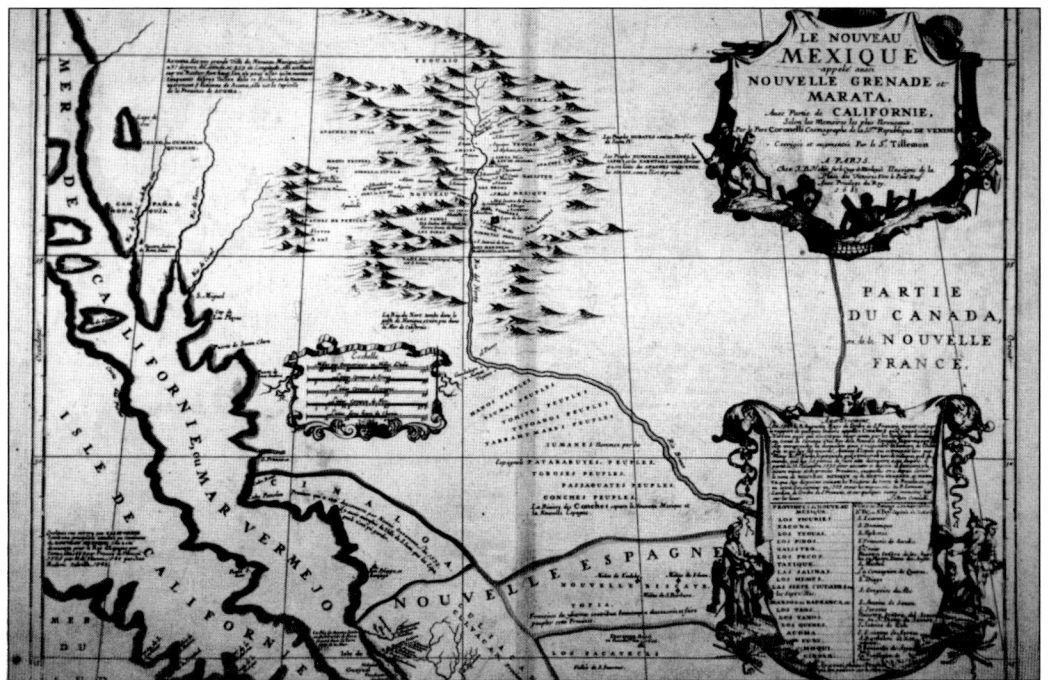

Spanish territory in the western United States is identified on this French map by Coronelli dating from about 1686–1688. The mountains east of Santa Fe are marked as the territory of "Apache Vaqueros" (Apache buffalo hunters). (Courtesy Museum of New Mexico.)

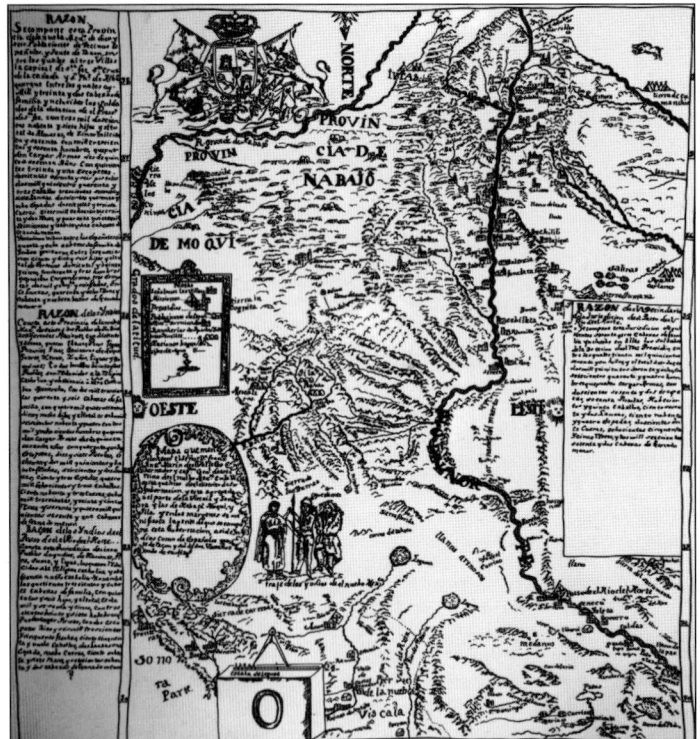

A buffalo lunges menacingly in the upper right corner of this 1758 Spanish map marking the villages of the fierce Comanche Nation. Extending slightly above Taos, the map designates the area around Abiquiu, west of Santa Fe, as the "province" of the Utes. The Apaches are now located on the plains east of Albuquerque, having been displaced by the Comanches. (Courtesy Museum of New Mexico.)

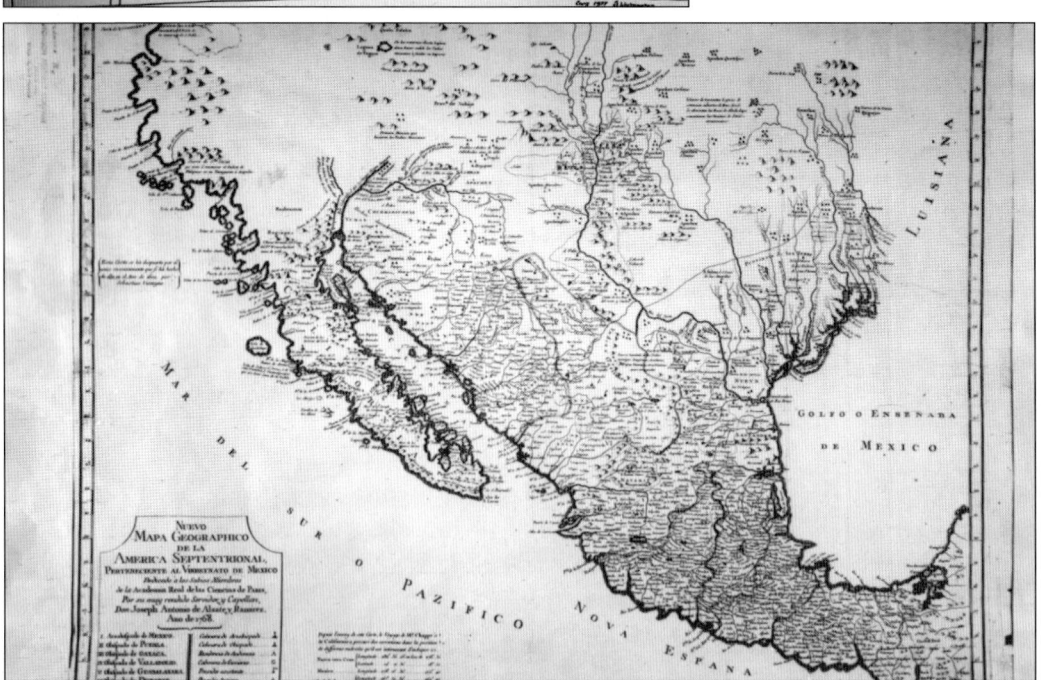

This 1768 map places the Jicarilla Apaches in a valley between the Rio Grande River (*Rio del Norte*) and the Taos Mountains (*Sierra de Taos*). They were first mentioned in 1700 by Gov. Pedro Rodriques Cubero, who impaled an Apache's head on a pole in Taos in order to warn the "apaches of la Xicarilla" against harboring Spanish fugitives. (Courtesy DPL.)

In 1779, some 200 Ute and Apache scouts joined Anza's 600-man army on a campaign against the Comanches, as first mentioned in chapter 2. This Apache warrior, like his ancient Comanche adversary, *Cuerno Verde* (Green Horn), wears a buffalo headdress with one horn painted green. Green Horn Mountain, southwest of Pueblo, is named for the famous Comanche chief. (Courtesy DPL.)

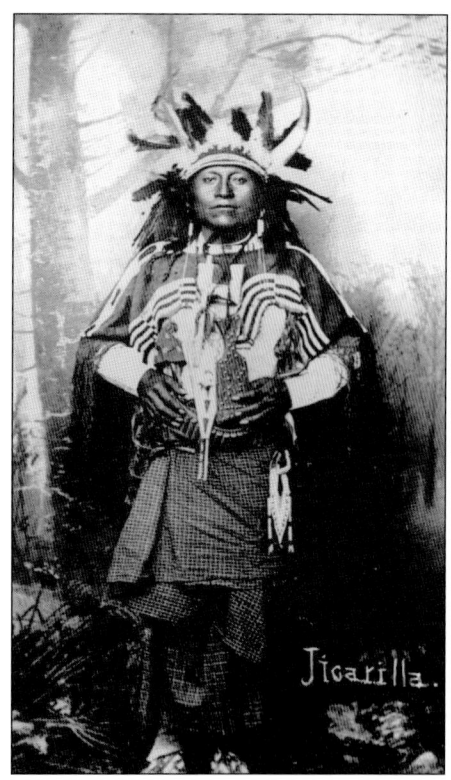

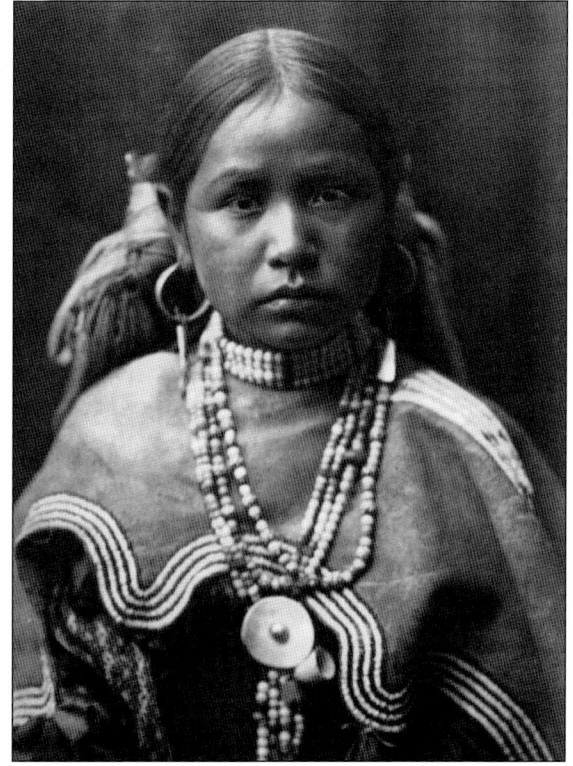

Federal officials issued woolen coats infested with smallpox to members of the Ute and Apache Nations in 1854. In December of that year, Moaches and Jicarillas launched a retaliatory raid against El Pueblo (Pueblo), killing 14 of the residents and taking the remaining 3 as hostages. New Mexico's governor, William S. Messervy, responded by calling for the extinction of the Apache people. (Courtesy DPL.)

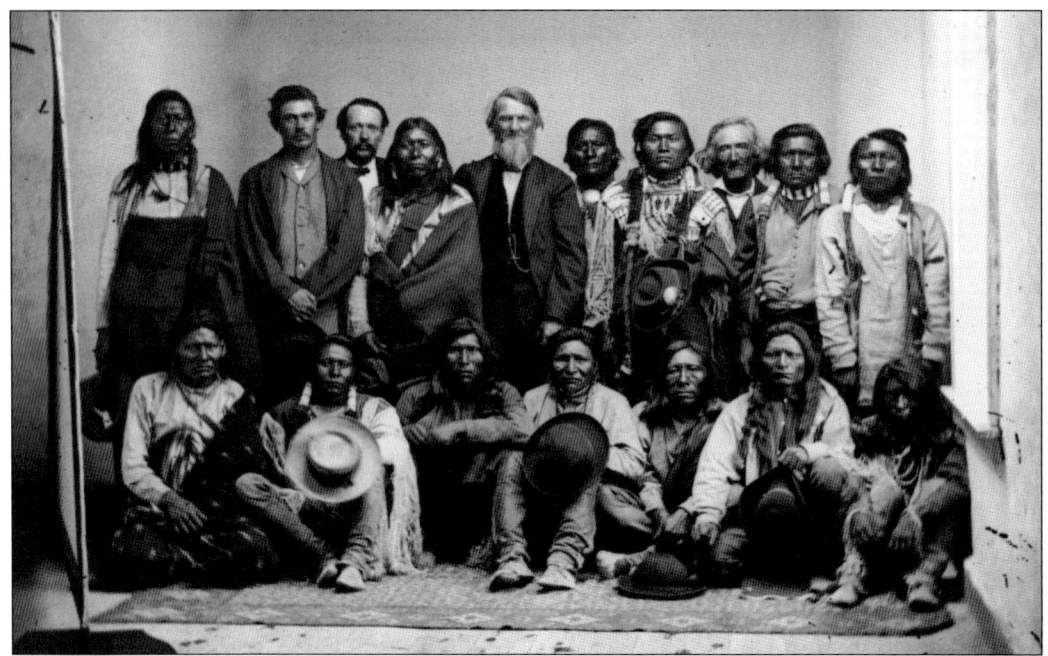

Indian agent William F. M. Arny (second row, fifth from left) poses with a delegation of Ute and Jicarilla Apache Indians in 1868. Appointed to the post by Pres. Andrew Johnson, Arny assumed his duties at Abiquiu in May 1867. His agency served about 1,100 Weeminuches, 700 Capotes, and 300 Jicarilla Apaches. (Courtesy Museum of New Mexico.)

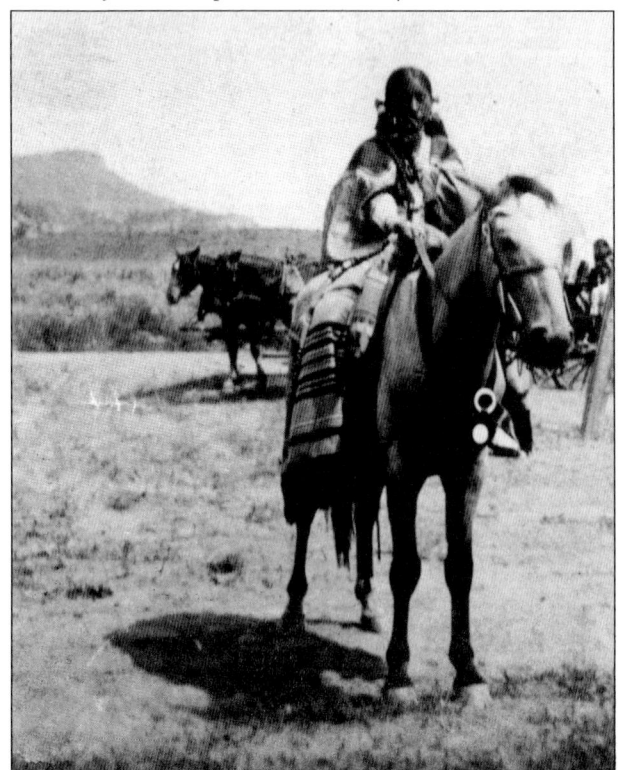

Alice, a young Apache woman, reflects the pride of her nation as people of the horse. Her mount is fitted with the finest regalia, including a beautifully woven blanket over its haunches. One of the most famous Apache warriors was a woman named Lozen. (Courtesy Pikes Peak Historical Society, Forster Collection.)

This beautiful young woman epitomizes Apache womanhood. One of her contemporaries, Lozen, remains larger than life to her people. Lozen was said to have the power of locating the enemy. She would hold out her arms and walk in a circle while praying to *Ussen*, the Creator. When facing the direction of the enemy, her hands would suddenly tingle and turn purple. (Courtesy DPL.)

Apache women attended council meetings with the men but seldom spoke unless they felt they could contribute something vital to the issue at hand. Generosity was a key element of leadership, as was consensus building. A chief was chosen based on his speaking ability and diplomacy, and he rarely went against the wishes of his people. (Courtesy DPL.)

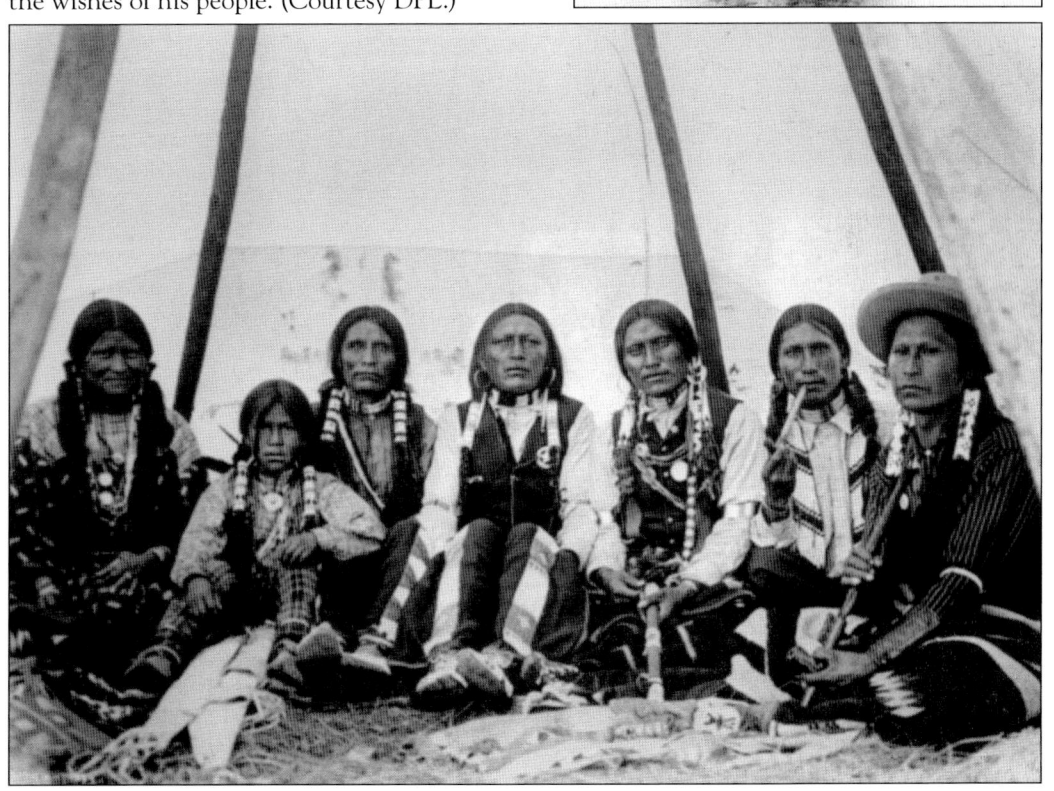

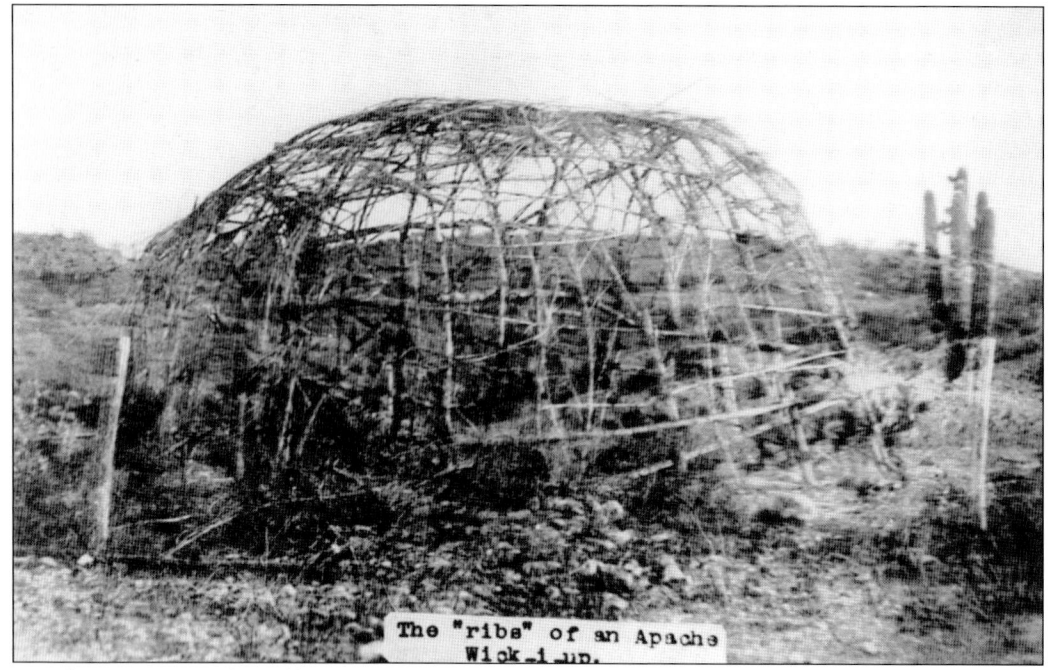

The "ribs" of an Apache Wick-i-up.

Apacherias, or Apache villages, consisted of a cluster of wickiups. These differed from the Ute structures of the same name in that they were dome-shaped rather than conical. Poles were bent and tied in the center and the circle covered with whatever natural materials could be found in the area. An Apache woman could construct this home in about four hours. (Courtesy DPL.)

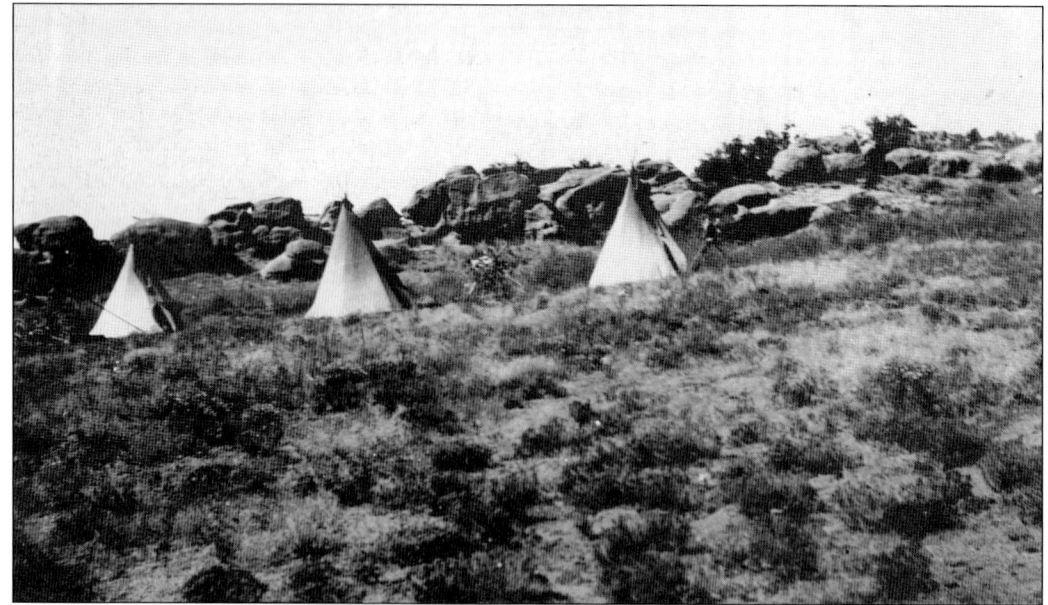

"In the beginning, everything that was to be [humans and animals] had a *hactcin* (a spirit)." In this creation story, Apaches say that "these spirits dwelt in the darkness of the underworld." Magically, light was created, but Sun and Moon escaped onto the Earth. Holy Boy led the people and animals up ladders made of sunbeams and onto Earth. For this reason, Apaches call themselves "the people who emerged from the underworld." (Courtesy Pikes Peak Historical Society.)

As one Indian agent described them in *The Jicarilla Apache Tribe* by Veronica E. Tiller, Jicarillas were "never disloyal to the government, lawless toward their neighbors, or unkind to him; they were trustworthy, although deprived of knowledge, moral teaching, and kind treatment." The agent goes on to say that they were devoted "to truth, attention to their young, kindness to their sick, and charity to their aged ones." (Courtesy DPL.)

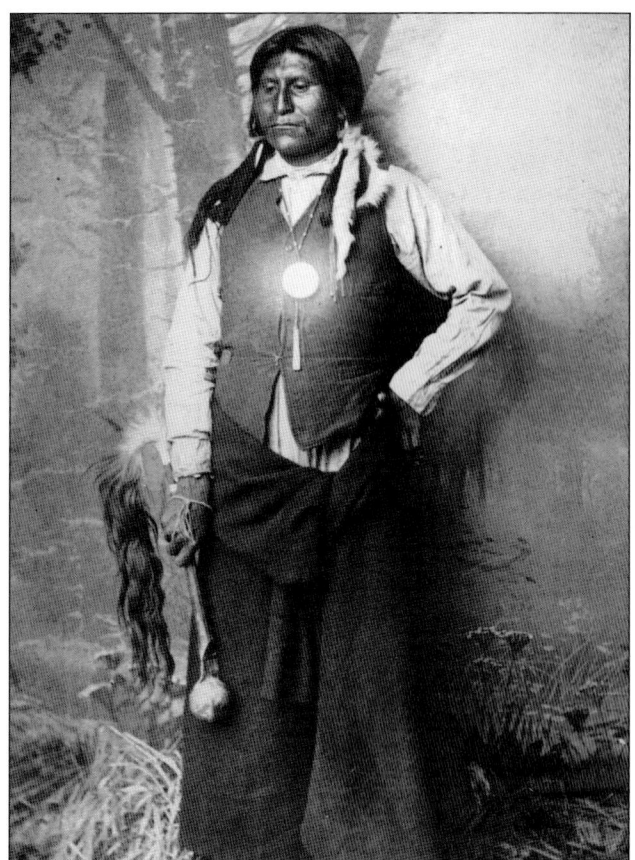

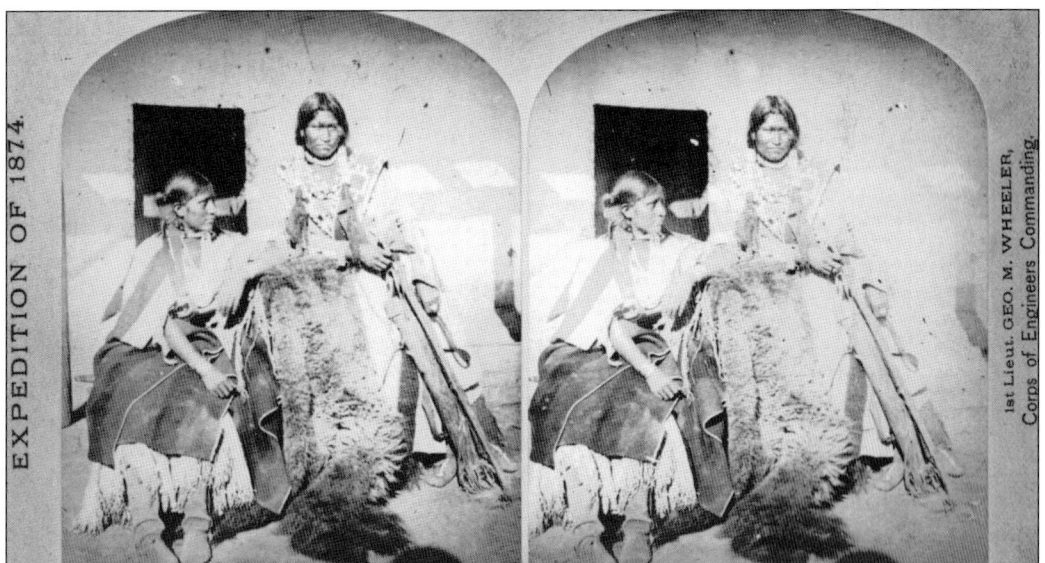

Newlyweds, such as this couple at Abiquiu in 1874, referred to one another as "you with whom I go about." Courtship consisted of the man killing a deer or other game and leaving it outside her tipi. The woman indicated her acceptance of him by cooking this offering and carrying it back to his camp. (Courtesy DPL.)

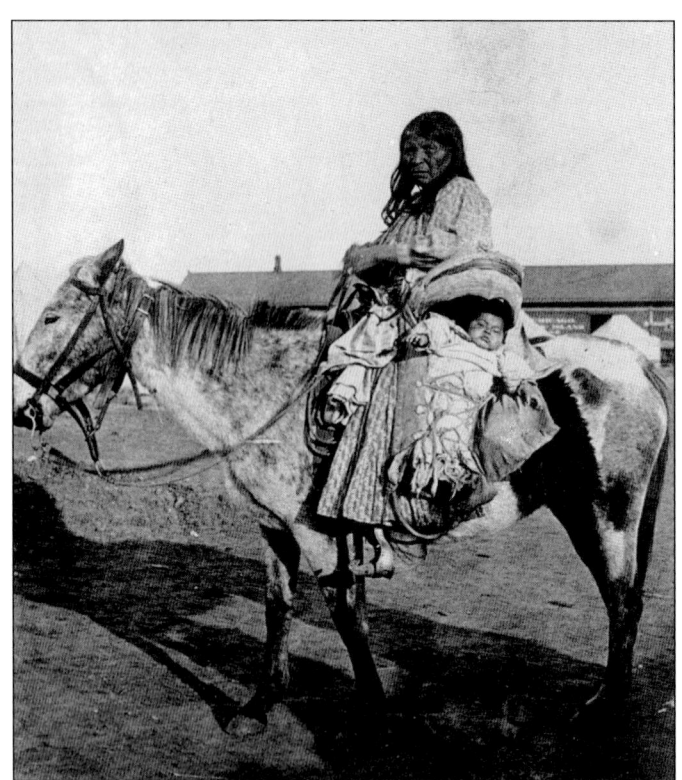

Apache grandmothers sang a sacred song while they made the cradleboard: "Good, like long life it moves back and forth. / Lightning dances alongside it, they say. / By means of Lightning it is fastened across. / Its strings are made of rainbows, they say. / Good, like long life the cradle is made. / Sun his chief rumbles inside, they say." These words are taken from *Apaches* by James L. Haley. (Courtesy DPL.)

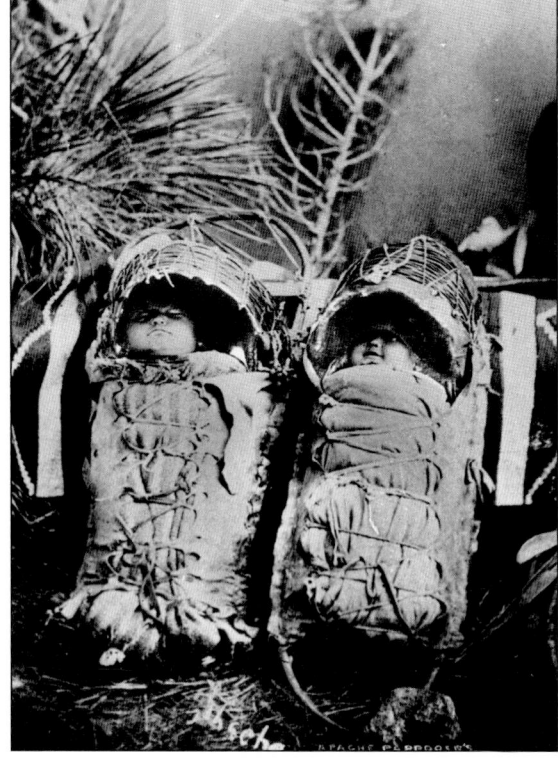

According to Haley's *Apaches*, "An infant's first name was usually given at birth, either for a peculiar characteristic or an unusual event attending its appearance. . . . This name was not expected to last beyond childhood. . . . One of the fiercest war leaders, . . . known to the whites and Mexicans as Geronimo (the Spanish for Jerome), had as a baby name Go-yath-khla, meaning Sleepy, or Yawns." (Courtesy DPL.)

Children were taught the Lifeways through fables and morality stories. One such story described a man who did not rub grease on his legs after eating. (Apaches felt that grease would nourish the legs.) This lazy man found himself in a dangerous situation one day and told his legs to run. They refused, instead telling him to "run with his belly." (Courtesy DPL.)

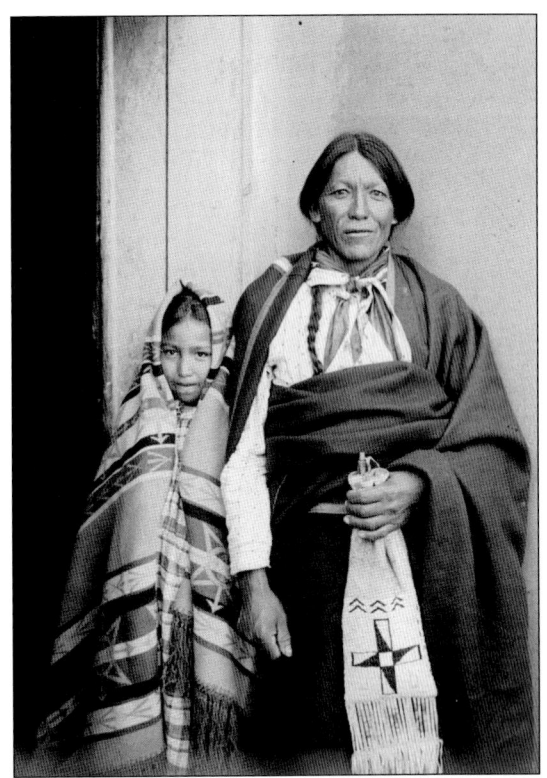

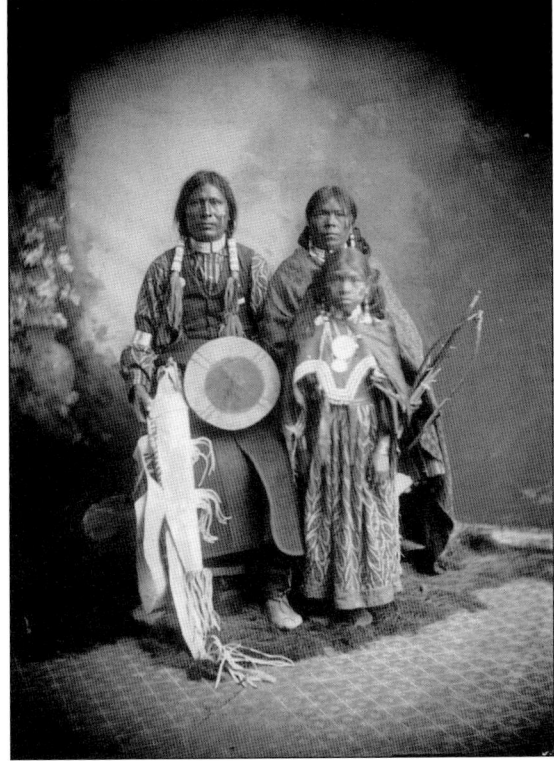

When a young girl reaches puberty, Apaches hold a Coming of Age Ceremony. The girl enters a ceremonial tipi clad in buckskins and accompanied by her mother and godmother. She carries a leather pouch of yellow pollen, which a medicine man uses to bless her. This same pollen is used by the girl to bless her people, wishing them peace, health, and happiness. (Courtesy DPL.)

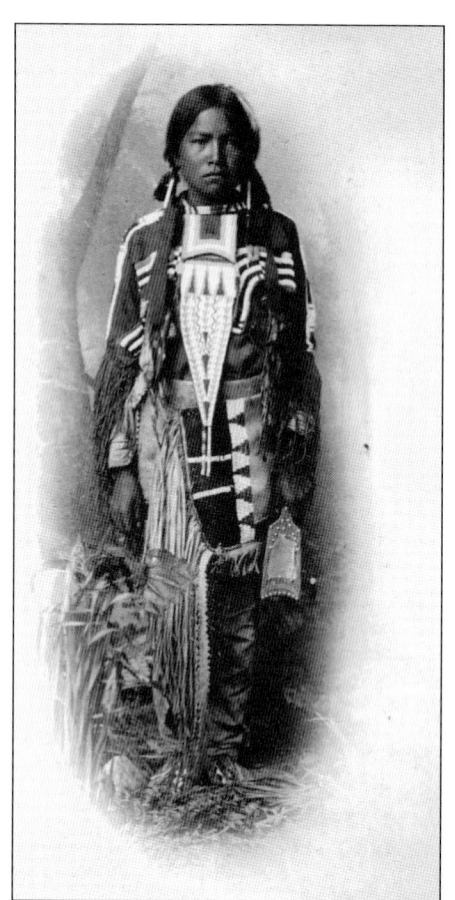

In 1893, Sen. Henry Teller forbade Indian agents from issuing rations or any kind of subsistence to any Apache family that did not send its children to boarding school. Jicarilla children were forced to attend school far from home, at Fort Lewis (near Durango) or Santa Fe. Finally, in 1902, a school was built on the reservation. (Courtesy DPL.)

Apache men, in the tradition of their ancestor warriors, take pride in their physical prowess. Geronimo told authorities that his warriors could run 40 miles a day without food and water. One of the principal feasts of the Jicarillas is the *Go Yii-Ya*, a relay race celebrated each fall. (Courtesy DPL.)

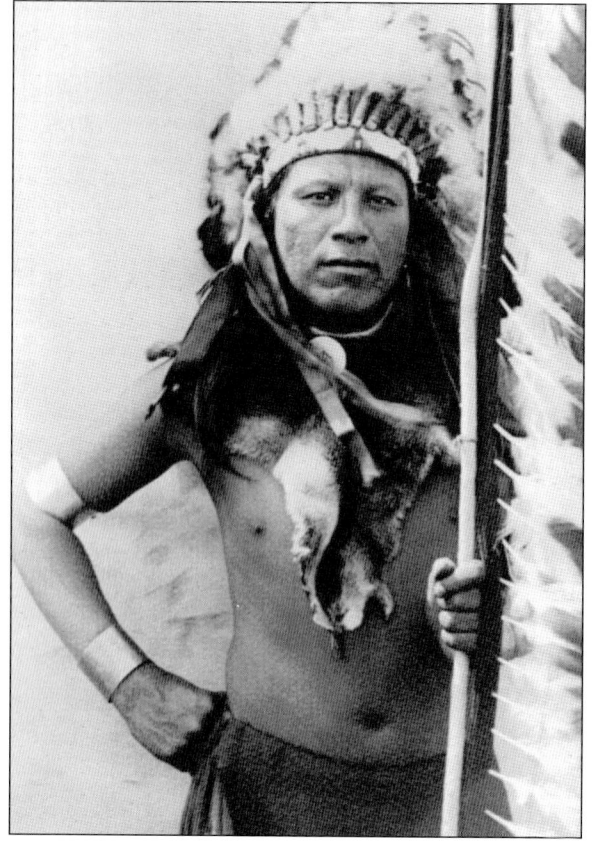

Four

NE'ME NE, THE COMANCHE NATION

"Lords of the Plains," these superb horsemen first appeared as their own nation along the Front Range of the Rockies in the early 1700s. Their dialect of the Uto-Aztecan language is related to the Utes but almost identical to the Shoshones. In the 1800s, they had five main bands totaling about 7,000: the *Penatuka*, "Honey Eaters"; the *Noyuka*, "Wanderers"; the *Kwaharu*, "Antelope Eaters"; the *Kuutsutuka*, "Buffalo Eaters"; and the *Yapaituka*, "Root Eaters."

Europeans corrupted *Penatuka* to *Padouca* and often referred to the entire nation by this name. In fact, the North Platte River was called Padouca Fork until 1805. Ne'me ne were fiercely nationalistic and determined to drive the Spanish back into Mexico—a feat they almost accomplished. With the help of their Ute and Apache allies, however, the Spanish won a decisive battle with the Comanches in 1779. They attacked a Ne'me ne village encamped at the confluence of Fountain and Monument Creeks in what is now Colorado Springs. In a running battle, the Spanish finally killed the Ne'me ne chief and his key men on the St. Charles River, southwest of Pueblo, Colorado. The nearby Green Horn Mountain commemorates this famous Ne'me ne chief, *Cuerno Verde*, or "Green Horn."

After their treaty with the Spanish in 1786, the *Ne'me ne* pushed on into Texas. Peace was still not on their agenda, and the famous Texas Rangers were organized as defense against their depredations. In an 1865 treaty, the Comanches were given a reservation in the Texas Panhandle and part of Oklahoma. This treaty was later amended, though, and in 1869, they were confined to a reservation in southwestern Oklahoma that they now share with Kiowas and Apaches. Current nation enrollment is approximately 13,391.

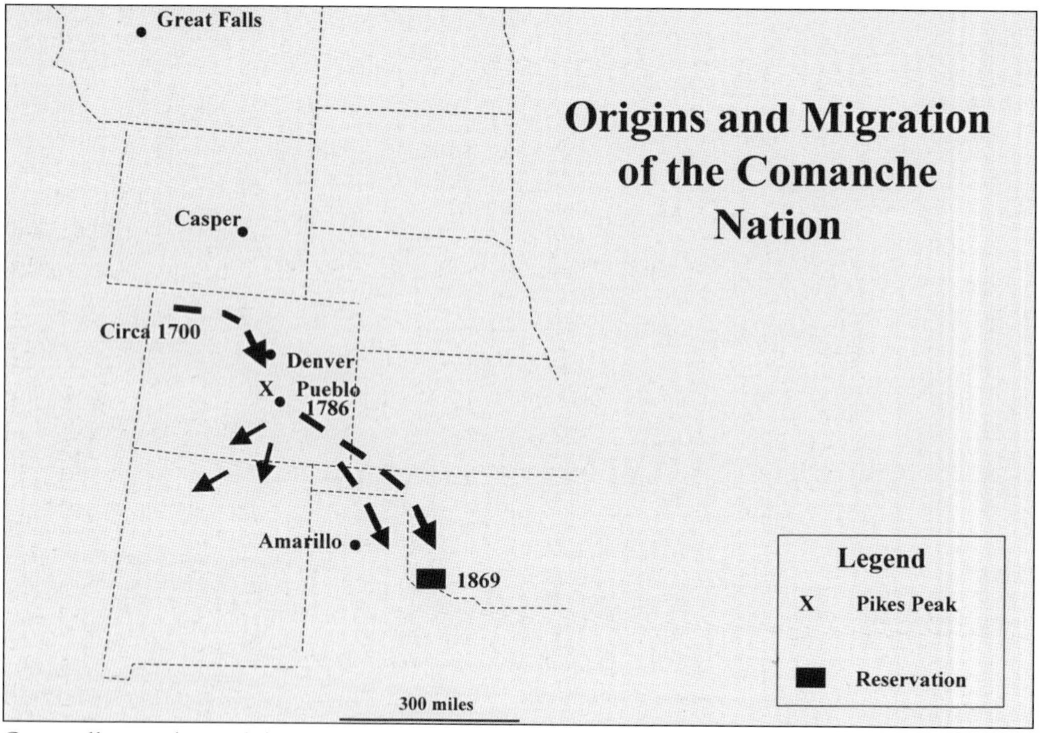

Origins and Migration of the Comanche Nation

Originally members of the Ute Nation, the Shoshone people splintered off around 1680, after they acquired the horse. Linguistically, Comanches are most closely related to these Shoshone cousins. When the two nations split sometime before 1730, Comanches ranged along the Wyoming border before spreading down along Colorado's Front Range.

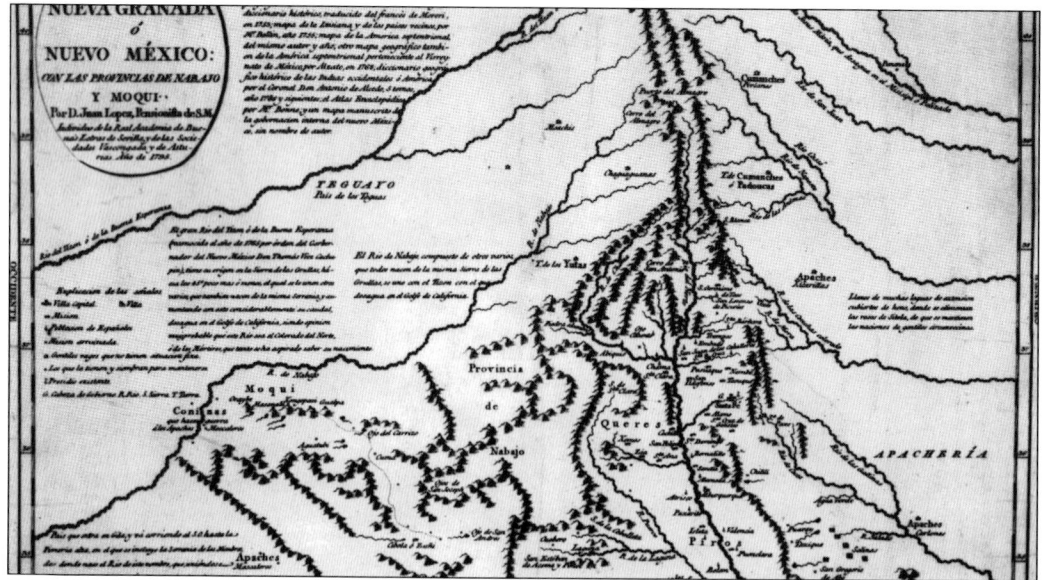

Cerro del Almagre (Pikes Peak) and *Puerto del Almagre* (Ute Pass) are shown for the first time on this 1795 Spanish map. This map was made after Gov. Juan Bautista de Anza's successful 1779 campaign against the Comanche. Anza's Ute scouts led him across South Park and down Ute Pass for the decisive battle at what is now America the Beautiful Park. (Courtesy Museum of New Mexico.)

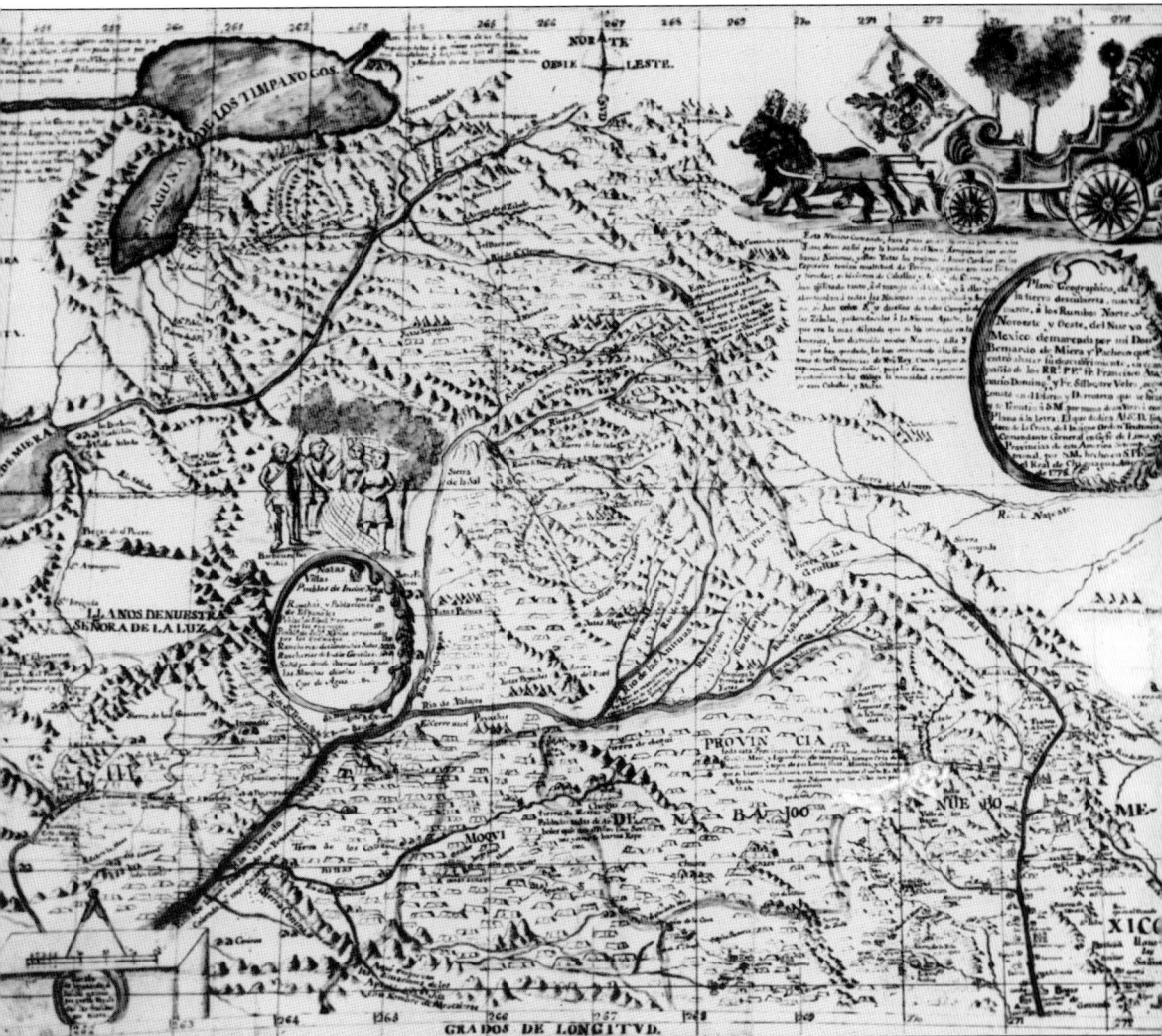

The caption in the upper right corner of this 1778 map of New Mexico translates as follows: "This nation of the Comanches, made just a few years ago [around 1703], first appeared among the Utes. They say they left the northern band [Yampaticas?], breaking their nations apart because the Utes cheated when they made trade with the Spanish, when they overloaded their dogs with pelts and items for sale, exchanging these items for horses and firearms and gaining knowledge in the handling of horses. That these Comanches raided other nations with agility and spirit. That they expelled the buffalo camps of the Apache Nation so that they now are the most extensive of the First Nations, having destroyed all the others until only they remain. They [Comanches] have been cornered on the [northern] frontier of the provinces of our king because their horses and mules suffer from the [Comanches'] lack of knowledge about their proper care." (Translated by Celinda Reynolds Kaelin in 2004; courtesy Museum of New Mexico.)

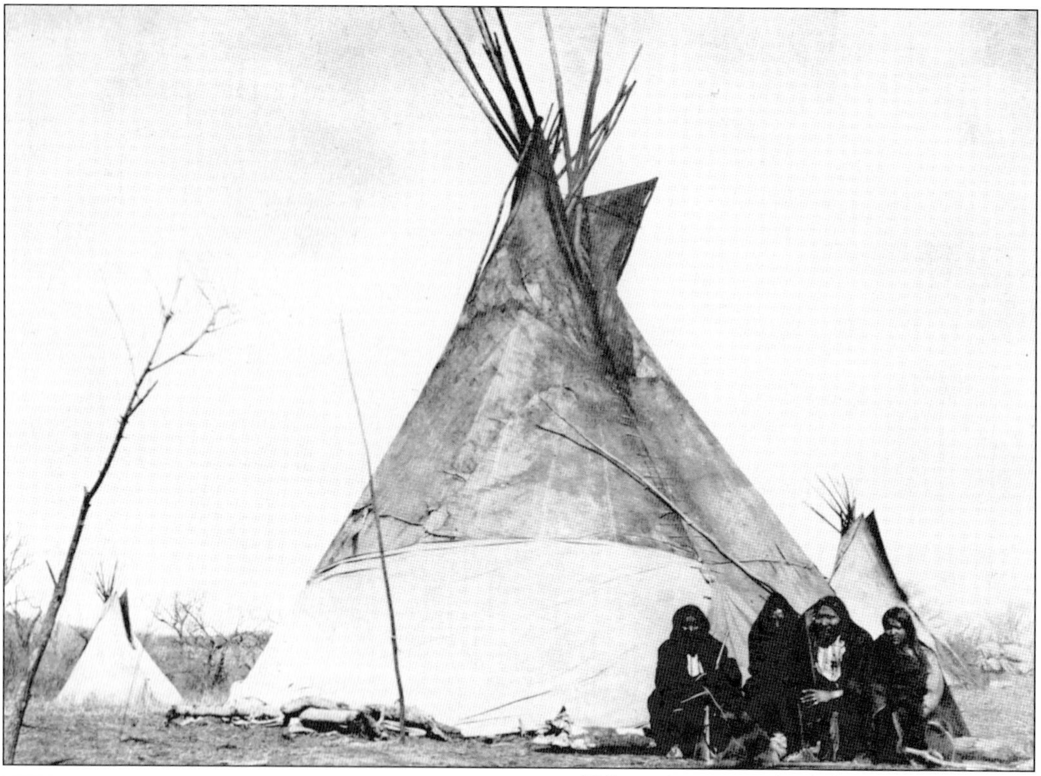

When Anza attacked the Comanche village on August 31, 1779, he wrote that he estimated Cuerno Verde's band at about 700 to 800 by "counting the tents [tipis] they were about to pitch, which are said to number more than 120. It is well known that six to eight warriors inhabit each." (Courtesy Library of Congress.)

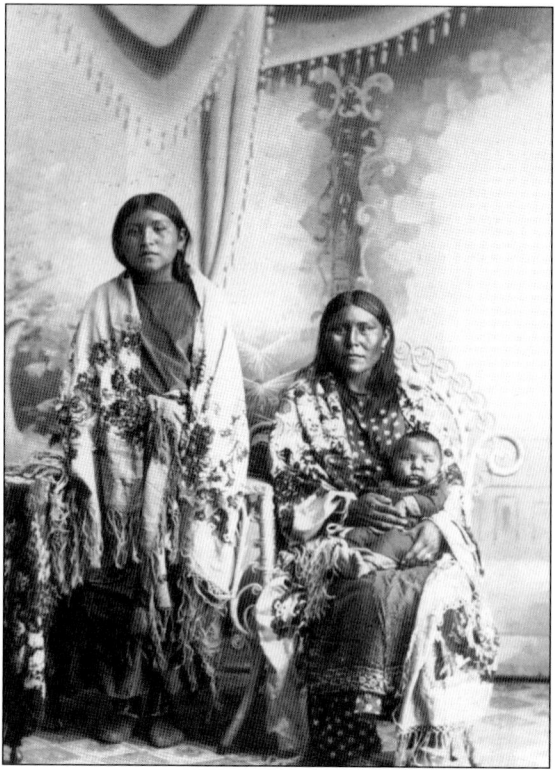

After he attacked the Comanche camp, Anza wrote, "Even the women and children took precipitous flight, . . . and in a running combat that lasted for about another league [three miles] . . . we managed to kill eighteen of the strongest [warriors]. . . . And it was necessary to kill more than thirty women and children who ran right along with their parents." (Courtesy DPL.)

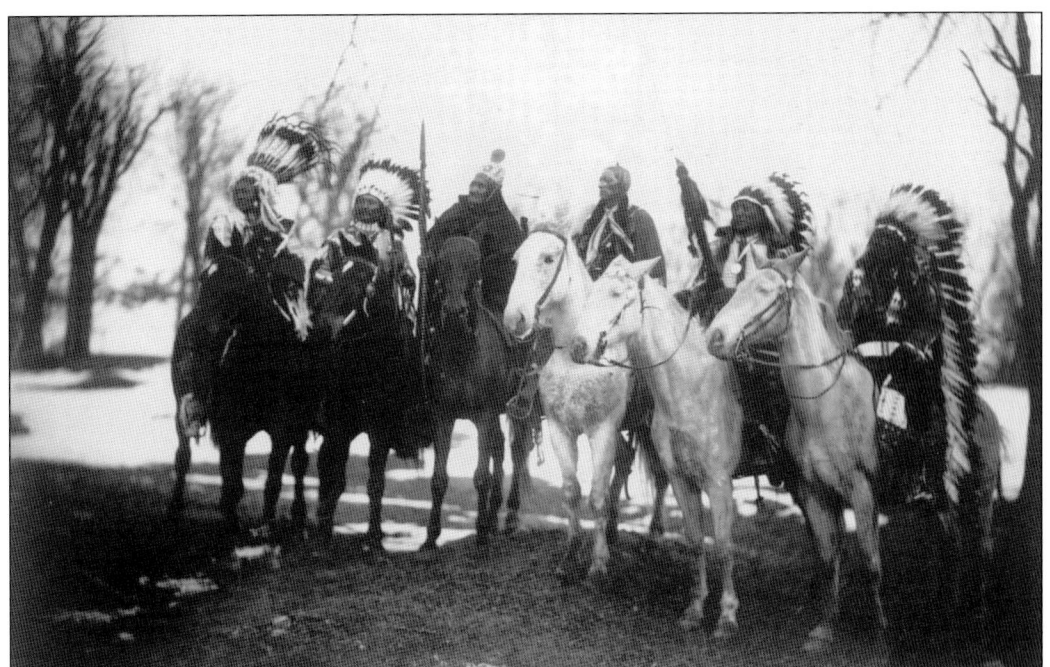

In 1905, E. S. Curtis managed to capture this image of leaders from six different nations. Among them are Southern Ute chief Buckskin Charley (second from left) and Comanche chief Quanah Parker (fourth from left), traditionally enemies. In 1977, some 200 years after the Utes joined Anza in his campaign against the Comanches, representatives of the Ute and Comanche Nations signed a peace treaty at Ignacio, Colorado. (Courtesy Library of Congress.)

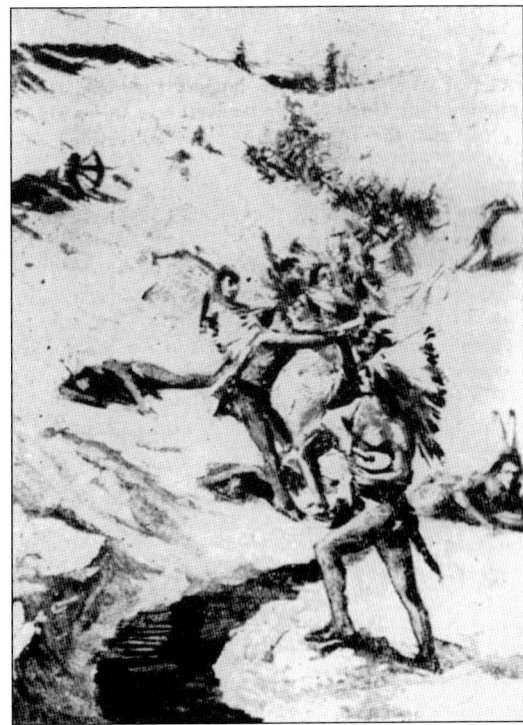

William Drannan and Kit Carson witnessed this battle in Florissant between the Utes and Comanches in 1852. Drannan wrote that "the war chief would take [his war drum] under one arm and beat it with a stick. . . . At the first tap the war-whoop could be heard, and in a few moments both tribes of Indians were down at the little stream, each formed in line on his own side." (Courtesy DPL.)

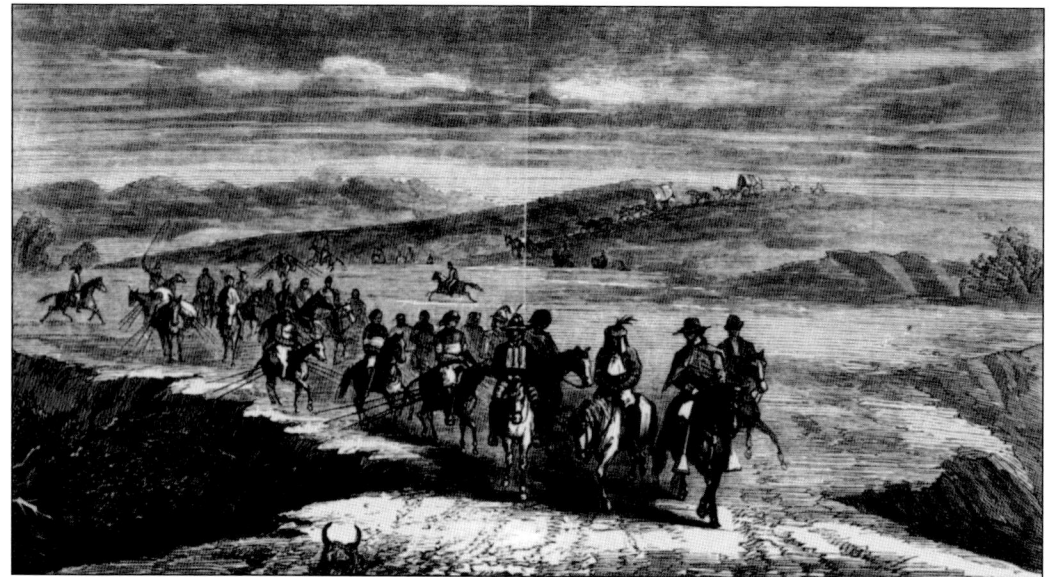

This illustration from Frank Leslie's 1867 newspaper shows the Comanches on their way to the Great Council on Medicine Lodge Creek. Before signing the treaty, Chief Ten Bears remonstrated, "When I was at Washington the Great Father told me that all the Comanche land was ours. . . . So why do you ask us to leave the rivers, and the sun, and the wind, and live in houses?" (Courtesy Library of Congress.)

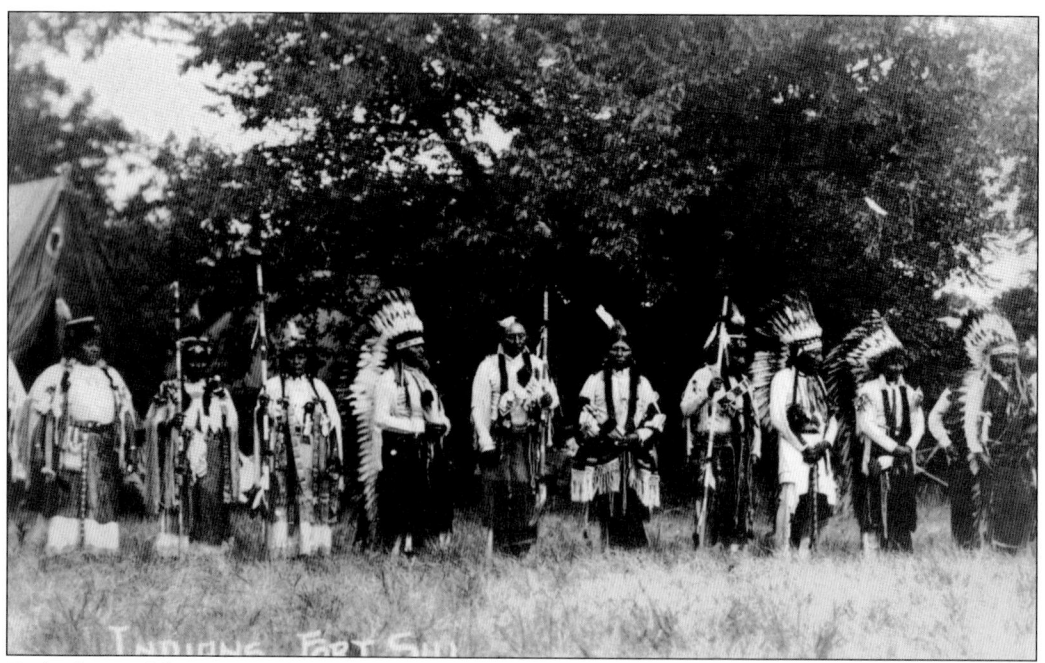

Only three of the Comanche bands—the Yep-eaters, Those Who Move Often, and the Wasps—signed the Medicine Lodge Treaty of 1867. The Meat Eater and Antelope bands refused. When the treaty bands joined the Kiowas and Kiowa-Apaches on their new reservation in Oklahoma, these Lords of the Plains became wards of the federal government. (Courtesy DPL.)

In 1871, Quanah Parker, chief of the Antelope band, led a blistering counterattack against Col. Ranald MacKenzie at Blanco Canyon. He succeeded in recapturing the Comanche horses—and all of the army's horses as well. Five years later, at Fort Sill, Parker offered to return MacKenzie's personal mount (a gray stallion), but MacKenzie declined. (Courtesy Library of Congress.)

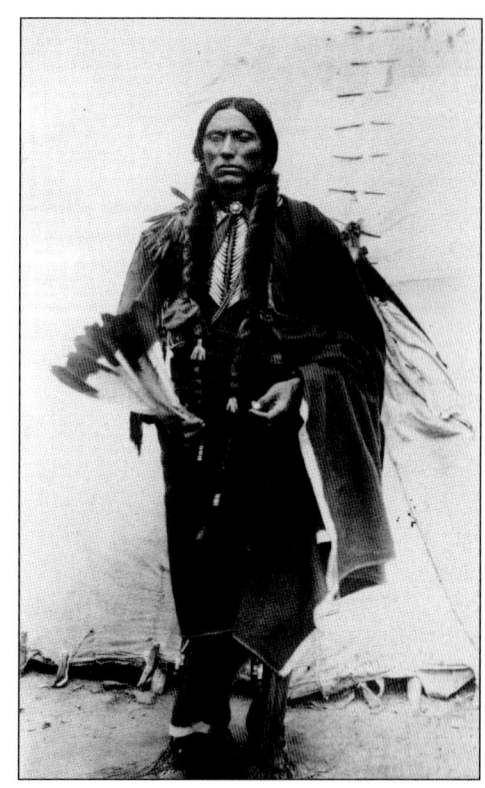

The last hostile Comanches suffered an overwhelming defeat at Palo Duro Canyon in 1874. These warriors were placed in a concentration camp at Fort Sill, where historian Ernest Wallace writes that "once a day a wagon pulled up by the walls and hunks of raw meat were pitched over the fence." Approximately 1,076 Kiowas and 1,597 Comanches resided at Fort Sill by 1875, housed in villages such as these. (Courtesy Library of Congress.)

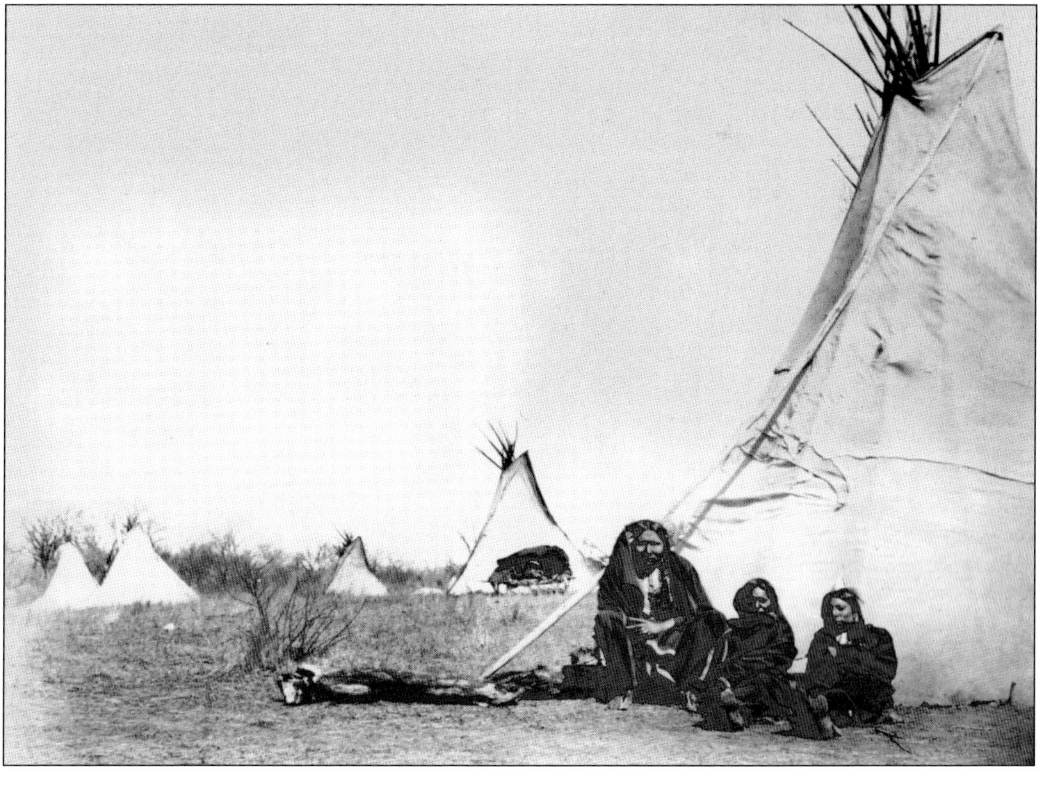

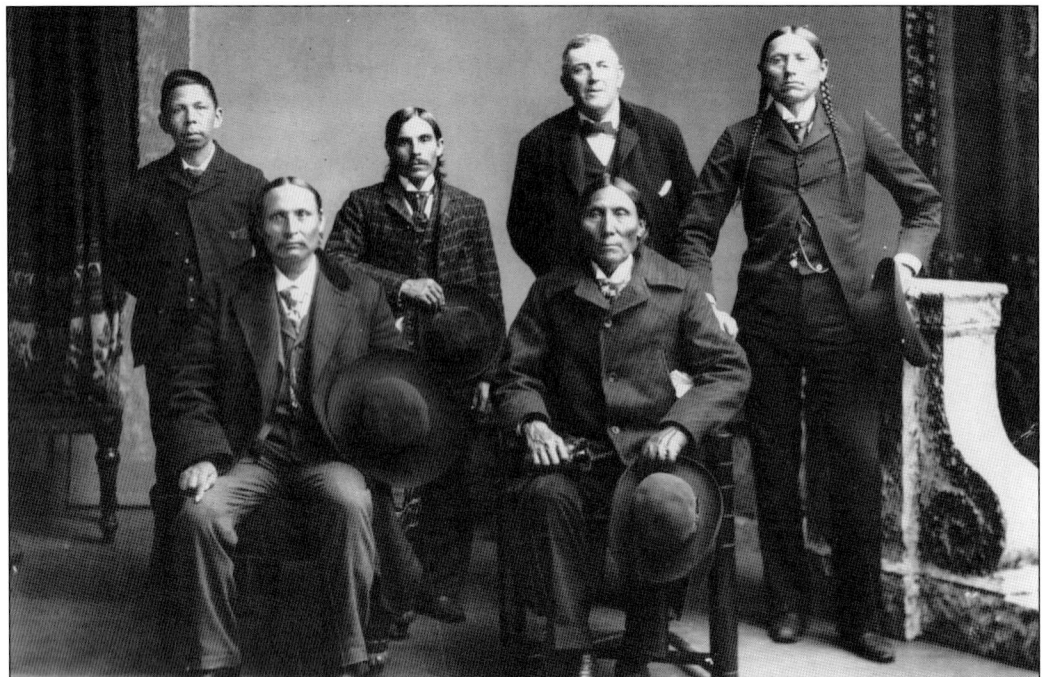

Encroachments on reservation land were a constant problem for the Comanches. In the 1890s, several delegations traveled to Washington in the hopes of solving the dilemma. Finally, they tried leasing the land as a solution. At one point, 1.3 million acres of Comanche reservation were under lease to stock growers. (Courtesy Library of Congress.)

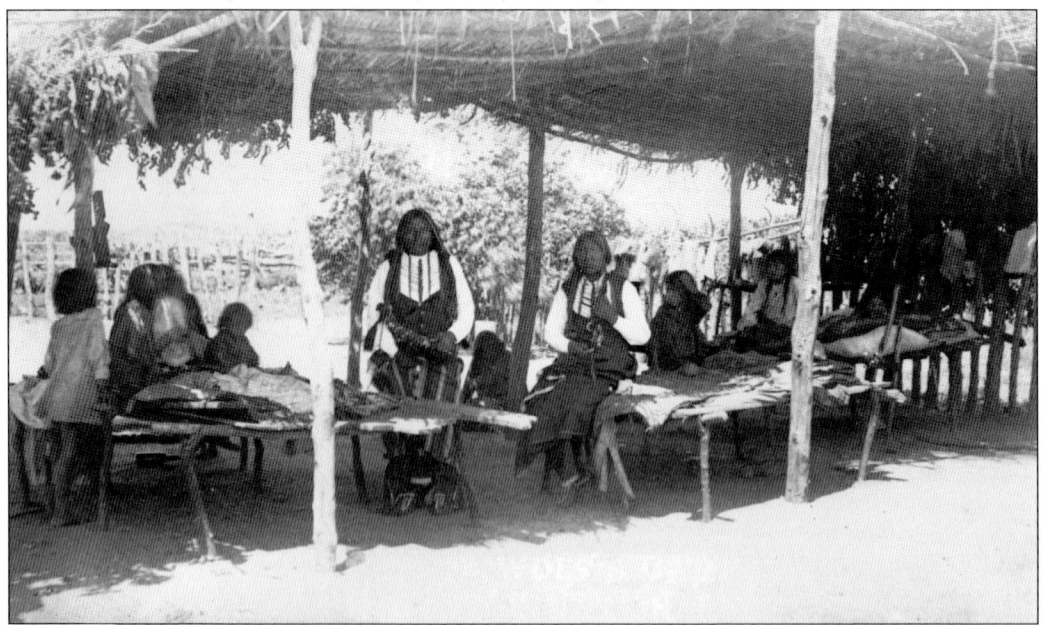

Chief White Wolf and his followers are sheltered under a brush shade. Comanche chiefs gained their status by personal bravery or an exhibition of courage and skill. As generosity was vital for leadership, chiefs always distributed the spoils of war evenly among the warriors. (Courtesy Library of Congress.)

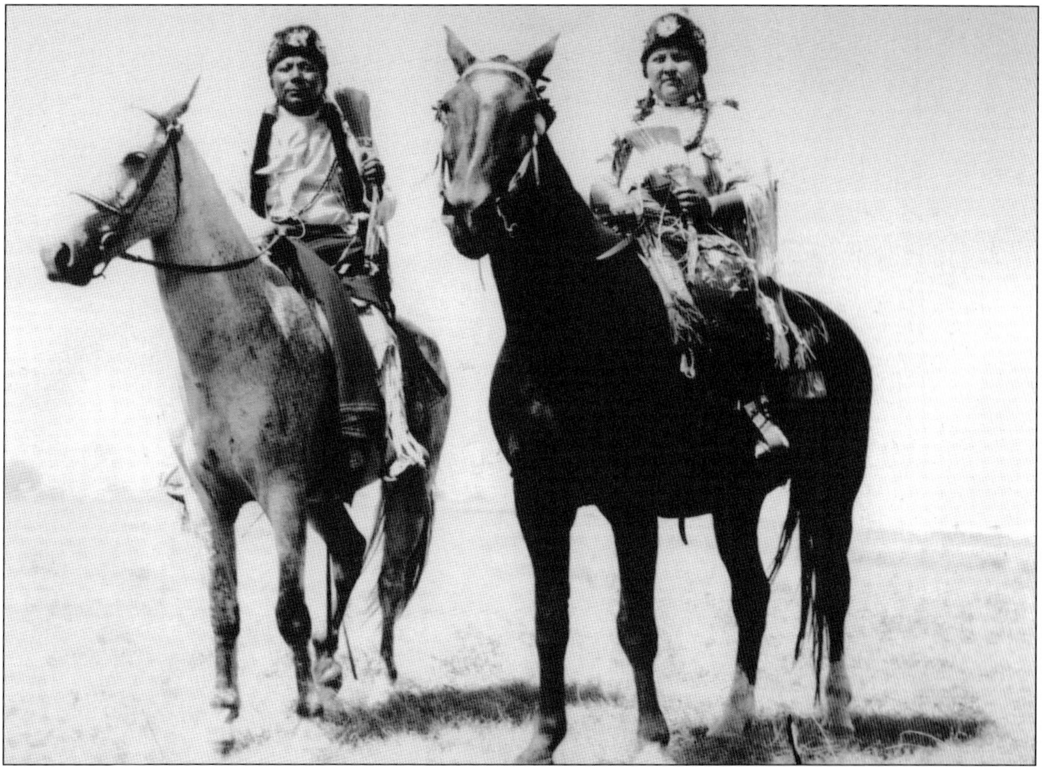

As the Comanche Nation became a horse culture, the impact was felt in such social customs as marriage. In the old Shoshonean way, a man and woman need only sleep together to be considered married. However, with the new prosperity of the horse, a bride was often won by the gift of horses to her family. (Courtesy DPL.)

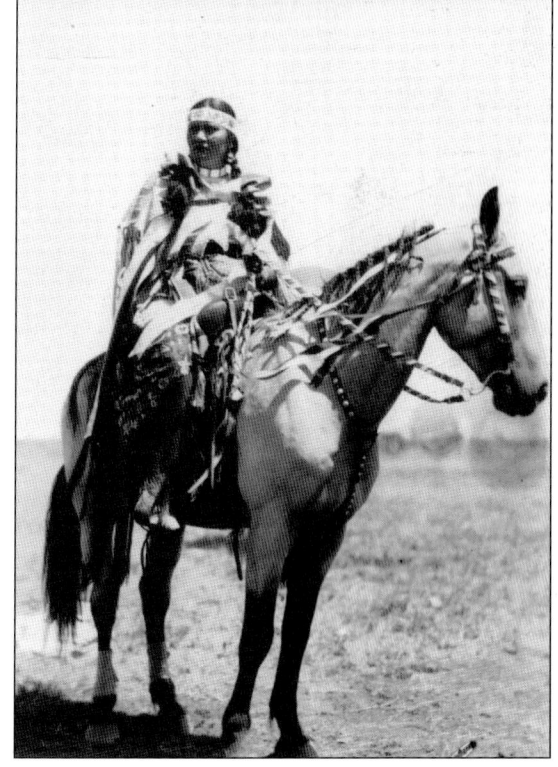

A young Comanche warrior returned to camp after his first horse raid. According to *The Comanches* by Wallace, the next morning, "some fine young maidens dressed up like warriors. They went over to the young brave's tipi. . . . They did the Shakedown Dance and sang the songs. The boy's father . . . was proud of his son, so he gave these girls what they wanted. He gave them two horses." (Courtesy DPL.)

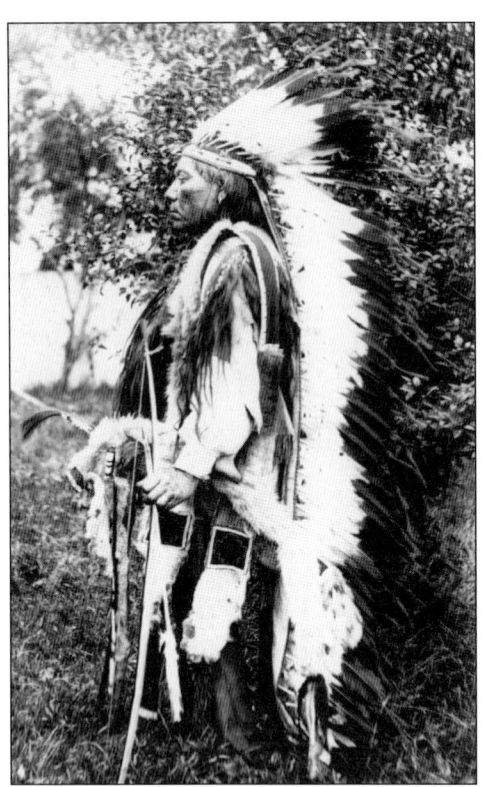

Historian Homer Thrall described Comanches as "half horse, half man," while others refer to them as Lords of the Plains. White Wolf, shown here, claimed that his buffalo horse saved many lives by signaling with his ears. If he waved one ear forward, a buffalo was close. The other ear meant coyote. Both ears forward indicated the approach of a human. (Courtesy Library of Congress.)

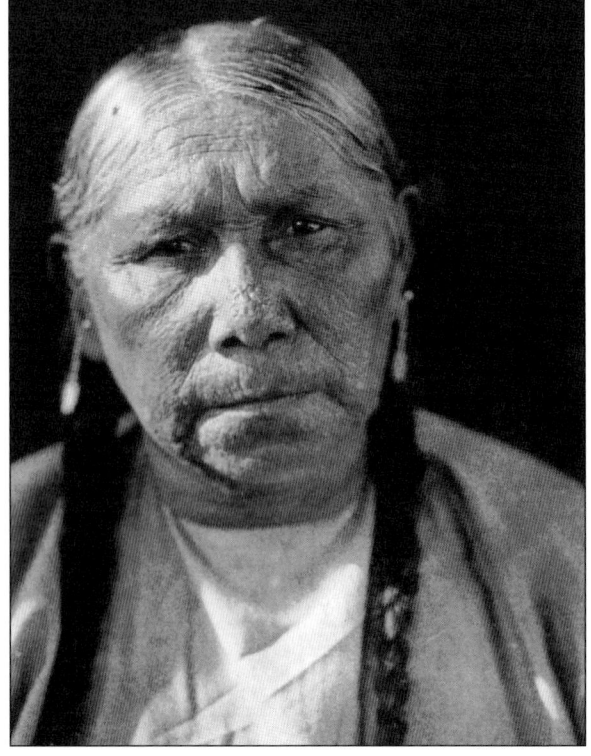

One has to wonder if this Comanche man's name, Kicha, is indicative of his true nationality. The Kichaies, of Caddoan stock, were strong allies of the Comanches. In the 1840s, they occupied the area from the Red River Valley all the way to Austin, Texas, and allowed the Comanches to freely live and trade among them. (Photograph by E. S. Curtis.)

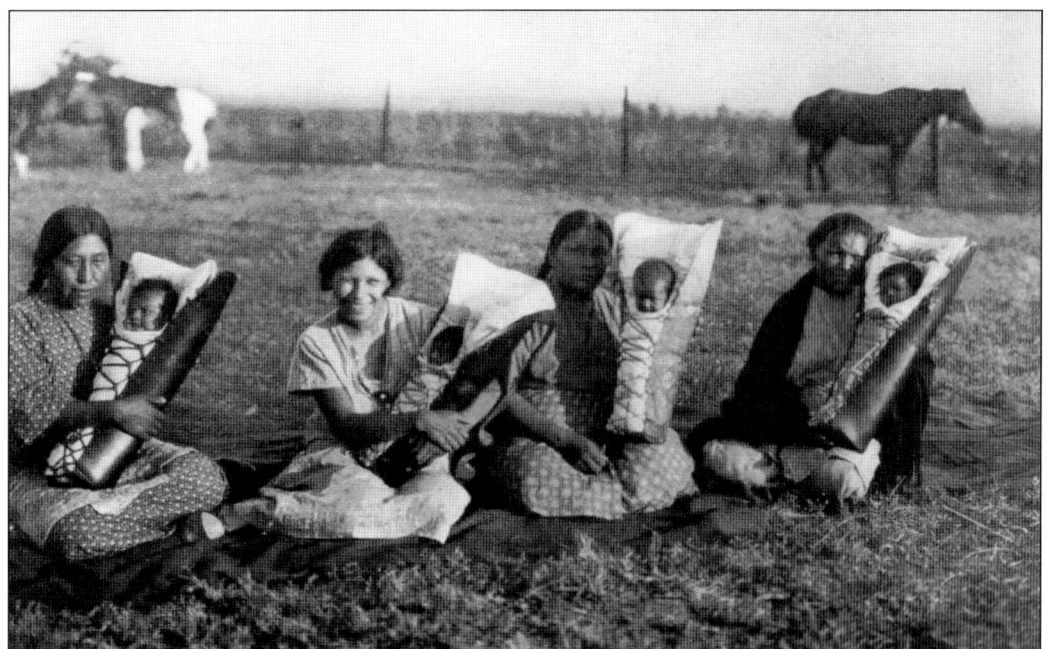

A Comanche woman kept her child tightly wrapped in soft buckskin that laced up the front and was anchored to a backboard. At night, he was rolled up in a stiff rawhide tube and placed beneath a buffalo robe between his parents. After 9 or 10 months, the child was allowed out of his cradleboard and given the freedom to crawl around. (Photograph by E. S. Curtis.)

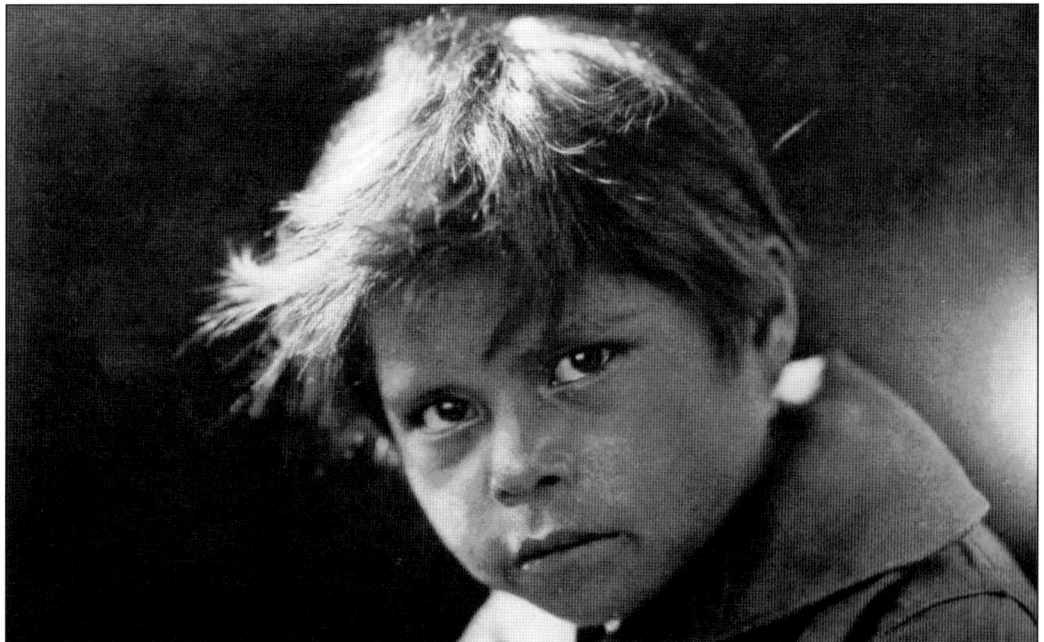

This young Comanche boy is at the age when his grandfather would give him a bow and arrows. The grandfather would then teach his young charge to ride, shoot, and hunt. He instructed the boy by telling stories of his own youth and passing on tribal history and traditions, along with legends and religion. The two affectionately called each other *tek*. (Photograph by E. S. Curtis.)

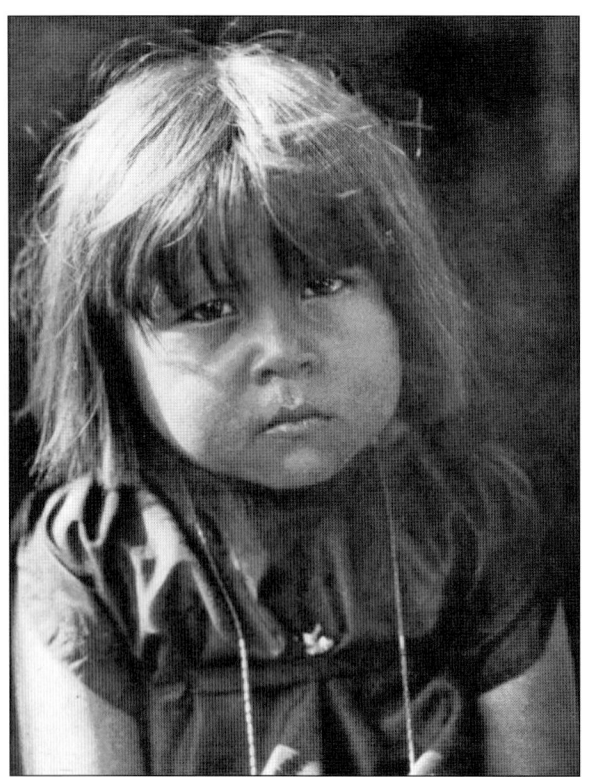

As with a boy and his grandfather, a girl and her grandmother formed a special bond, calling each other *kaku*. At first, the grandmother would give the girl small tasks like carrying water or gathering firewood. As she grew older, kaku would teach her to sew moccasins, cook, dress hides, and set up her own tipi. The girl would likely marry by the age of 16. (Photograph by E. S. Curtis.)

Pakewa, now a *tsukup*, or "old man," probably belonged to the Smoke Lodge, a special tipi where all the old men smoked the peace pipe and talked each evening. When he was too old to be useful or when he became a burden, an old man would dispose of all his property and go off alone to die. (Photograph by E. S. Curtis.)

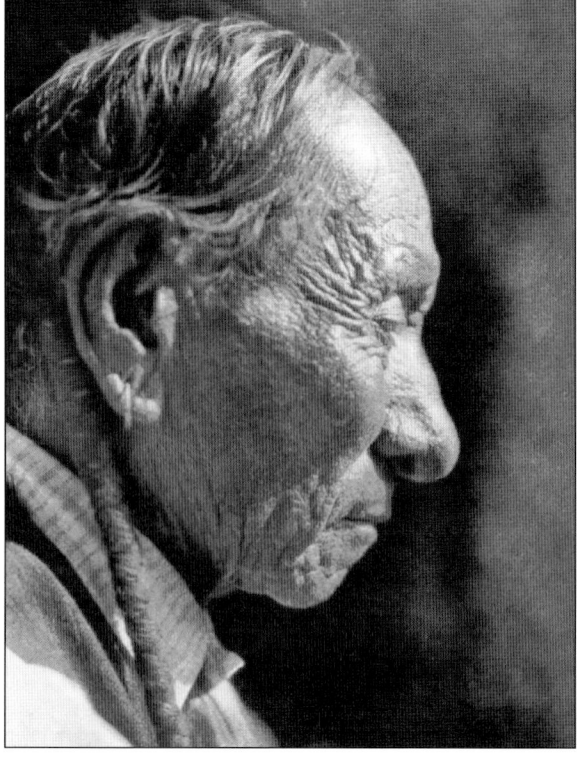

Five

INUNA-INA, THE ARAPAHO NATION

Plains Indians gave this nation its common name, Arapaho, which is a derivative of the Pawnee word for "he buys or trades," *tirapihu*. Members call themselves *Inuna-ina*, "Our People," and are part of the Algonquin language family. The Inuna-ina seem to have been originally located in the Red River Valley of northeastern Minnesota and then moved southwest across the Missouri River in the early 1800s, just ahead of their future allies, the Cheyennes.

Not long after acquiring the horse, the Inuna-ina divided into northern and southern bands. Half of the people hunted along the Bighorn and Powder Rivers, while the other half ventured along Colorado's Front Range and into the Pikes Peak region. In 1835, Col. Henry Dodge found a large encampment of the Inuna-ina near the mouth of Fountain Creek, near present-day Pueblo. Unfortunately for the Inuna-ina, Americans found gold in Colorado in 1858. Chief Left Hand barely avoided an unfortunate conflict with miners who had built log cabins in Boulder Valley near his people's winter encampment. The collision of cultures inevitably came, even though the Inuna-ina were more inclined to trade than war.

After the Sand Creek Massacre in 1864, the Arapahos joined the Cheyennes and Sioux on the warpath. In October 1867, these allies of the First Nations met with representatives of the federal government in southern Kansas, where they signed the Medicine Lodge Treaty. This agreement provided a reservation for the Inuna-ina between the Arkansas and Cimarron Rivers in Kansas. Today the Inuna-ina and the Cheyennes share a reservation in Oklahoma on the Canadian River created by presidential proclamation in 1869. About 3,000 of Our People live there at this time.

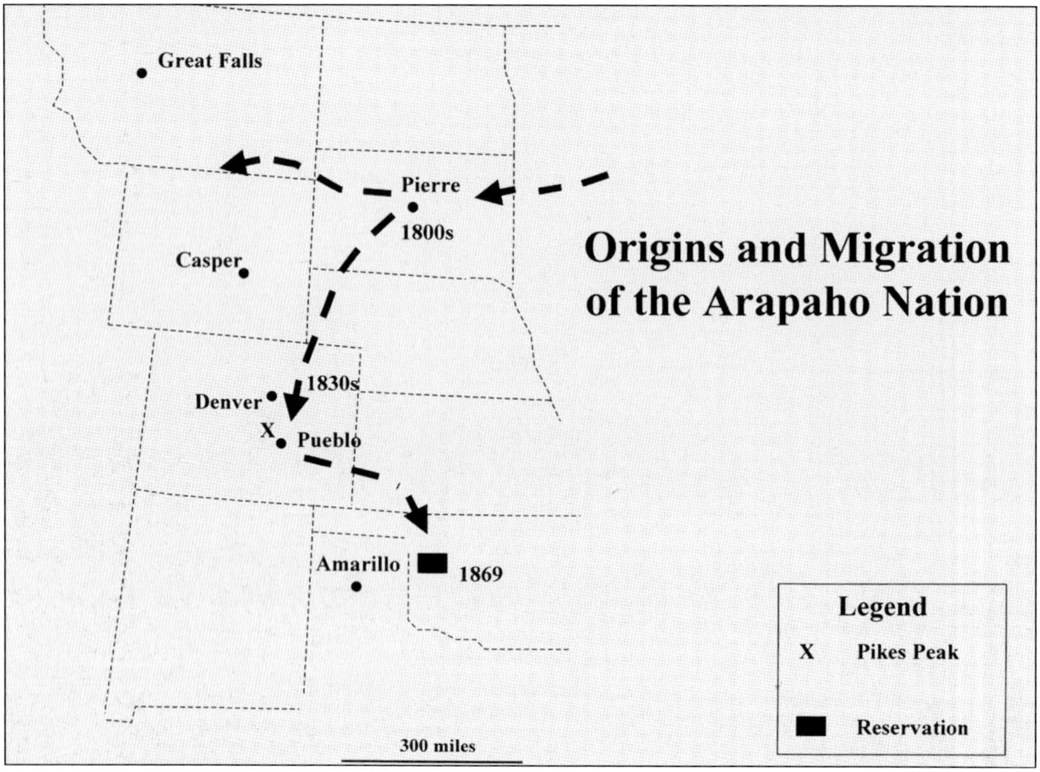

Origins and Migration of the Arapaho Nation

Legend
X — Pikes Peak
■ — Reservation

Most of Canada (except for the western coastal area) is populated by people who speak the Algonquin language. These people migrated across the Bering Strait, as recorded in the *Wallam Olum* of the Delaware, the mother culture of the Arapahos. The Arapahos left the Red River Valley in Minnesota and crossed the Missouri River in the 1800s, arriving in Colorado around 1830.

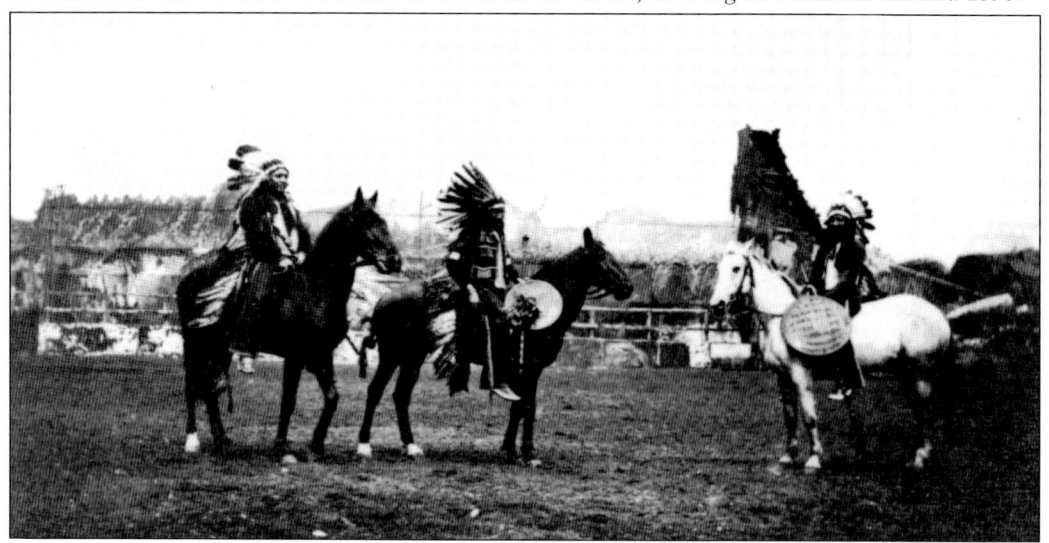

When the Arapahos first encountered white people in the early 1800s, they called them *nih'a'ca*, or spider. Some historians feel that the Arapahos first acquired horses from these early meetings; others say that they captured wild horses. Here several Arapahos ride in Buffalo Bill's Wild West Show about 1892. (Courtesy DPL.)

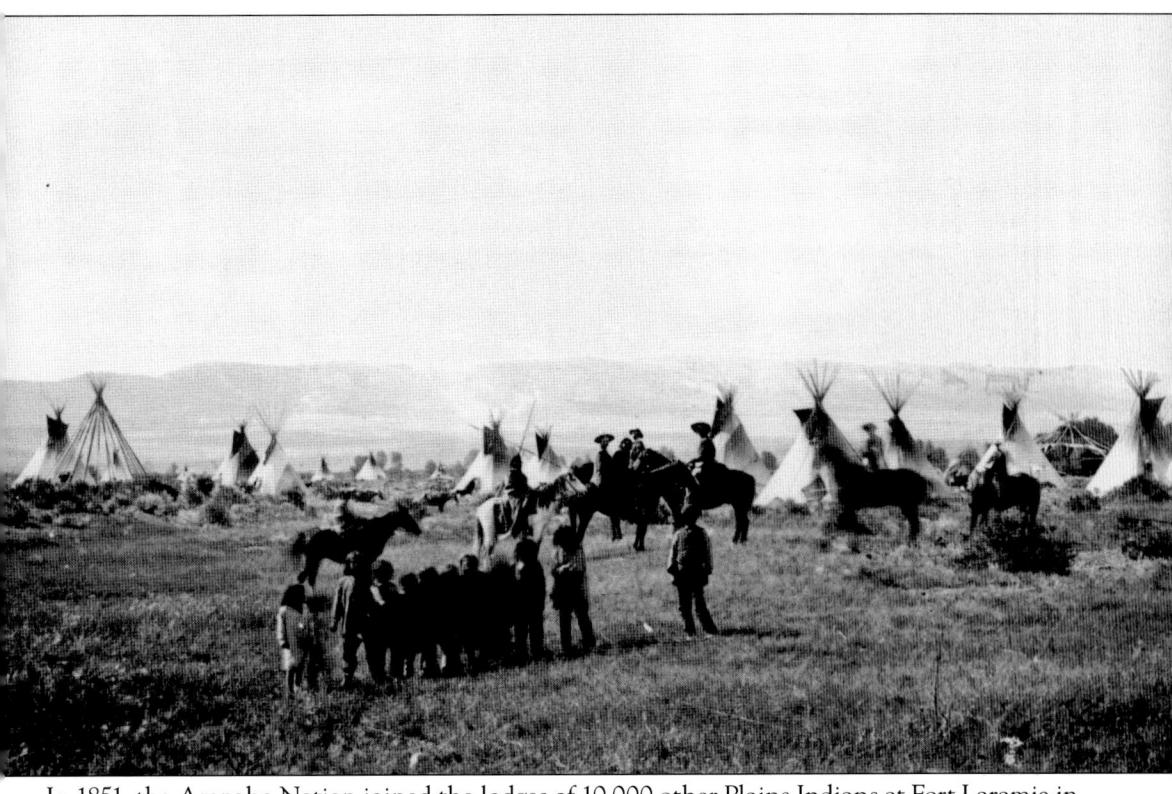

In 1851, the Arapaho Nation joined the lodges of 10,000 other Plains Indians at Fort Laramie in a peace effort. Indian agent Thomas Fitzpatrick, who was married to an Arapaho woman, worked tirelessly at bringing the nations together for this treaty. The final agreement was signed by the Arapaho, Sioux, Cheyenne, Crow, Assiniboine, Gros Ventre, Mandan, and Arikara Nations on September 17, 1851. It established a promise of peace between these nations, as well as boundaries for each nation, in return for annuities. In the treaty, the chiefs also gave permission to the federal government to build roads and military posts on American Indian land. Later, when troops marched across these ancestral lands, the chiefs protested, saying they were "strongly adverse to the establishment of military posts in their midst." The stage was thus set for conflict, as streams of white settlers continued to flood onto their lands in addition to the military. (Courtesy DPL.)

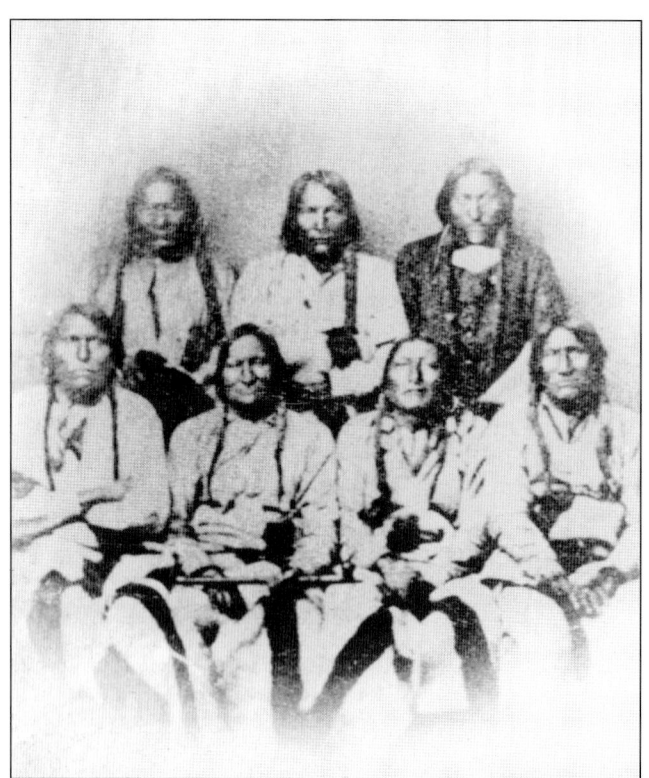

In the early fall of 1864, Maj. Edward Wynkoop brought these Cheyenne and Arapaho chiefs to Camp Weld, on the southwest edge of Denver, for a meeting with Gov. John Evans. Black Kettle (first row, holding the peace pipe) told Evans, "All we ask is that we may have peace with the whites. We want to hold you by the hand. You are our father." (Courtesy DPL.)

Arapaho chief Left Hand and Cheyenne chief Black Kettle camped with 500 Arapaho and Cheyenne people at Sand Creek in November 1864. They flew the American flag and a white flag of peace over their encampment. At dawn on November 29, their sleeping village was attacked by Col. John Chivington and his 700 troops. More than 150 were killed in this massacre—mostly women and children. (Courtesy DPL.)

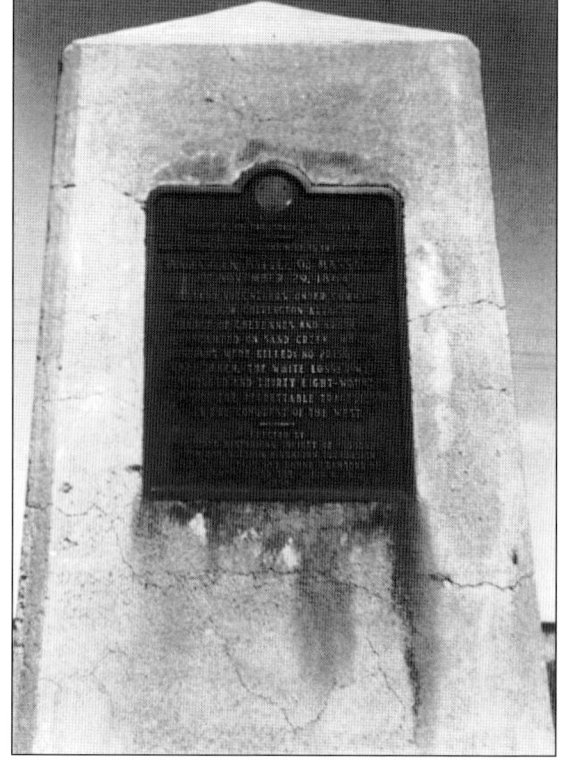

This photograph by McKinney is titled "Only Child Saved out of Sand Creek." An 1867 congressional committee wrote, "The fact which gives such terrible force to the condemnation of the wholesale massacre [at Sand Creek] . . . was, that those Indians were there encamped under the direction of our own officers, and believed themselves to be under the protection of our flag." (Courtesy DPL.)

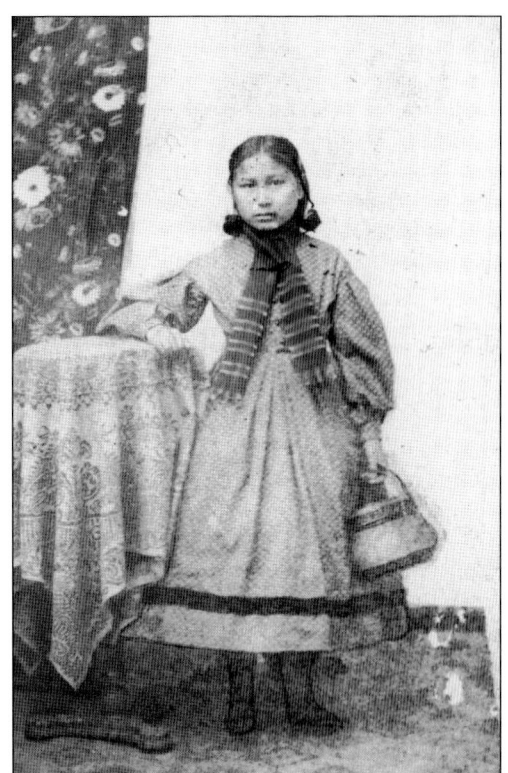

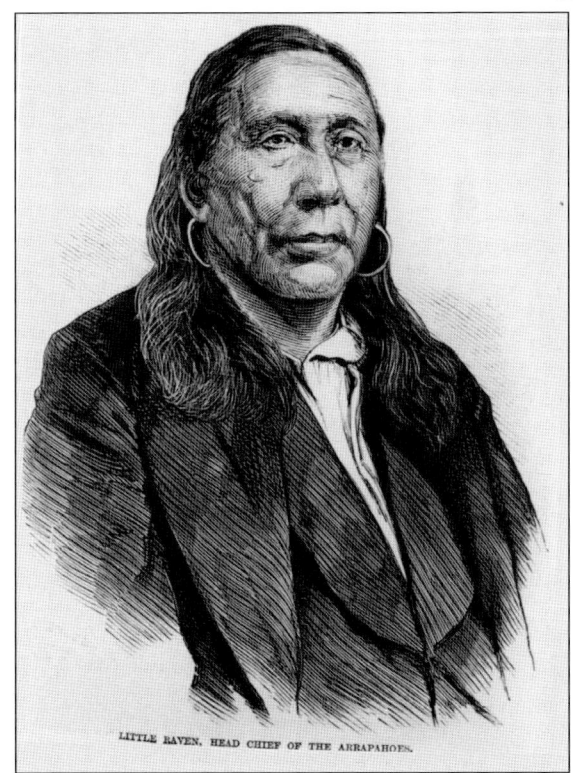

After Sand Creek, the federal government sought to extinguish all aboriginal land rights of the Arapahos and Cheyennes in the treaty of 1865. Little Raven responded, "It will be a very hard thing to leave. . . . We hate to leave these grounds [at Sand Creek]. . . . There is something strong for us—that fool band of soldiers cleared out our lodges and killed our women and children." (Courtesy DPL.)

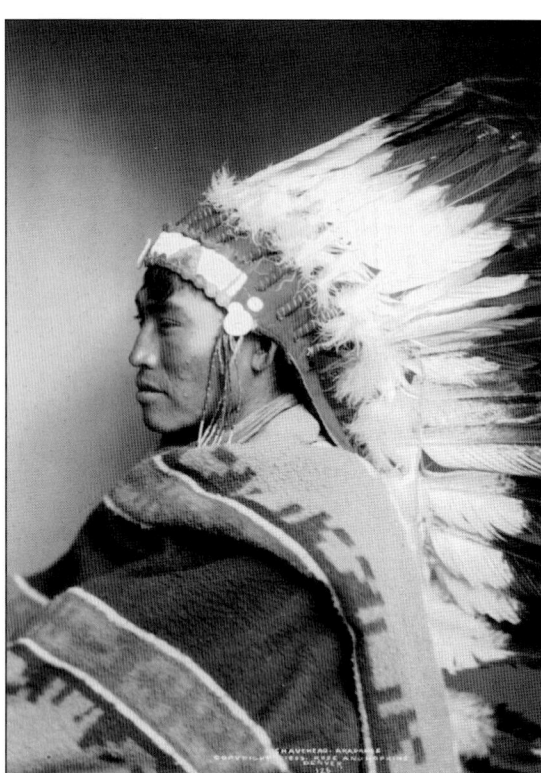

Arapaho chiefs such as Shave Head (pictured) were chosen from among the *hecawawu*, or Dog Society. Only the most valiant warriors belonged to this group, as they never fled the scene of battle even when in imminent danger. (Courtesy DPL.)

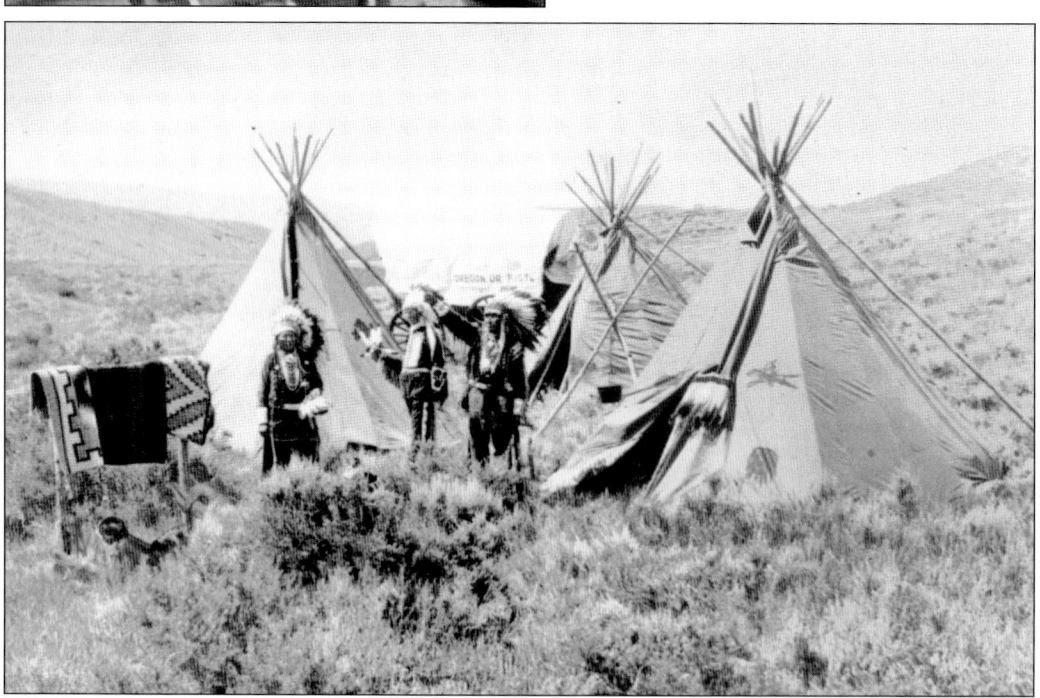

With the 1867 Medicine Lodge Treaty, the Southern Arapahos and Cheyennes were assigned a reservation in northwest Indian Territory (Oklahoma). This effectively ended their days as a nomadic people, and camps such as this one in Wyoming became only a memory. (Courtesy DPL.)

Arapaho warriors, still enraged by the atrocities at Sand Creek, joined the Cheyenne and Sioux Nations on the warpath. In their anger, they killed 18-year-old Charlie Everhart near Platte and Cascade Avenues in Colorado Springs and the 8- and 10-year-old sons of Thomas Robbins near Shooks Run in 1868. This stone monument at Boulder-Cascade Park in Colorado Springs memorializes the event. (Courtesy DPL.)

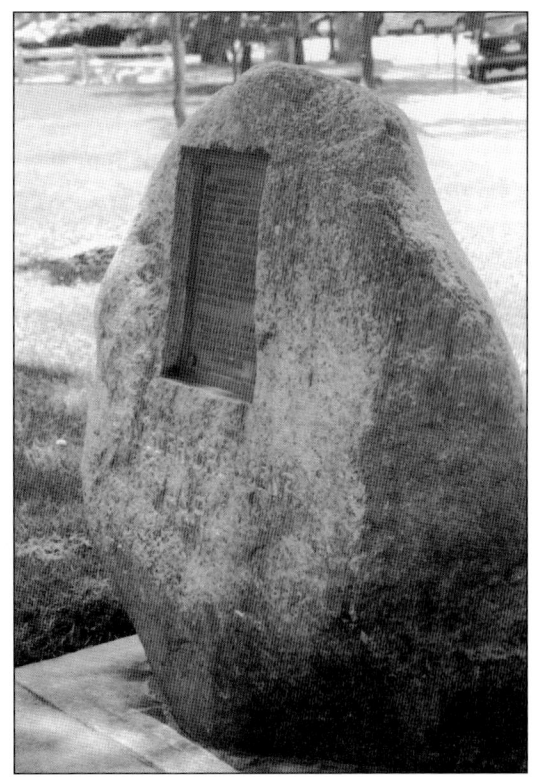

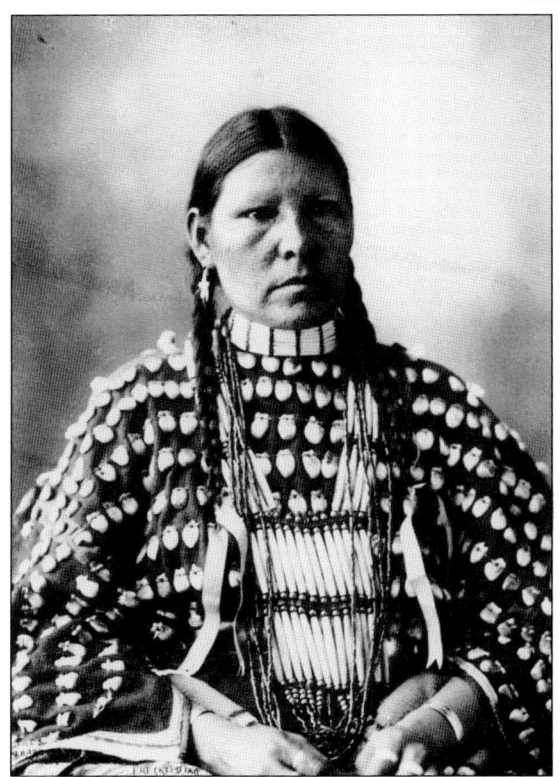

Freckle Face, an Arapaho woman, wears a trade cloth dress ornamented with hundreds of elk teeth. Only two teeth are used—the bull elk's whistling teeth, which have a small hole that creates the haunting sound when a bull bugles for a mate. The sheer numbers of these teeth on Freckle Face's dress attest to her husband's prowess as a hunter. (Courtesy DPL.)

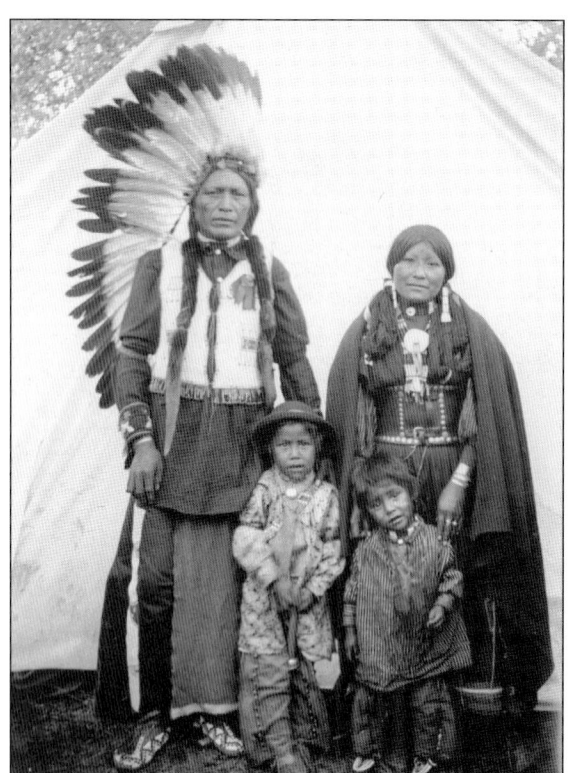

Arapaho marriage customs were simple and straightforward. When a young man was interested in a girl, he sent a female relative to her family with his request. If her brothers approved, then her mother, sisters, and aunts would build a new tipi for the couple. As soon as the young man set foot in the lodge, he and the girl were considered married. (Courtesy DPL.)

The Arapaho Sundance is held in a circular lodge that is open to the sky except for the log rafters that radiate from a forked cottonwood trunk set in the center. This lodge is open on the east side, and the dancers form an arc facing the tree on the west side. (Courtesy DPL.)

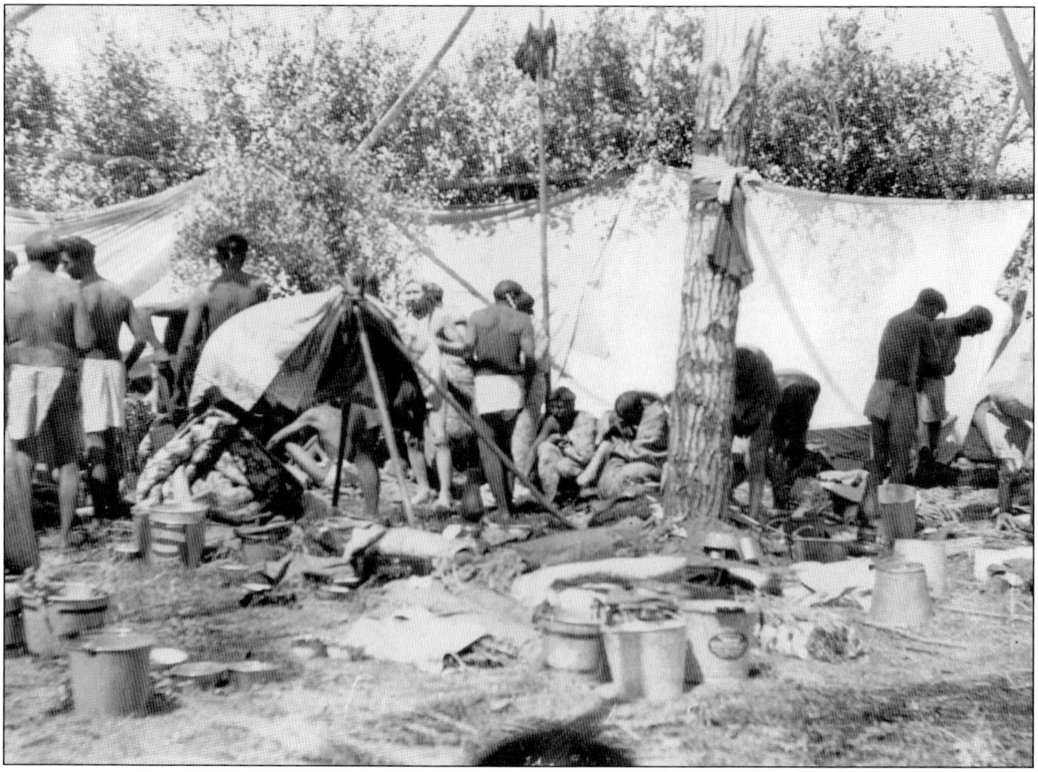

Weensizeneet, an Arapaho boy, carefully examines his pistol for the photographer. These children were indulged by their parents, who patiently taught them about acting the right way and living the right way. They were never beaten or spanked, for the act might have broken their spirit. (Courtesy DPL.)

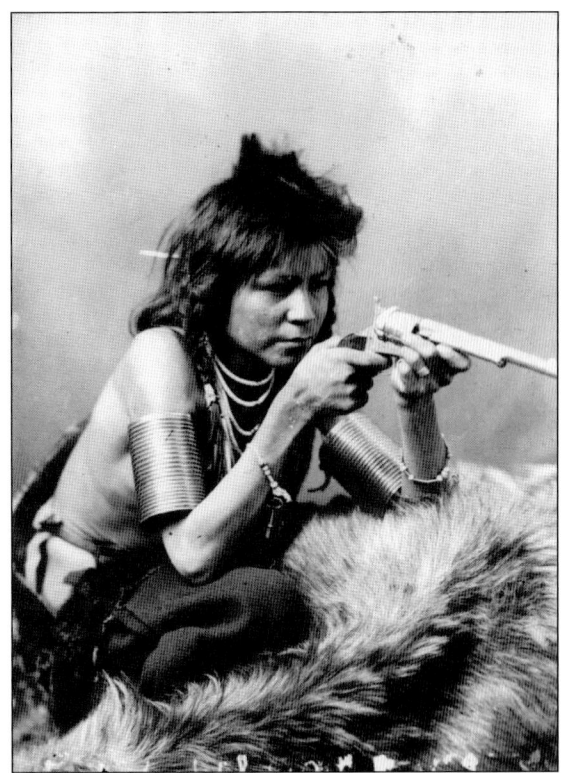

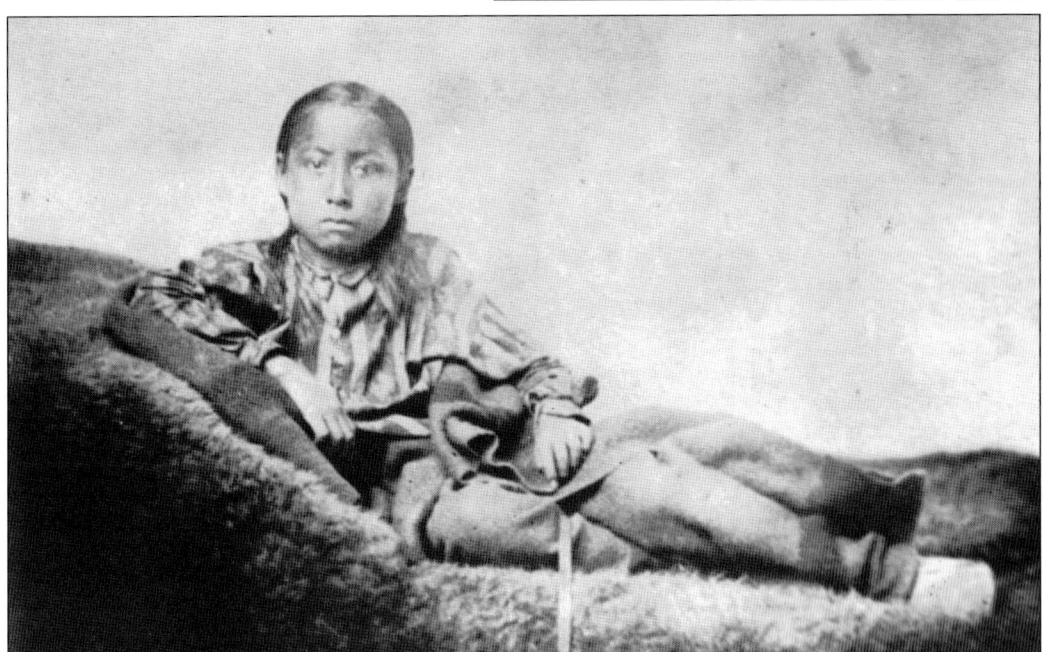

Chief Little Raven's child reclines on a buffalo blanket. These robes provided a warm, cozy bed at night when the children were tucked in on the north side of the tipi. During the day, the robes covered the floor or were rolled and used for seating. To be cleaned of vermin, they were placed on an ant hill. (Courtesy DPL.)

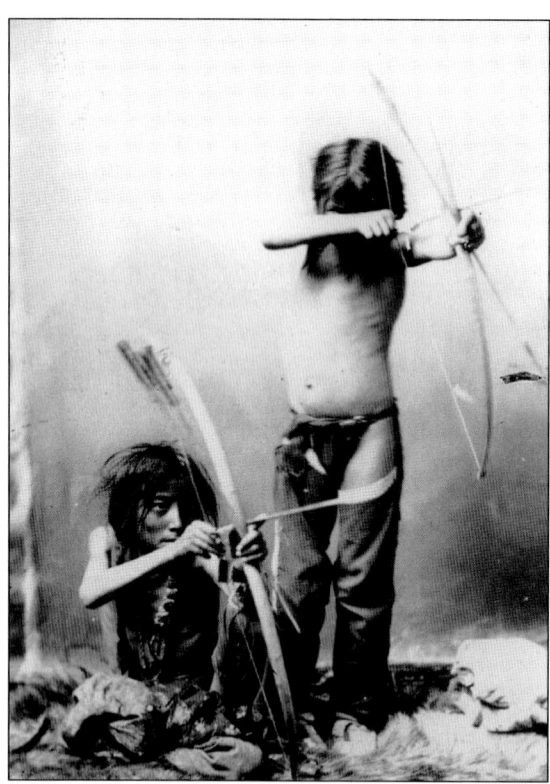

Little boys were given bows and arrows with blunt tips at about four years old. Taught to sit a horse, they became expert riders within a year. An Arapaho maxim cautioned, "Always have fat horses no matter how poor your saddle." (Courtesy DPL.)

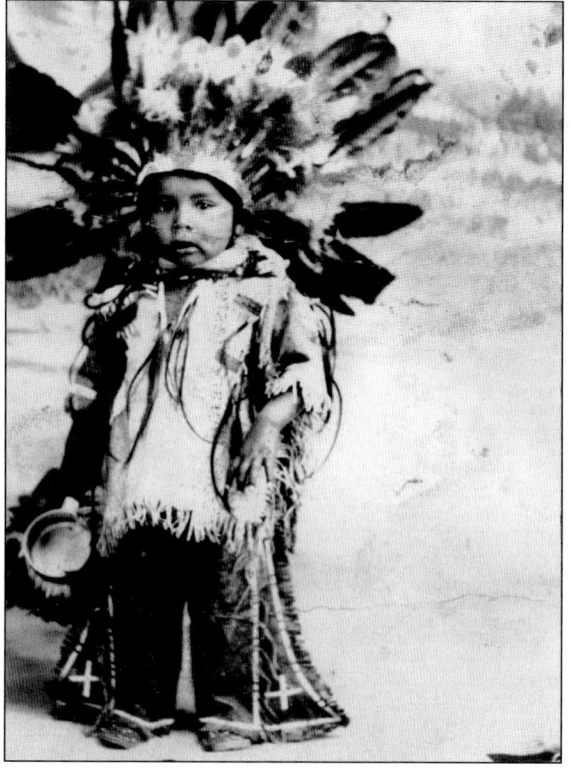

Blue Cloud, an Arapaho child pictured in 1880, probably never saw the traditional life of his people. Carl Sweezy writes that, prior to the reservation, villages were idyllic places where "ponies grazed in open spaces; children romped with the dogs and climbed on the ponies." (Courtesy DPL.)

Six

DZITSI'STAS, THE CHEYENNE NATION

Their language was one of the most unique among the Algonquin speakers, so the Dakotas christened them the *Cheyenne*, "People of Alien Speech." Members of the nation call themselves *Dzitsi'stas*, "Like-hearted People."

Originally agriculturalists, the Dzitsi'stas abandoned their pottery-making and Minnesota cornfields in the 1600s due to conflicts with the Dakotas and Chippewas. By the late 1600s, they had settled in the Chicago area and visited Fort Crevecoeur in 1680. By 1700, they were living in eastern North Dakota along the Cheyenne River, and by the mid-1700s, they had acquired the horse and become buffalo hunters.

Around 1830, the Dzitsi'stas split into two united tribes: north and south. The northern people are called Sotaeo'o. The other half, the Dzitsi'stas, moved southward to take advantage of the trading opportunities afforded by William Bent's new fort along the Arkansas River. As they arrived in the Pikes Peak region, they formed an alliance with the Arapahos. After the Sand Creek Massacre in 1864, Dzitsi'stas, Arapaho, and Lakota warriors waged a retaliatory war against the Americans. Hostilities finally ceased in 1867, when the Dzitsi'stas signed the Medicine Lodge Treaty. In 1868, a rogue band of about 75 Dzitsi'stas and Arapahos passed through Colorado City on their way up Ute Pass to South Park. About four days later, they reappeared eight miles northeast of Colorado City, where they killed two cowboys near H. M. Teachout's ranch. Then they killed Charley Everhart and Thomas Robbins's two little boys.

Under the terms of the 1867 treaty, the Dzitsi'stas share a reservation in northwestern Oklahoma with Arapahos. Today there are about 11,000 people in their nation.

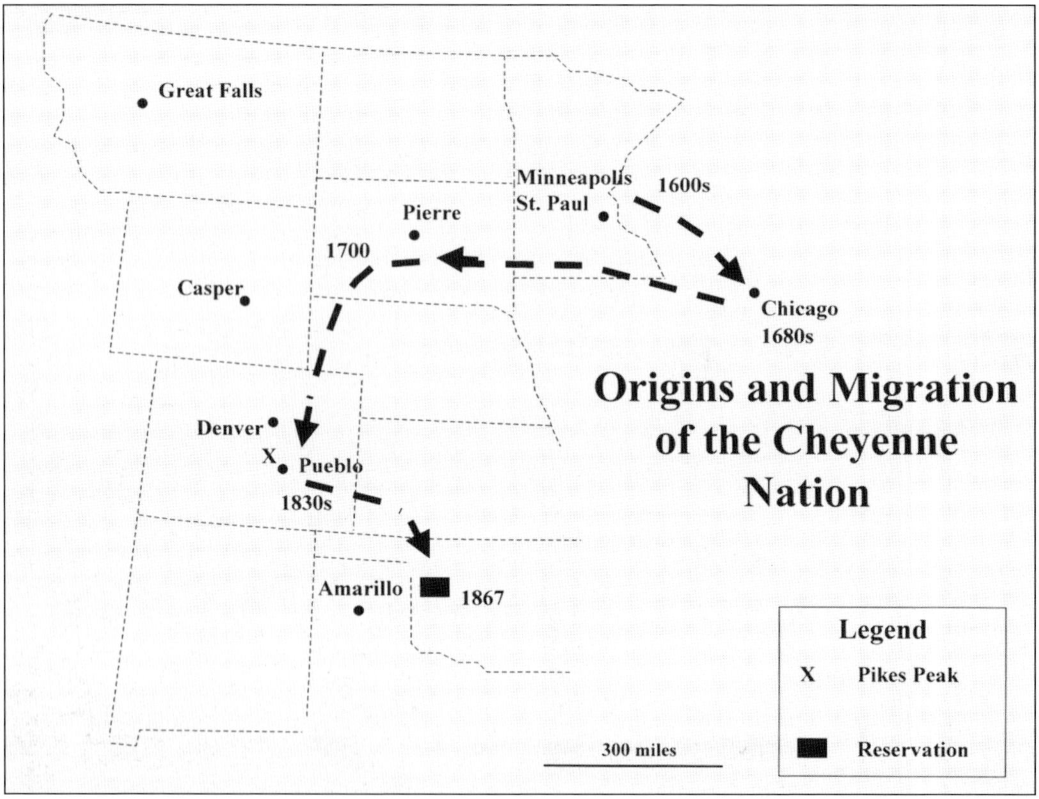

Origins and Migration of the Cheyenne Nation

Like their linguistic cousins, the Arapahos, the Cheyennes are a product of the Delaware mother culture. They were agriculturalists in Minnesota until the Dakotas and Chippewas launched relentless attacks and drove them into Illinois. From there, they traveled west, crossing the Missouri River just ahead of the Arapahos. The Cheyennes arrived in Colorado around 1830.

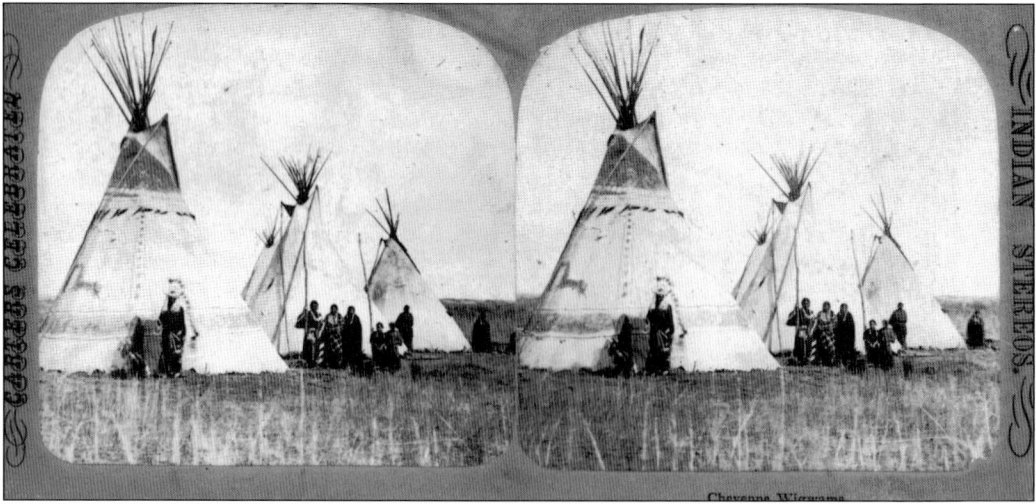

The Cheyenne Nation moved southward down the Front Range and onto the Arkansas River in the 1830s to trade at Bent's Fort. They established their villages near the fort and lived peaceably. This ended in 1864, when Little Chief and his warriors were returning stolen livestock for a reward and were mistakenly attacked by the army as hostiles. (Courtesy DPL.)

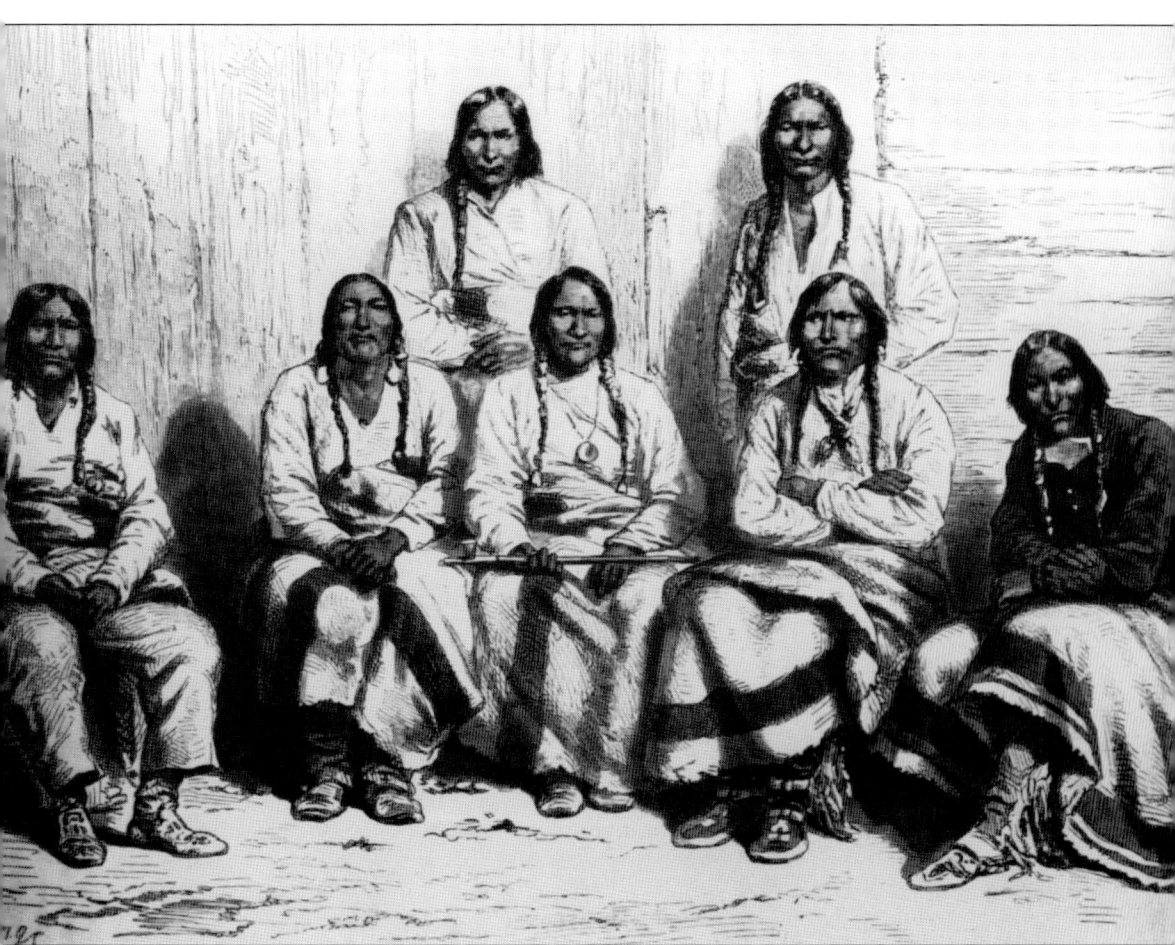

After meeting with representatives of the Arapaho and Cheyenne Nations, Governor Evans issued an official report in 1863 stating that the tribes were friendly and there would be no war. Unfortunately, Evans later chose to believe the unfounded stories of a white man named North, who said they were going on the warpath. In his ignorance, Evans authorized Colonel Chivington to form his infamous militia. When *Motavato* (Black Kettle) learned of Evans's hawkish inclinations, he protested. "We want to take good tidings home to our people, that they may sleep in peace. I want you to give all the chiefs of the soldiers here to understand that we are for peace, and that we have made peace, that we may not be mistaken by them for enemies." (Courtesy DPL.)

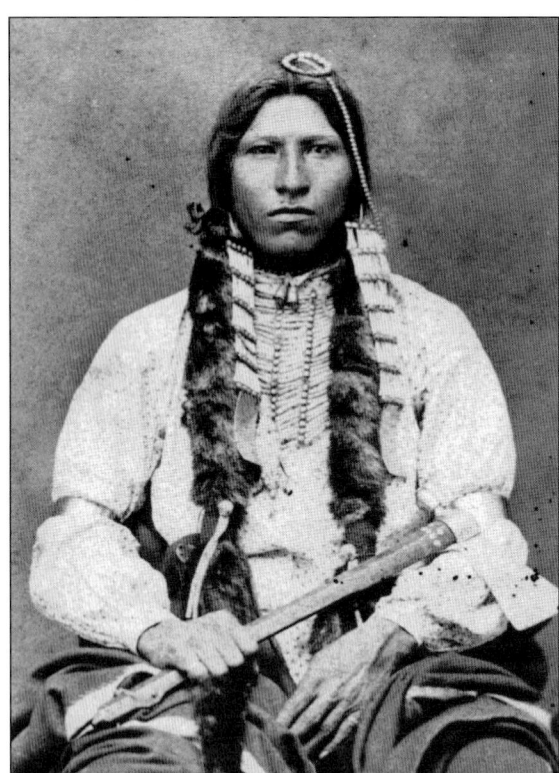

After leaving Bent's Fort in 1847, Lt. J. W. Abert and his small party were approached by a band of Cheyennes. The chief complained that he and his band "had had nothing to eat for three days, as the snow that covered the country had driven the buffalo off." Abert and the men continued their journey unmolested, even though they had refused to share provisions and were outnumbered. (Courtesy DPL.)

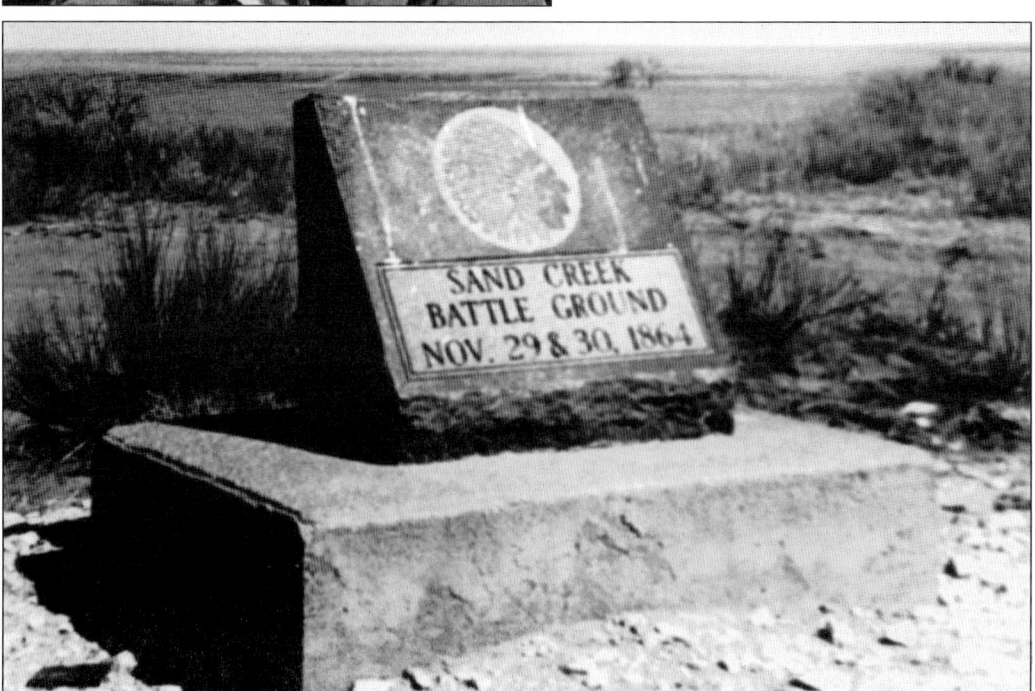

This marker observes the Sand Creek Massacre of November 29, 1864. After Chivington's attack, the Cheyennes lamented, "What do we want to live for? The white man has taken our country, killed all of our game, . . . killed our wives and children." (Courtesy DPL.)

Dog Soldiers were a Cheyenne warrior society. In battle, these men staked themselves to the ground with a rope and fought to the death. They were often wild and reckless and got the rest of the tribe into trouble with their mischief. After the Sand Creek Massacre, Dog Soldiers led the defense of their people. (Courtesy DPL.)

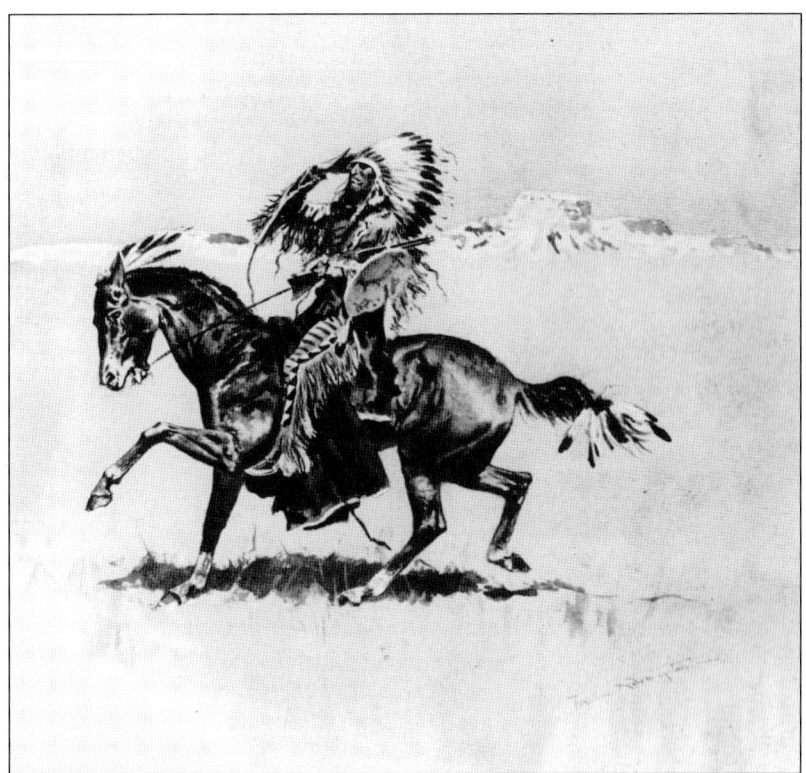

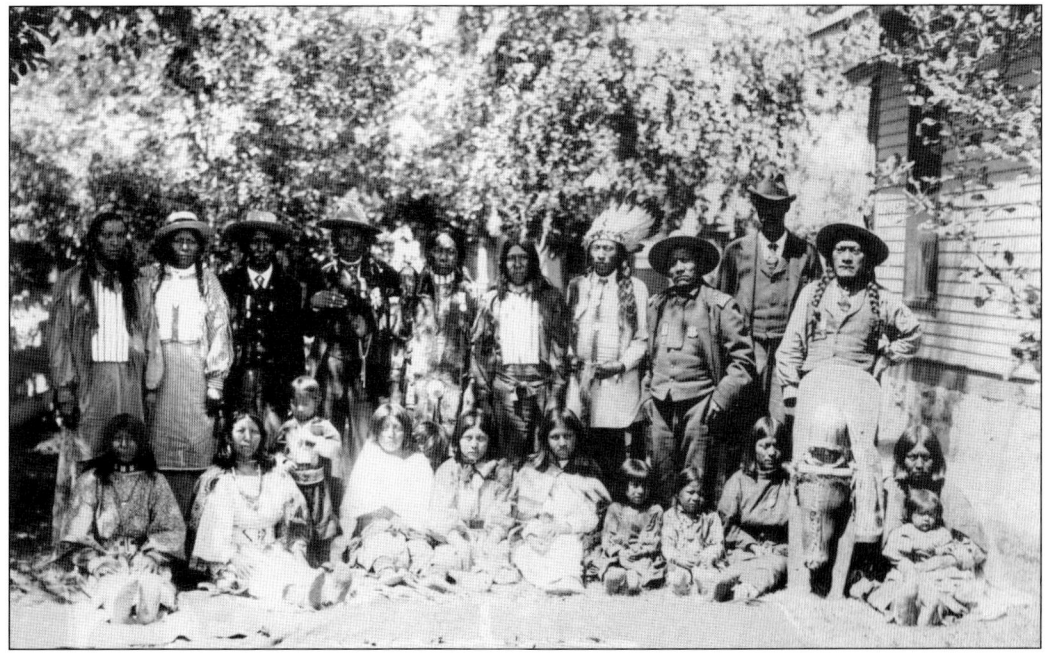

Magpie Bent (first row, far right) is shown here with a group of Utes at the Broadmoor in Colorado Springs. Her husband, George, was the son of William Bent (of Bent's Fort) and a Cheyenne woman. After Sand Creek, George gave himself fully to his Cheyenne heritage and vented his anger on the warpath. (Courtesy Pikes Peak Library District, Poley.)

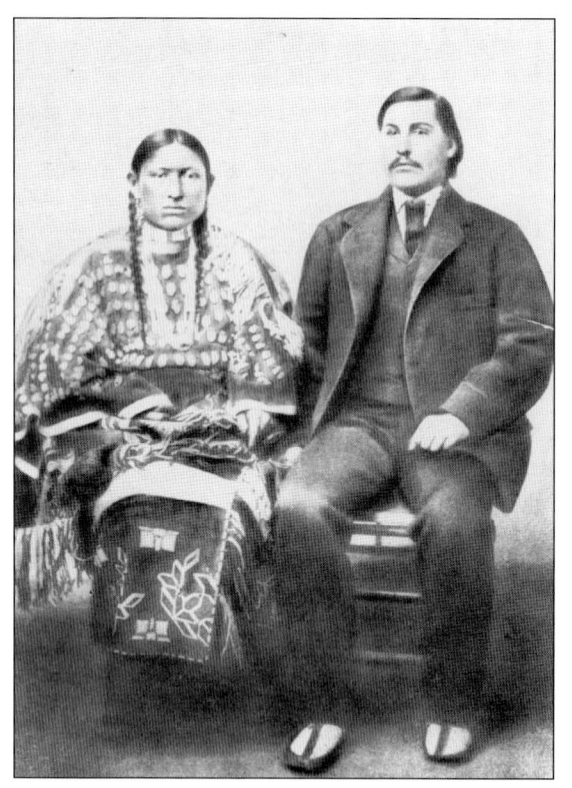

Though badly wounded, George Bent (pictured with Magpie) survived the massacre at Sand Creek and was able to refute Chivington's testimony concerning the battle. He also joined the Dog Soldiers as *Hi-my-ike*, "Beaver." Later he became an instrument of peace when Col. Jesse Leavenworth asked him to "gather up these Indians" for the Medicine Lodge Treaty of 1867. (Courtesy DPL.)

Roman Nose secured his place in history during the Beecher Island Fight in September 1868. His band attacked at daylight, driving 51 army scouts onto Beecher Island in the Republican River, where they were pinned down for three days. Roman Nose claimed to have taken medicine that made a person bulletproof. A metal fork touched his food, thereby destroying his power, and he was killed in the battle. (Courtesy DPL.)

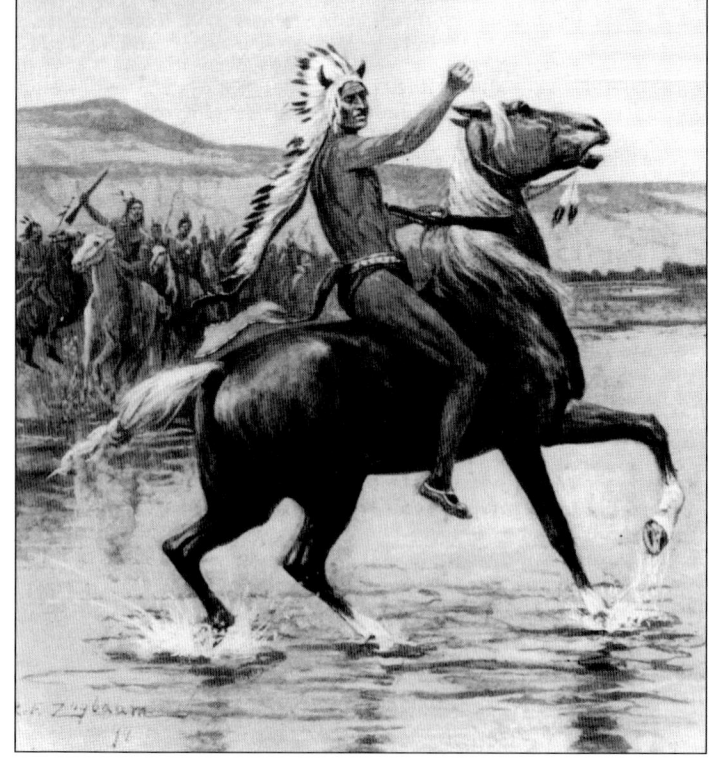

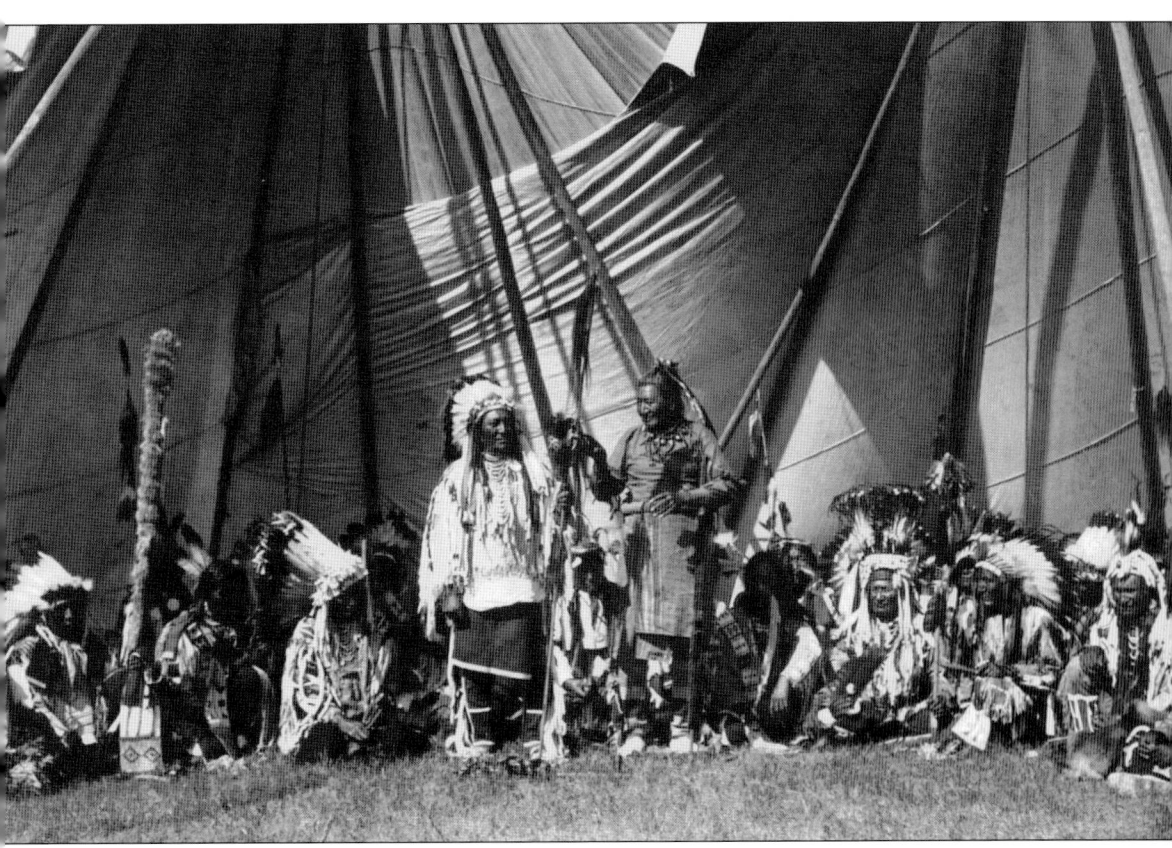

Ish Hayu Nishus, Cheyenne chief Two Moons, surrendered to Gen. Nelson A. Miles at Fort Keogh in 1877. He and the Northern Cheyennes fought against Custer at the Little Big Horn in 1876. In his account of the battle, Two Moons told historians, "I went to water my horses at the creek, and washed them off with cool water, then took a swim myself. I came back to the camp afoot. When I got near my lodge, I looked up the Little Horn towards Sitting Bull's camp. I saw a great dust rising. It looked like a whirlwind. . . . I saw flags come up over the hill to the east. . . . Then the soldiers rose all at once. . . . The Sioux rode up the ridge on all sides, riding very fast. The Cheyennes went up the left way. Then the shooting was quick, quick. . . . We circled all round, . . . swirling like water round a stone. . . . All the soldiers were now killed, and . . . were left where they fell." After the battle, the Sioux and Cheyenne Nations scattered to the north and south. (Courtesy DPL.)

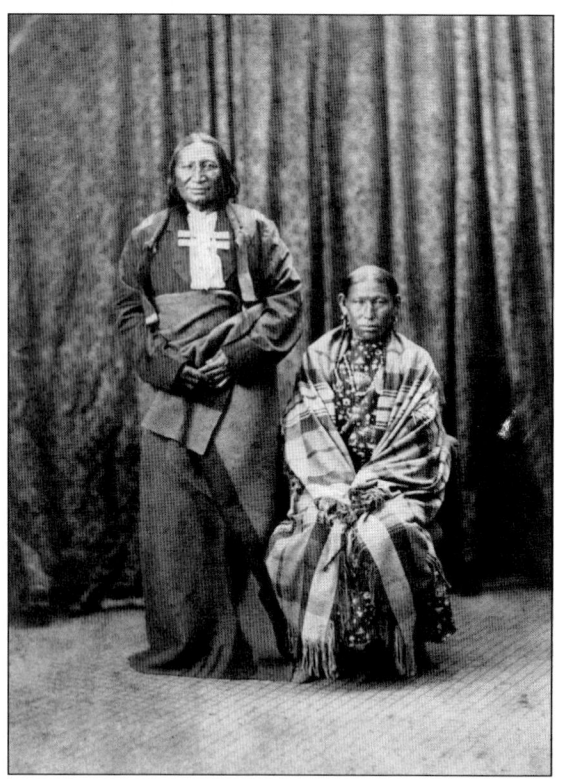

Chief Stone Calf and his band joined Arapaho, Kiowa, Apache, and other Cheyenne warriors under the leadership of a Comanche medicine man. I Sa Tai' assured them that his medicine made white people's guns useless. After their defeat at Adobe Walls, angry Cheyenne warriors attacked a party of immigrants and captured their four daughters. Stone Calf returned the girls when he surrendered in 1875. (Courtesy DPL.)

Facing sickness and starvation at the reservation in Oklahoma, several hundred Northern Cheyennes left for their homelands in 1879. They were intercepted and made prisoners at Fort Robinson. "We have been without food and fire for seven days; we may as well die here as be taken back south and die there," they said. In a desperate escape, almost half were killed—mostly women and children. (Courtesy DPL.)

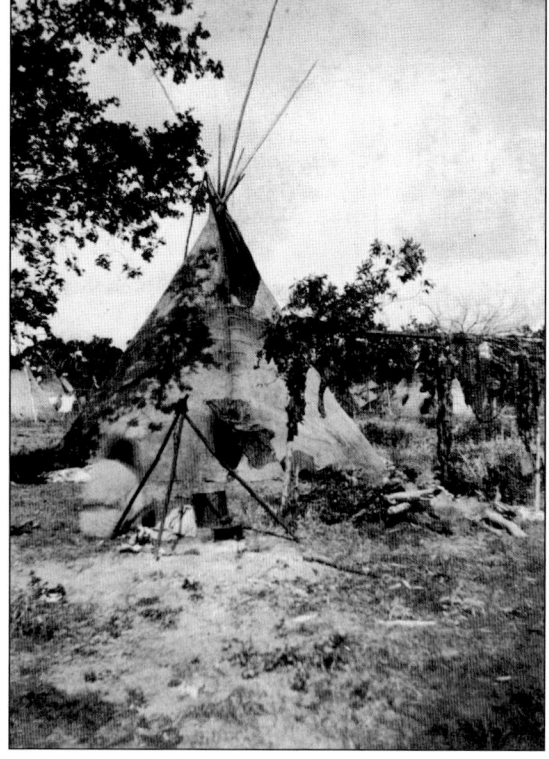

Sweet Medicine, prophet of the Cheyenne Nation, was the son of a virgin. He performed many miracles for his people, including bringing them the buffalo. As he was dying, he warned his people that light-colored "Earth Men" would soon be coming. He warned his people to "follow nothing these Earth Men do, but keep your own ways." (Courtesy Coffrin's Old West Gallery.)

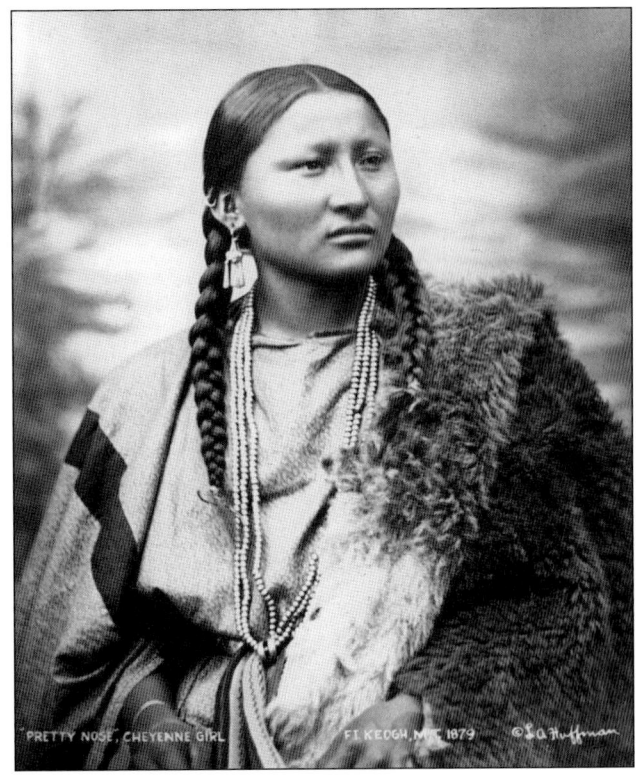

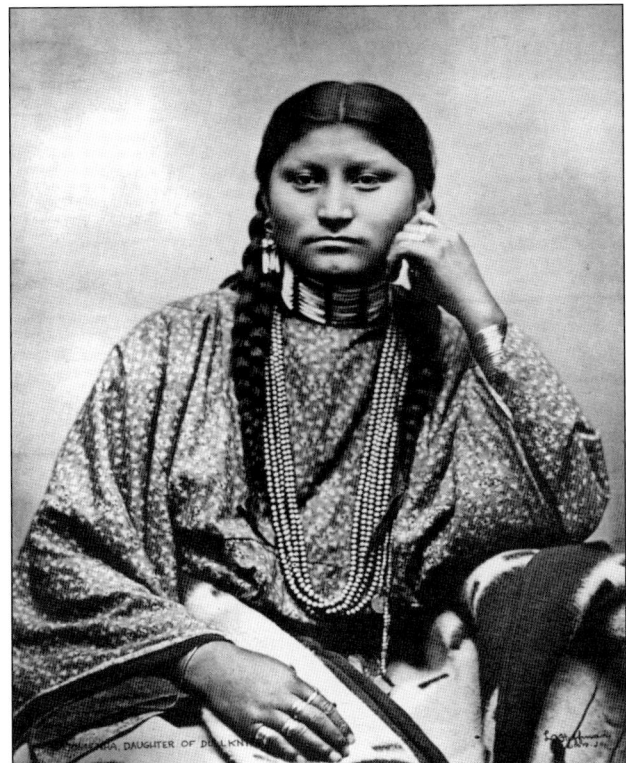

Chief Dull Knife's daughter Comenha epitomizes the beauty and quiet dignity of Cheyenne women. Young men could not court women until proving their courage. These women taunted the warriors by chanting, "If you had fought bravely I would have sung for you." Cheyenne men felt it was better to fight than to face their women. (Courtesy Coffrin's Old West Gallery.)

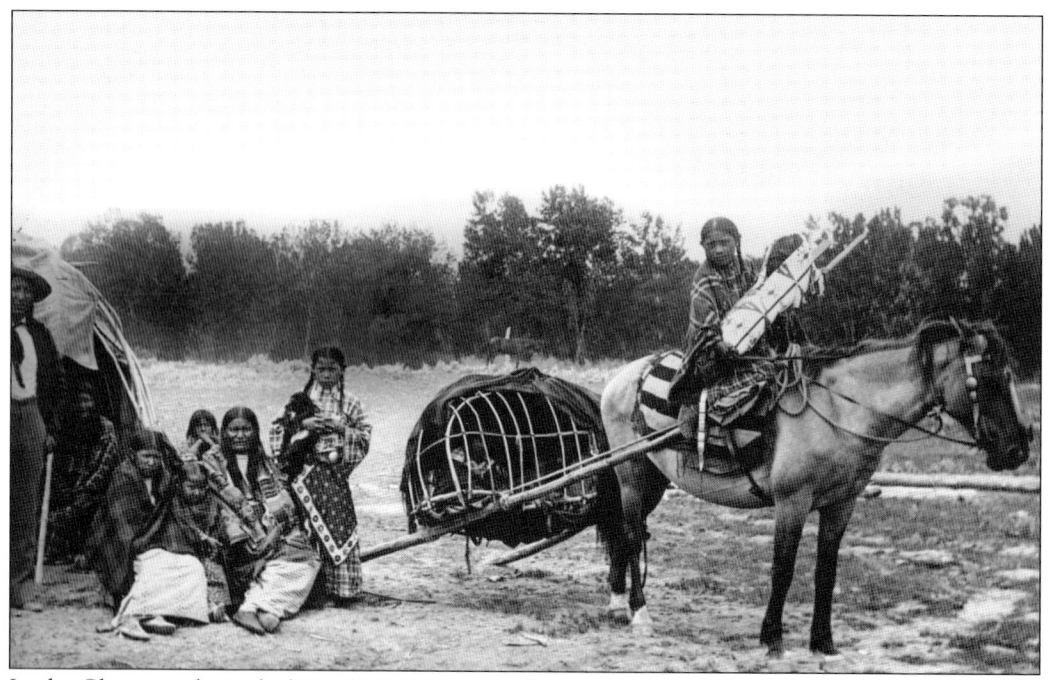

In the Cheyenne legend of Devil's Tower, a girl adopts seven boys as brothers. The buffalo people demand that the brothers surrender their sister. When they refuse, the buffalo charge their tipi. One brother shoots a magic arrow into a tree, and it grows up to the stars. The children climb the tree and find safety as the seven stars of the Pleiades. (Courtesy Coffrin's Old West Gallery.)

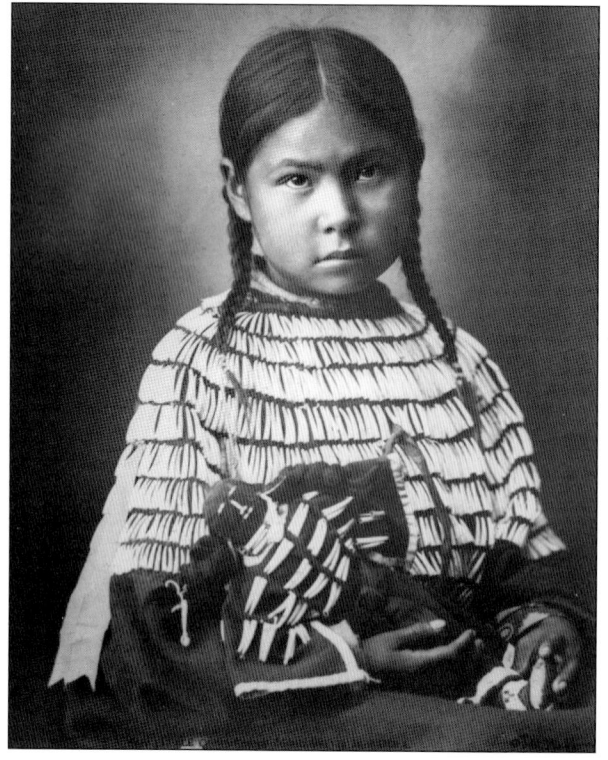

This little girl will probably become a strong, proud Cheyenne woman. One story tells of an old woman captured by 50 Assiniboine warriors who demand to be fed. Lifting a sheet of back fat from the fire, she flings it around the lodge, burning the men. She then flees, throwing her torch over a cliff. The warriors follow the light and are killed. (Courtesy Coffrin's Old West Gallery.)

Seven

Tepki'nago, the Kiowa Nation

The Kiowa people are an anomaly among American Indians because they are commonly called by their own name, meaning "Principal People." However, they did have another ancient name they used for themselves: *Tepki'nago*, "People Coming Out."

Their language is another mystery. Kiowa-Tanoan belongs to the Aztec-Tanoan language family and is most closely related to the Puebloans of the Rio Grande Valley in New Mexico, even though the people originated in the Kootenay region of British Columbia. In the late 1600s, the Tepki'nago migrated from this area into western Montana. In the late 1700s, the Cheyennes and Lakotas pushed them farther south into Nebraska, Oklahoma, Colorado, and New Mexico. By the mid-1800s, they had settled in the Texas Panhandle.

Skilled diplomats, the Tepki'nago made a fateful alliance with the Comanche Nation at an encampment near Las Vegas, New Mexico, in 1790. Soon they also affiliated with the Plains Apaches and became known as the Kiowa-Apaches. These powerful warriors made long-distance raids over incredible distances—from Canada to the Grand Canyon and into Mexico and Central America. In 1840, they further allied themselves with their former enemies, the Cheyenne Nation.

Kiowa forays into the Pikes Peak area mainly involved hunting, trading, and raiding parties. Zebulon Pike met the trader James Purcell in Santa Fe in 1806. Purcell (Pike calls him Pursley) told of being part of a trading party of more than 2,000 "Paducahs and Kyaways" (Comanches and Kiowas), who were driven into South Park by the Lakotas in 1805. Most hostilities ended, though, with the previously mentioned Treaty of Medicine Lodge in 1867.

By 1879, Kiowas were mainly settled on their reservation in Oklahoma, where they now live. According to the 2000 census, this nation includes 8,559 members.

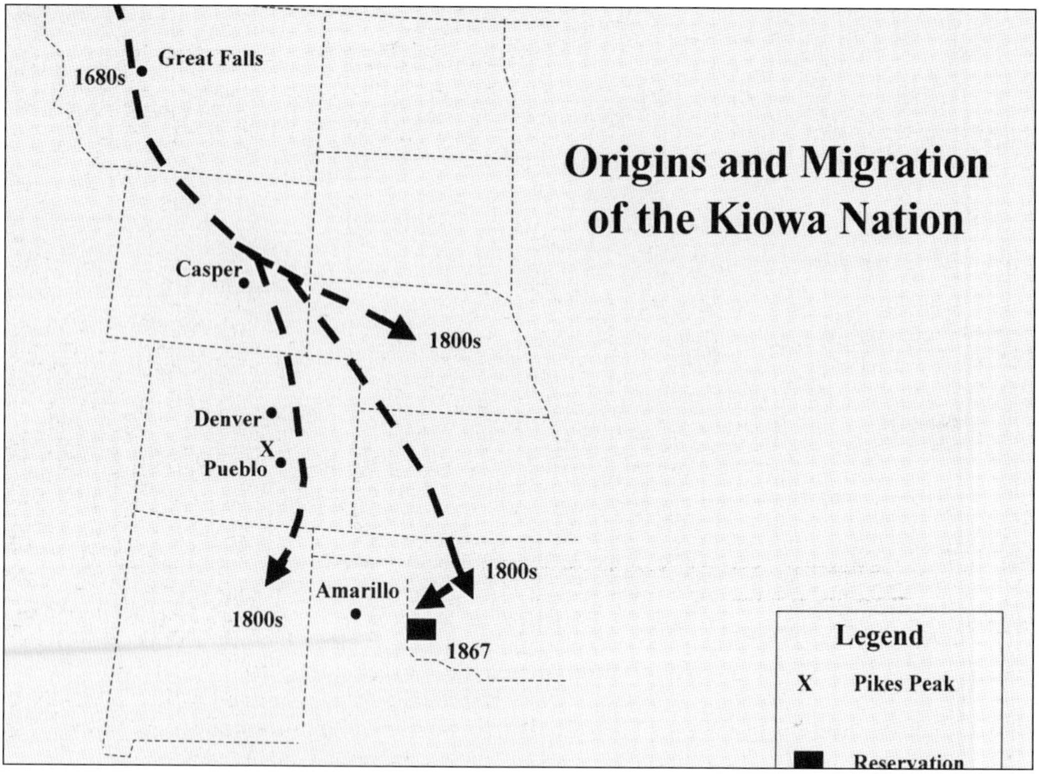

Origins and Migration of the Kiowa Nation

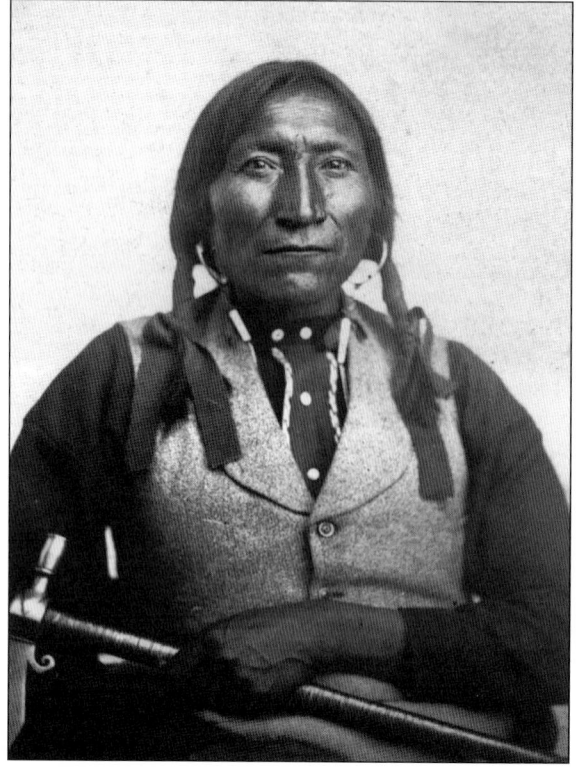

How did these linguistic cousins of the Pueblo and the Ute find their way into Canada? Kiowa people were originally documented in the Kootenay region of British Colombia. In the 1680s, they arrived in Montana and were forced farther south by their enemies, the Cheyennes and Lakotas. They had come to Colorado and northern New Mexico by the late 1700s, as shown on this migration map.

Lone Wolf, a Kiowa chief, told George Bird Grinnell of a battle between Kiowas and 14 Cheyenne warriors. One man, Mouse's Road, fought so bravely that Lone Wolf decided to let him live. "No, . . . I should be crying all the time—mourning for these men. You must kill me." Mouse's Road fiercely attacked Lone Wolf until he fell to the ground, feigning death. (Courtesy Library of Congress.)

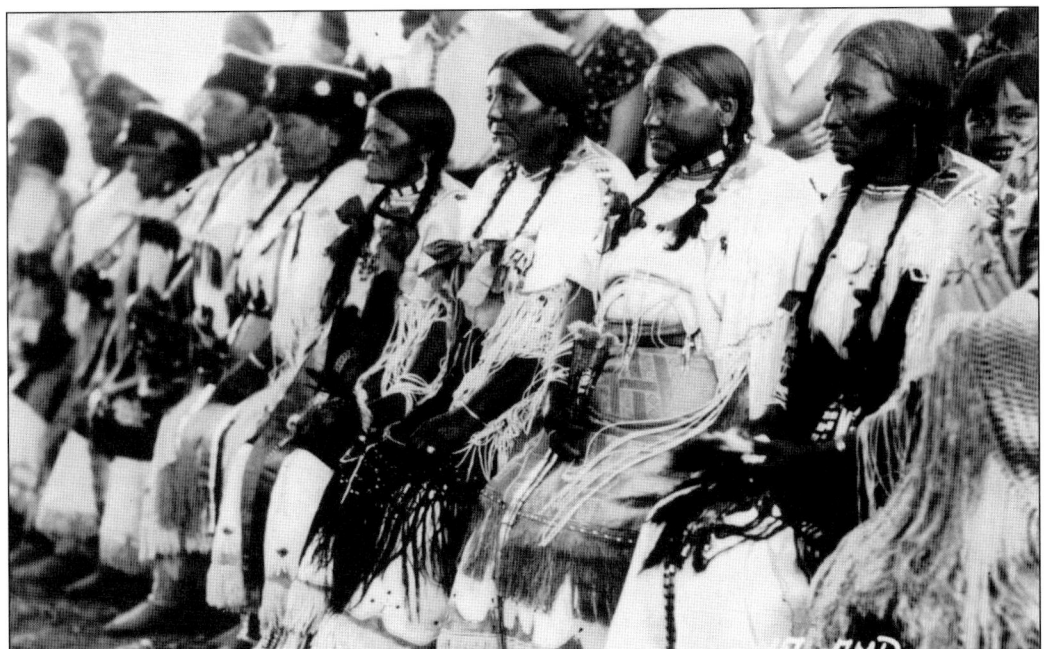

War with the Cheyenne and Lakota Nations forced the Kiowas south into Colorado and adjacent areas. They astutely made peace with the Comanches in 1790 at a council in Las Vegas, New Mexico. Then, around 1840, they formed an alliance with the Cheyennes. In an 1837 treaty, the Kiowas provided safe passage for Americans through their lands. (Courtesy DPL.)

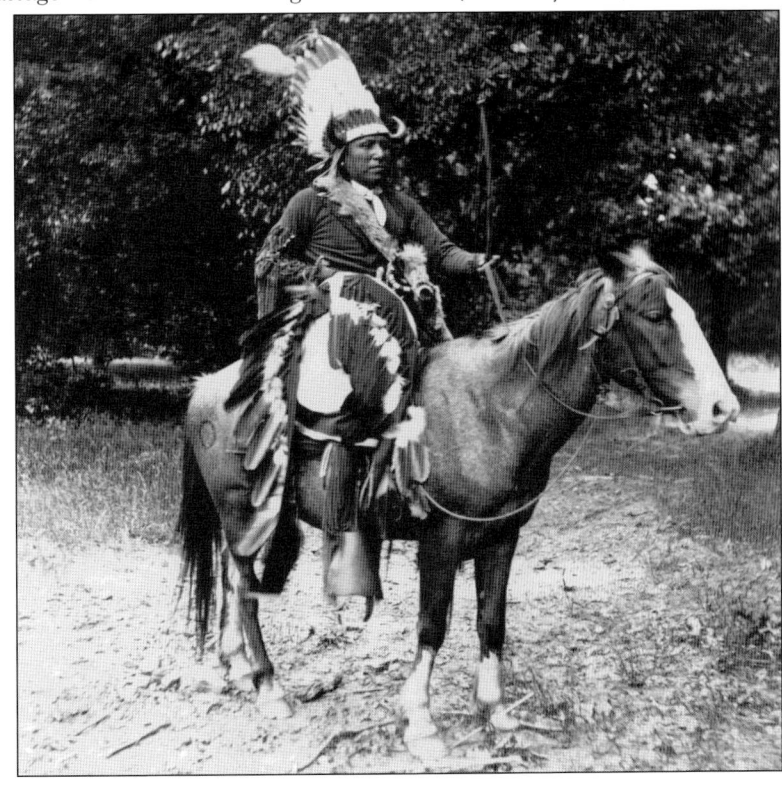

Kiowa warriors like Elk Tongue, seen here, were great horsemen. Under the leadership of Satanta, they successfully stole the horse herd from Fort Larned in 1864. The wily chief entered the post and engaged the drunken commander, Capt. J. W. Parmeter, in conversation. While the Kiowa women held a dance to distract the soldiers, Satanta's warriors quietly ran off with 240 horses and mules. (Courtesy Library of Congress.)

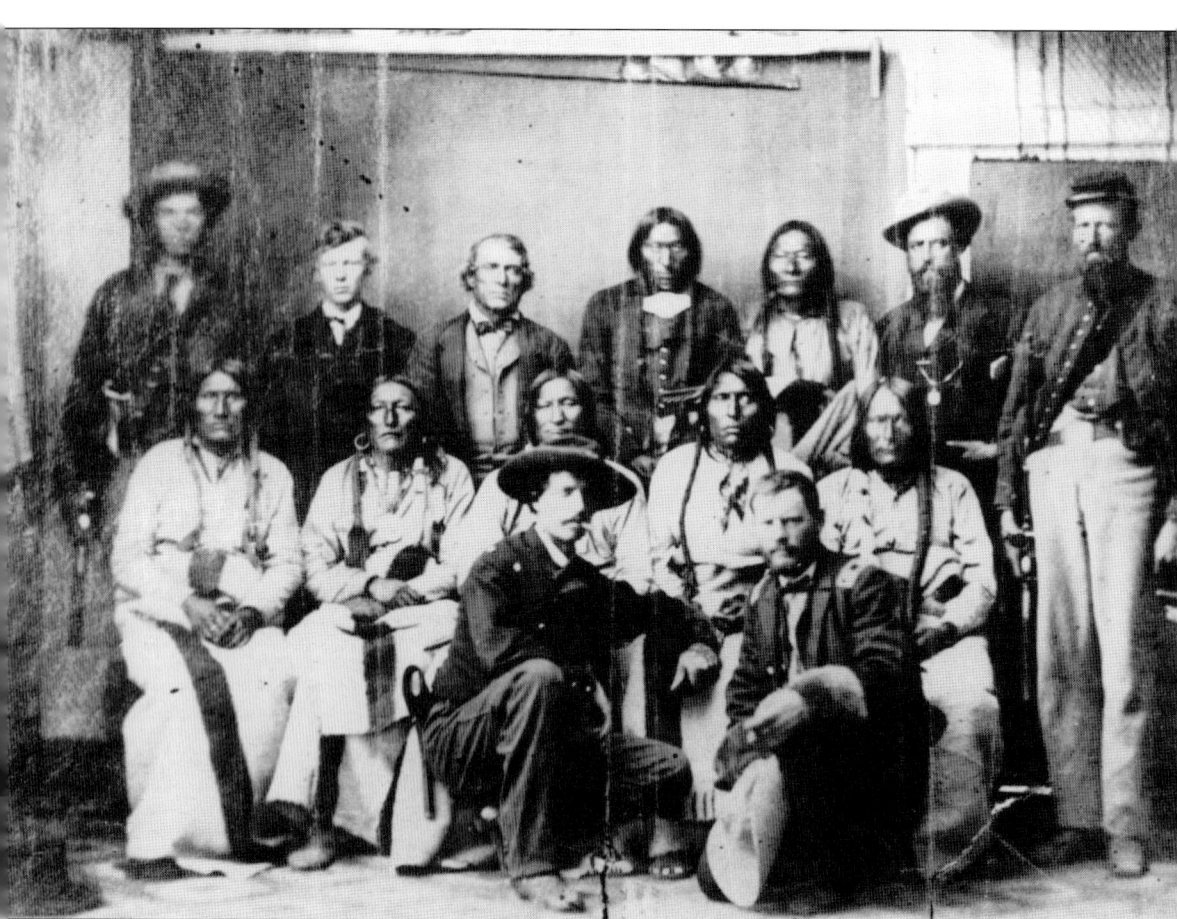

Kiowa chief White Wolf (standing, fourth from left) joined Cheyenne and Arapaho allies to sign the treaty at Camp Weld in Denver in 1864. Witnesses at the council said that "time and again the chiefs tried to tell of the outrages committed by whites against their people," but Governor Evans had no ears. Major Wynkoop later reported Evans as saying, "The regiment [Chivington's] was ordered to be raised upon his [Evans's] representation to Washington that they were necessary for the protection of the Territory, and to fight hostile Indians; and now, if he made peace with the Indians, it would be supposed at Washington that he had misrepresented matters in regard to the Indian difficulties in Colorado and put the government to a useless expense." The massacre at Sand Creek was the inevitable outcome. (Courtesy DPL.)

In September 1874, Col. "Bad Hand" MacKenzie and his troops attacked 200 lodges of Kiowas, Comanches, and Cheyennes in their secret Palo Duro Canyon hideaway. There were very few casualties on either side, but almost all the pony herd was captured. MacKenzie ordered more than 1,400 of these horses killed. (Courtesy DPL.)

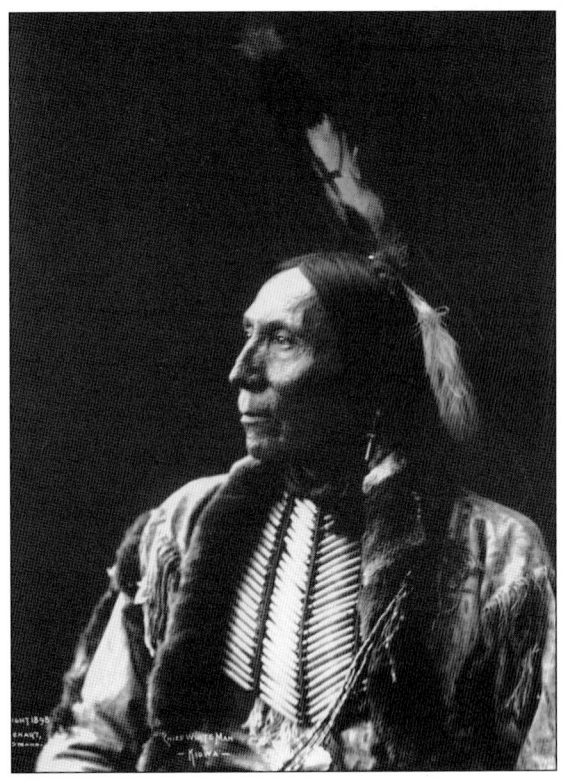

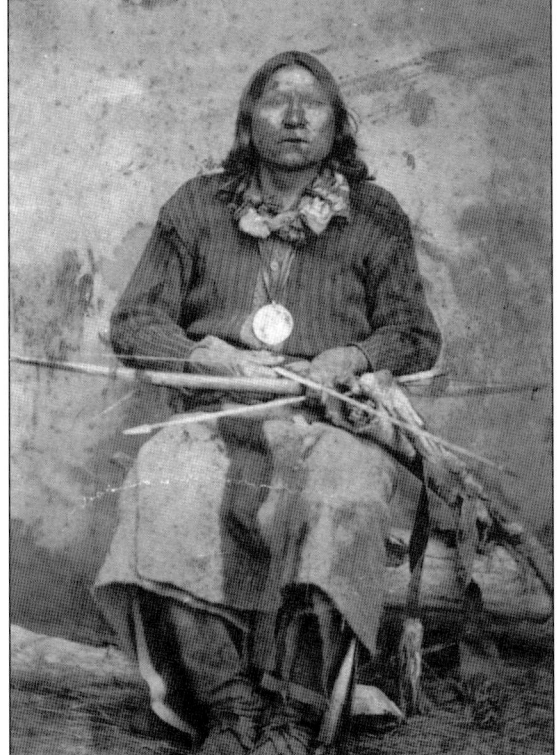

Satanta, pictured here, was sarcastically called the "orator of the Plains" by government officials. He complained that white leaders told his people "to be gone, as the offended master speaks to his dog." Satanta also protested that by accepting peace, "I have been made poor. Before, I was rich in horses and lodges. Today I am the poorest of all." (Courtesy Library of Congress.)

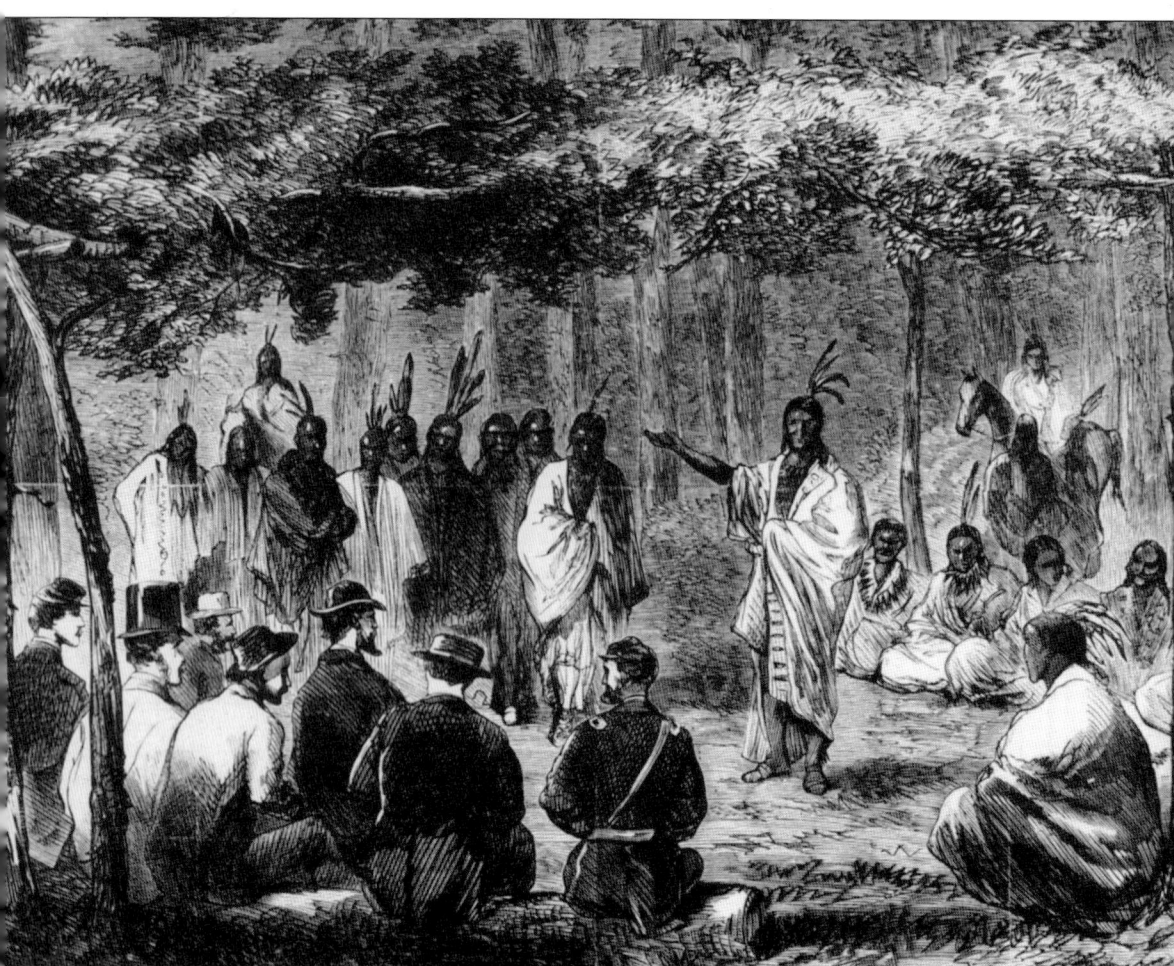

Kiowa chief Black Eagle and 150 lodges of his people joined 100 Comanche lodges, 171 Arapaho, 85 Kiowa-Apache, and 250 Cheyenne on the banks of Medicine Lodge Creek to sign a treaty in October 1867. The peace commissioners wanted to settle the Kiowas on the Red River, near the Wichita Mountains, in exchange for food, clothing, and other goods. The next day, 10 Kiowa and 10 Comanche chiefs signed the treaty. When the gifts were distributed after the council, they were too many to carry away. Piles of clothing, blankets, and other items were left on the ground. The Kiowas exited the camp on foot, leading their heavily laden horses. (Courtesy DPL.)

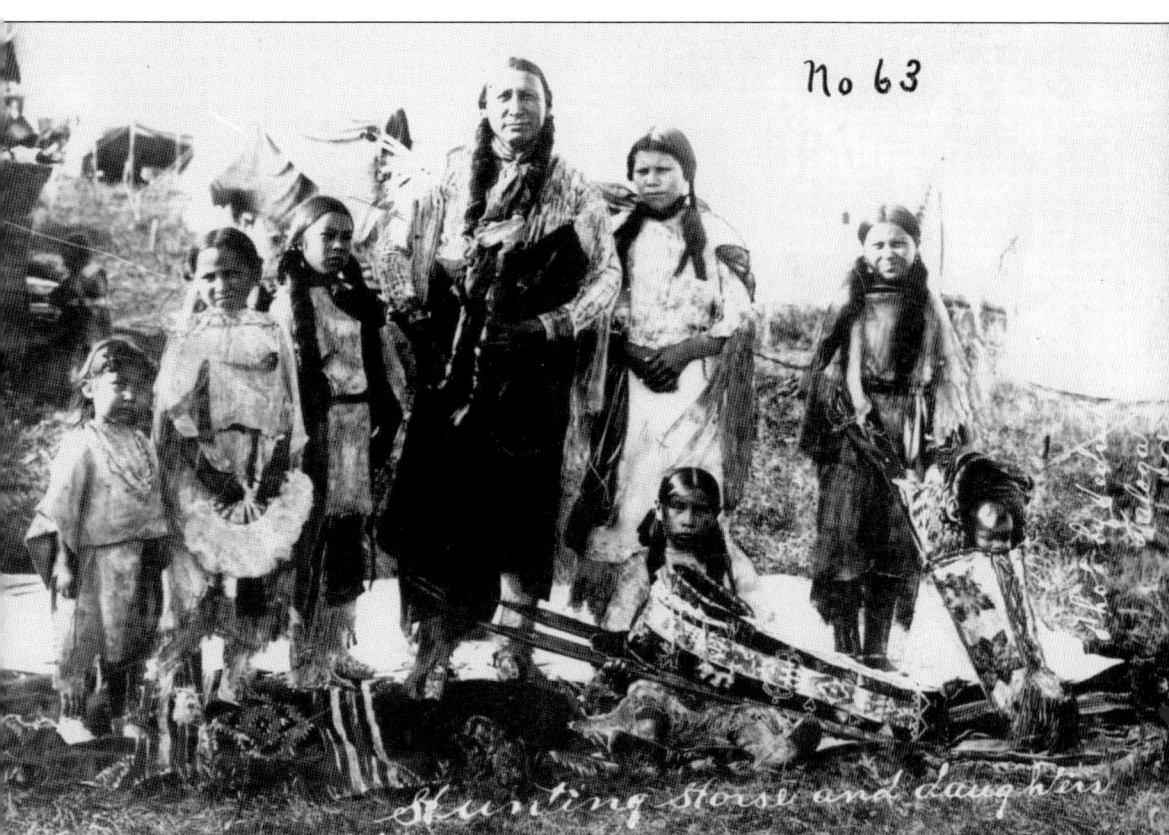

Kiowas, like other Plains Indians, have their legend of Devil's Tower. "Before the Kiowa came south," there were many bears in the place where the people camped. Seven little girls were playing near their village when bears began to chase them. They jumped on a large boulder and begged it to have pity and save them from the bears. As the girls said this, the rock began to grow. It rose higher and higher in the sky as the bears clawed at it. The bears' claws broke on the hard stone but left deep grooves on its sides. Enraged, the bears continued to jump, trying to reach the girls while the rock carried them higher into the sky. When the rock reached the stars, the girls climbed off and became the seven little stars of the Pleiades. Devil's Tower is called *Tso-aa*, "Tree Rock," by Kiowas because of how it grew. The grooves along its sides are evidence of the bears' attack. (Courtesy Library of Congress.)

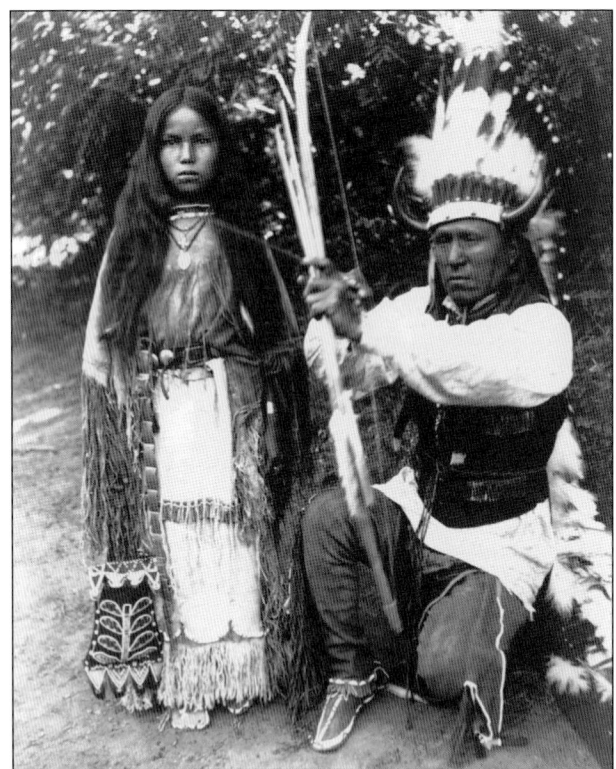

Kiowa people were notorious wanderers. Perhaps this is why their Aztec-Tanoan language is most closely related to the Pueblo Indians of New Mexico, yet they came from southwestern Canada. Long-distance raids carried the Kiowas into the Grand Canyon region and south into Mexico and Central America. (Courtesy Library of Congress.)

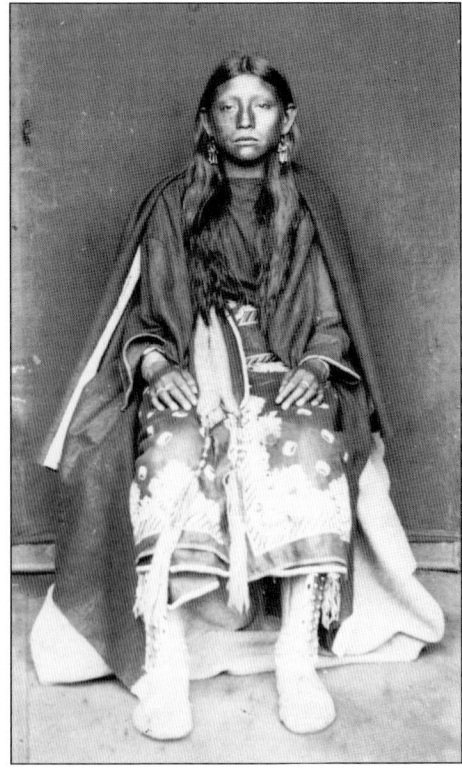

In a wonderful legacy for future generations, the Kiowa Nation left a record of events using pictographic signs. These symbols, painted on the hides of deer, antelope, and buffalo, provide a calendar of events. The Kiowas later adapted this for the white man's record books, producing beautiful ledger art. (Courtesy Library of Congress.)

Eight

Lakota, the Sioux Nation

This is arguably the most famous of the First Nations. Lakota is the western, or Teton, dialect of the word *Dakota*, meaning "allies." Their common name, Sioux, is an abbreviation of the Chippewa word *Nadouessioux*, a pejorative meaning "adders" or "enemies."

Lakota is a dialect of the Macro-Siouan language family, which also includes the Crow and the Mandan. This First Nation was originally documented by the Jesuits in 1640 in Minnesota, but the tribe is thought to have originated in the area of North Carolina. Again, with the domino displacement of First Nations after the European invasion, the Lakotas were pushed westward, reaching the Black Hills in the early 1700s. On the other hand, ancient Lakota star maps (verified by archaeo-astronomers) place them in the Black Hills by at least 896 BCE. Marking the southernmost region on their sacred star map is Pikes Peak, where Lakota holy man Black Elk had his famous vision in 1873.

This nation was primarily in the Pikes Peak area on hunting and raiding parties. As mentioned in the last chapter, Lakotas chased a band of 2,000 Comanches and Kiowas and over 10,000 horses up Ute Pass and into South Park in 1805. Allied with the Cheyennes and Arapahos, they waged a major battle against the Utes about six miles north of Colorado City in 1859. Irving Howbert stated that these allies made frequent forays up Ute Pass to battle with the Utes. In 1874, Colonel Dodge wrote that Ute warriors stole 200 ponies from a Lakota hunting party, members of which then chased the Utes from the Republican River to the edge of Ute Pass.

The Sioux Wars ended in 1877, when Lakotas began their reservation era on lands in North and South Dakota. Today their nation numbers about 108,000.

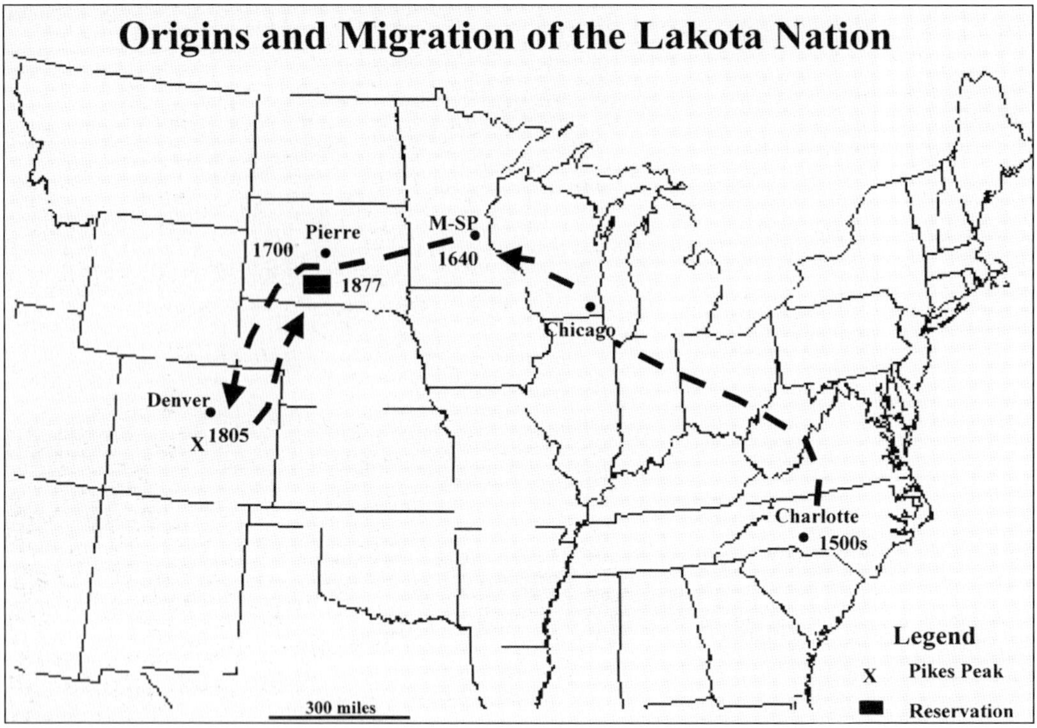

Origins and Migration of the Lakota Nation

The Siouan language group carves a jagged, oval-shaped area in the heart of Canada and the United States. It is something of a mystery, then, that the Lakotas are first documented in North Carolina. In the early 1600s, they migrated northwestward into Minnesota, where they displaced the Cheyennes. Buffalo hunting forays brought them into Colorado in the early 1800s.

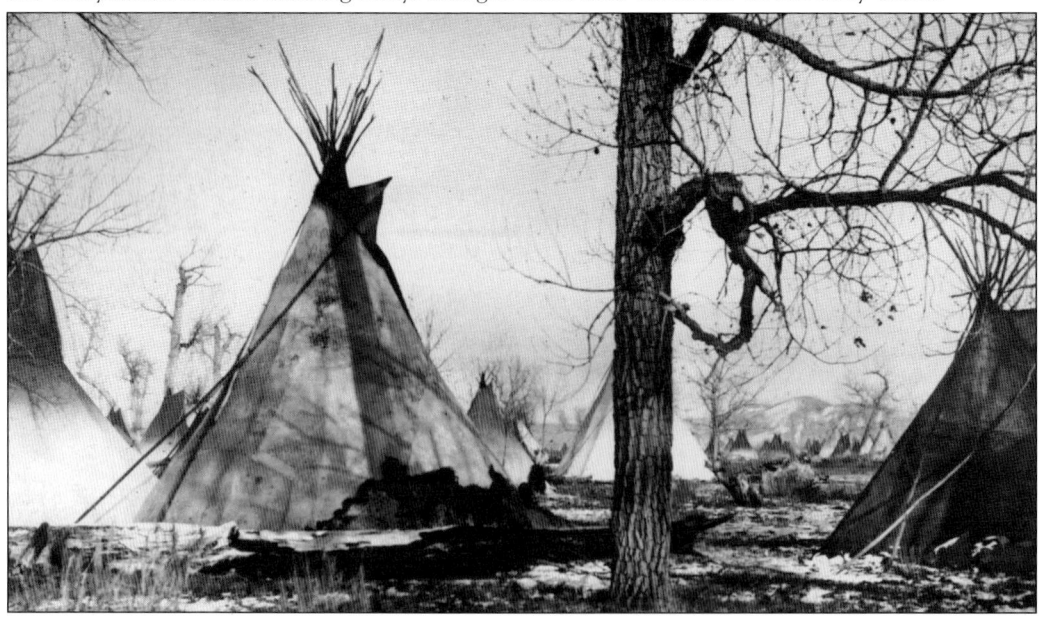

After the European invasion, the Lakota people migrated northwestward. Their winter count places them in the Black Hills in the late 1870s. They quickly adapted to Plains Indian culture, and life soon evolved around the buffalo. (Courtesy Coffrin's Old West Gallery.)

After gold was found in California, miners flooded into Lakota lands, scattering the buffalo herds and disrupting life. Chief Red Cloud, shown here, led his warriors in repelling these invaders. In 1868, he signed the second Fort Laramie Treaty, a document he thought would protect Lakota lands. (Courtesy Coffrin's Old West Gallery.)

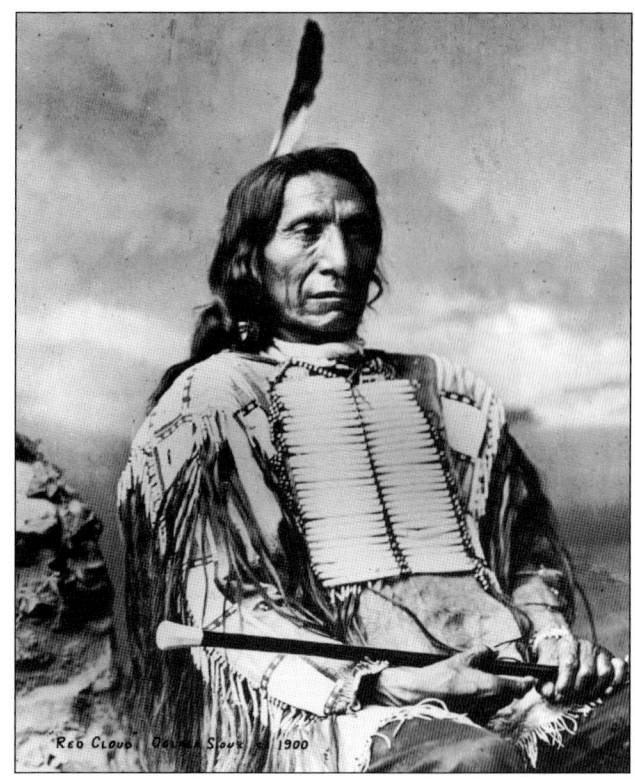

In 1874, Gen. George A. Custer and 1,200 troops marched into the Black Hills in search of gold—a clear violation of the Treaty of Fort Laramie. This triggered the Sioux War, culminating in the Battle of the Little Big Horn in 1876. (Courtesy Coffrin's Old West Gallery.)

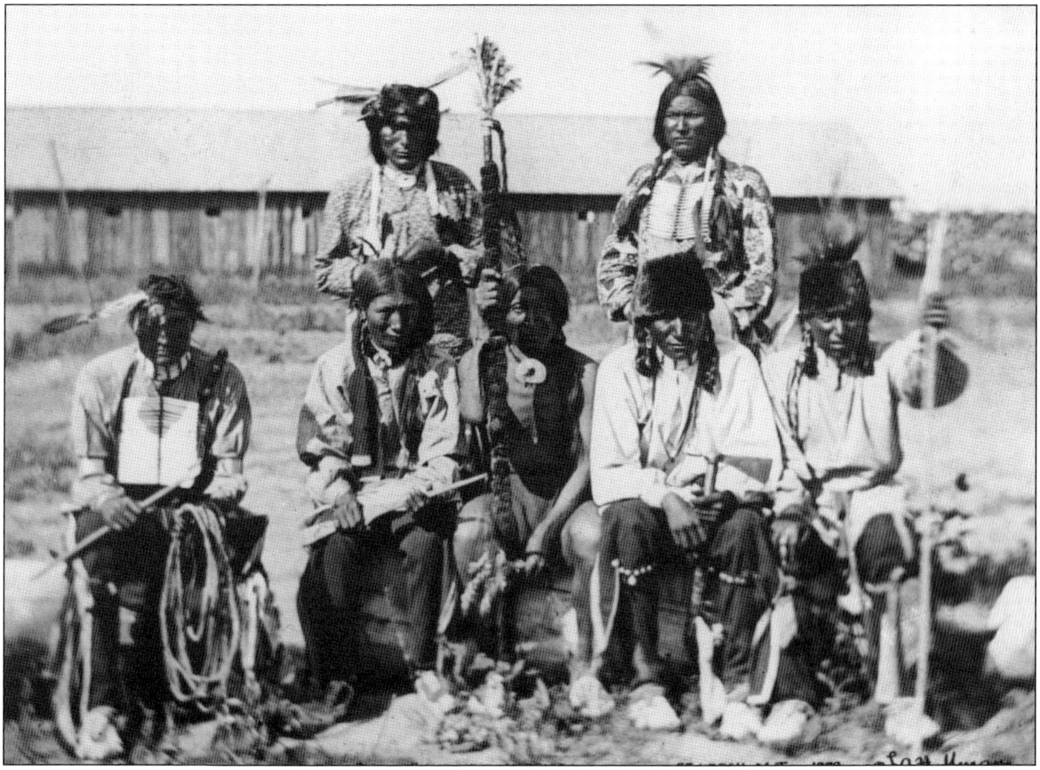

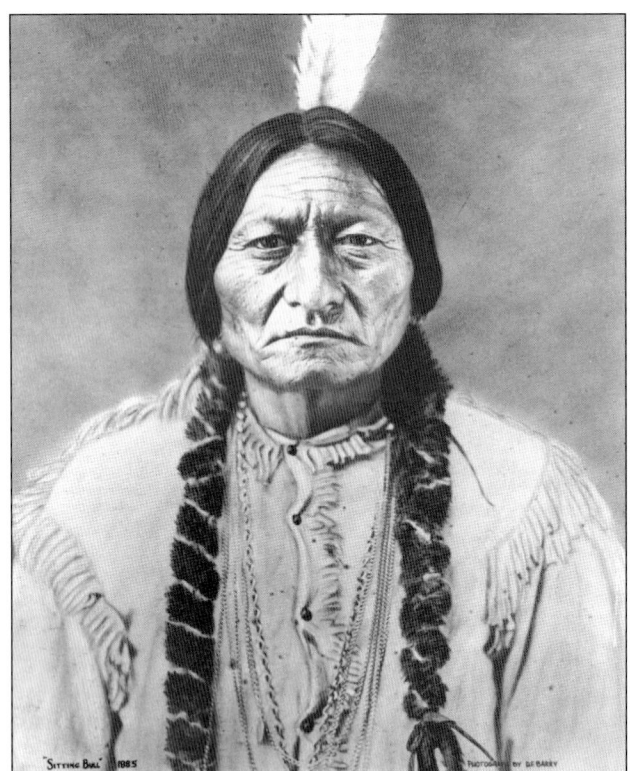

Sitting Bull remonstrated, "Look at me, and look at the earth. . . . It does not belong to us alone: it was our fathers', and should be our children's after us. . . . What is this white soldier doing here? What did he come for? To spy out the land, and to find a good place for a fort and a road, and to dig out gold." (Courtesy Coffrin's Old West Gallery.)

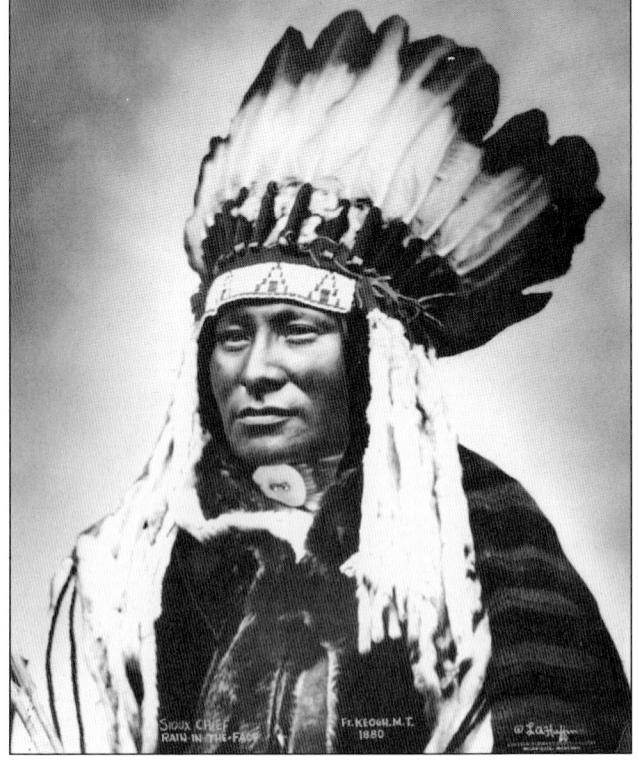

Rain-in-the-Face, shown here, was with Sitting Bull when they defeated Custer on the Little Big Horn. He was also beside Sitting Bull during the harrowing escape into Canada. When Sitting Bull surrendered five years later, Rain-in-the-Face was still with his leader. (Courtesy Coffrin's Old West Gallery.)

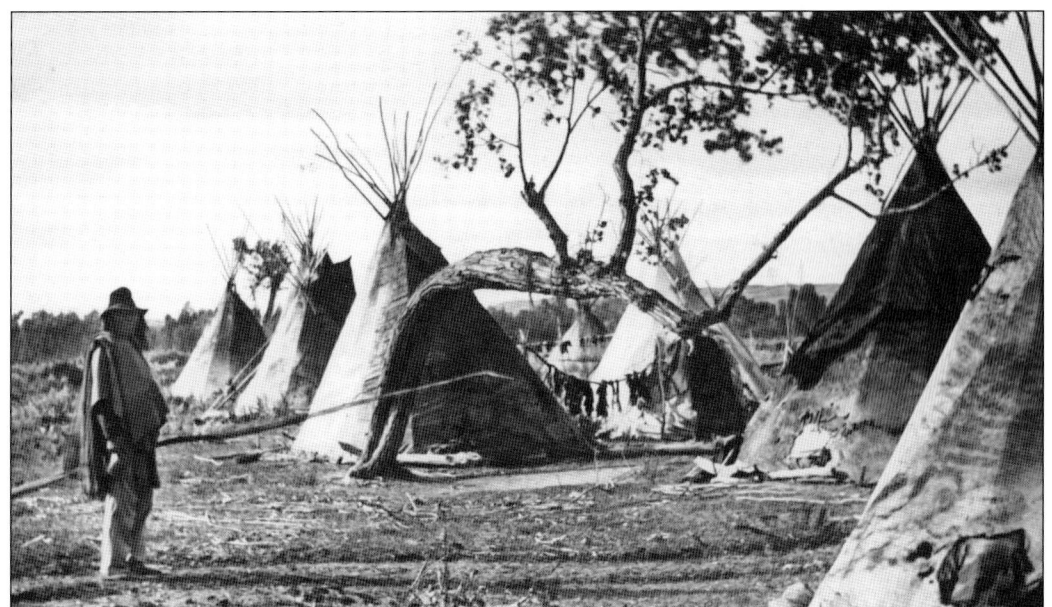

After Sitting Bull's surrender, the Lakota people were settled on reservations in North and South Dakota. The Oglala band was settled on Pine Ridge Reservation in South Dakota, while the Hunkpapas were located at Standing Rock in North Dakota. The Minniconjou were given the Cheyenne River Reservation in northern South Dakota. (Courtesy Coffrin's Old West Gallery.)

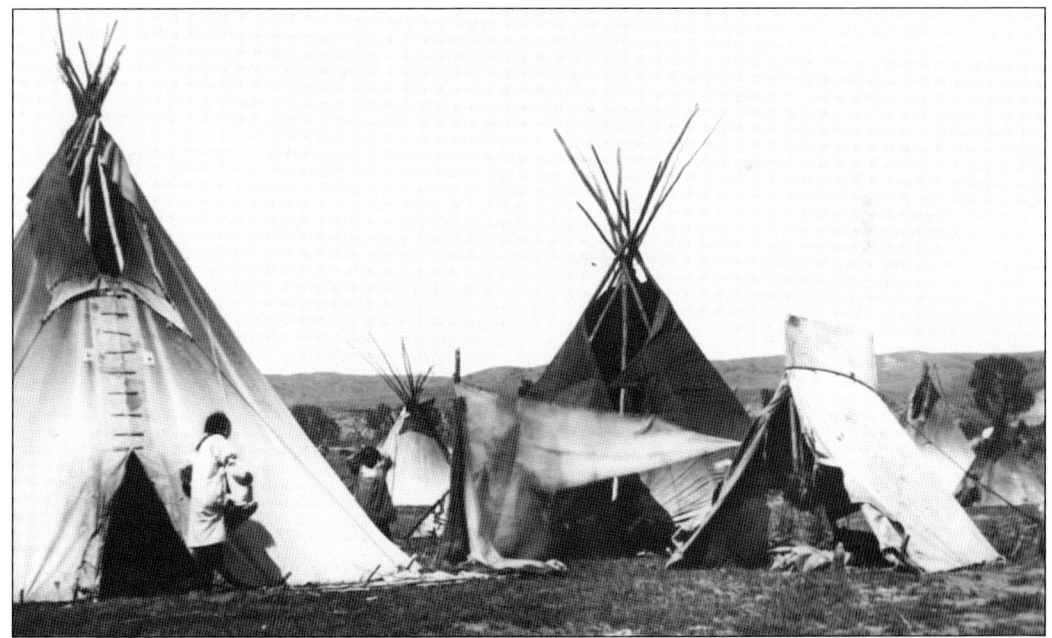

The dark-colored tipi (probably red) in the center belongs to Rain-in-the-Face, a Lakota medicine man. In the spring of 1890, Indian agents reported that the Lakota had adopted the new Ghost Dance religion, which purportedly brought all dead ancestors to life and made dancers immune to bullets. Government fear of the ceremony led to the tragedy at Wounded Knee that December. (Courtesy Coffrin's Old West Gallery.)

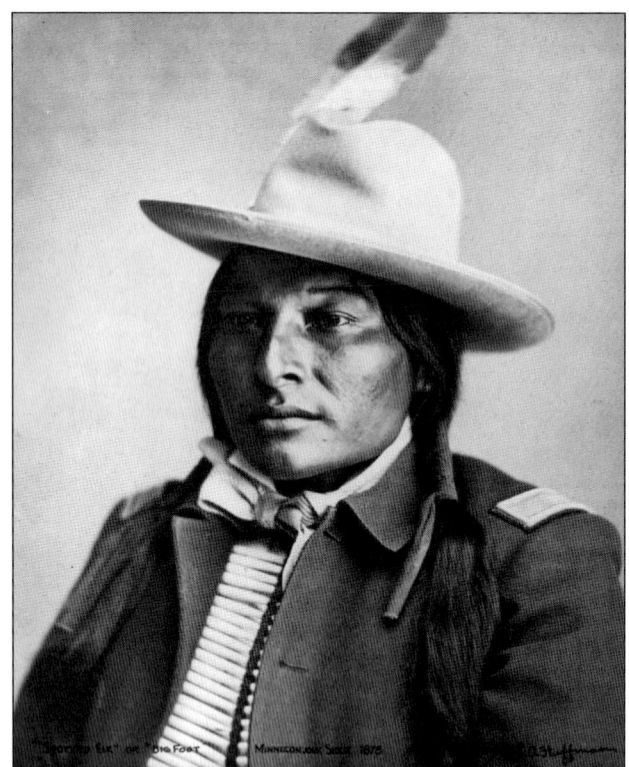

Sitanka, "Big Foot," and his band of Minniconjou left the Cheyenne River Reservation in December 1890 for Pine Ridge. On the morning of December 29, soldiers opened fire at their village on Wounded Knee, killing more than 150—mostly women and children. (Courtesy Coffrin's Old West Gallery.)

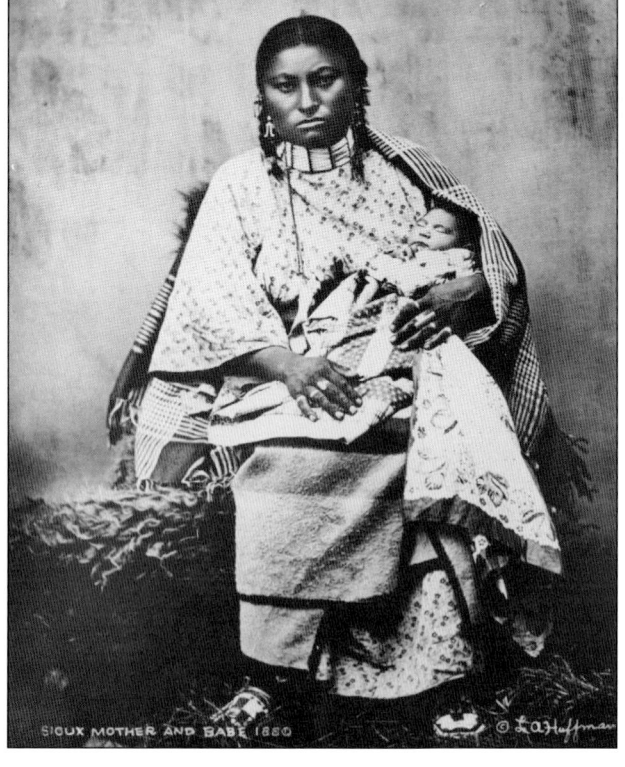

Lakotas called children "sacred star beings" because they were newly arrived from the spirit world. They also regarded *winkte*, two spirits (gay men), as sacred. *Winkte* were thought to have special powers, and if they gave a child a secret name, that child would grow up without sickness. (Courtesy Coffrin's Old West Gallery.)

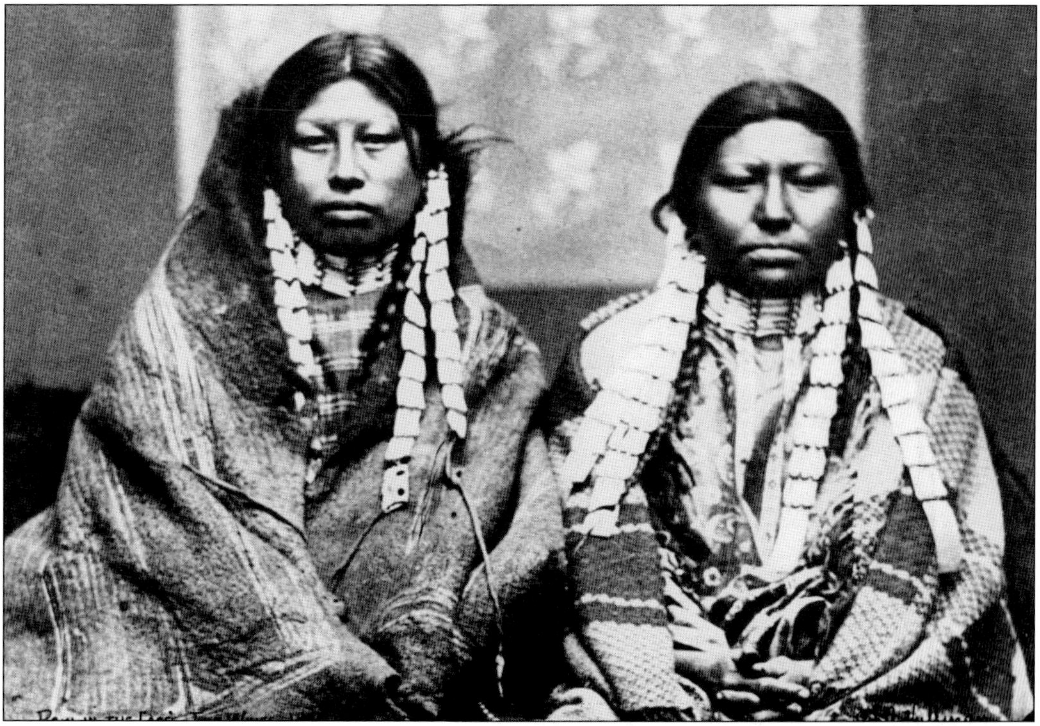

Truthfulness was integral to Lakota culture. There was no privacy within a village, and everyone knew everyone else's business. Talk was a powerful control on the behavior of the band, and women excelled at it. This created an esprit de corps, reminding people of the correct way to "walk the red road." (Courtesy Coffrin's Old West Gallery.)

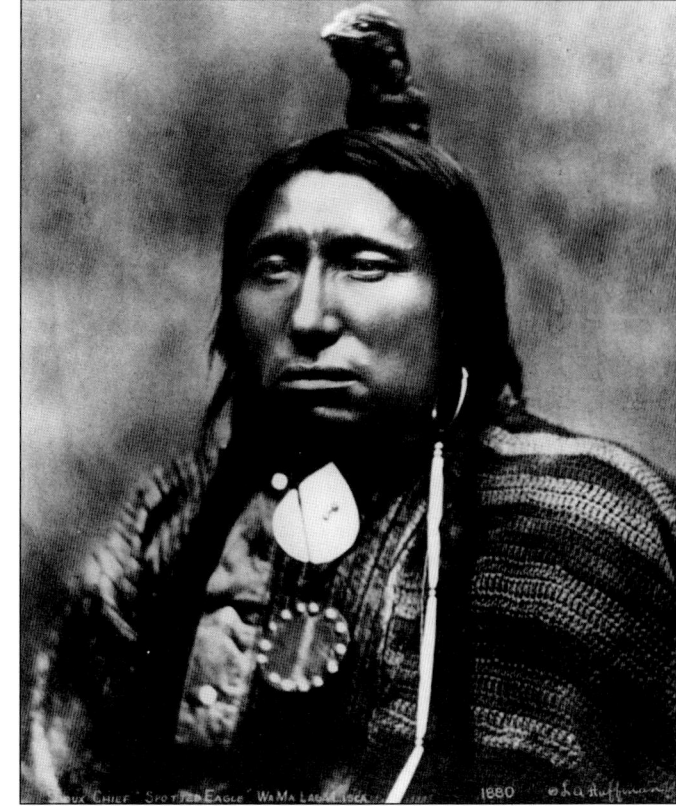

In Lakota cosmology, the spotted eagle, which flies higher and faster than any other bird, is thought to be one of the special messengers from *Wakan Tanka*, the Creator. Lakota chief Spotted Eagle wears the powerful talisman of his namesake. (Courtesy Coffrin's Old West Gallery.)

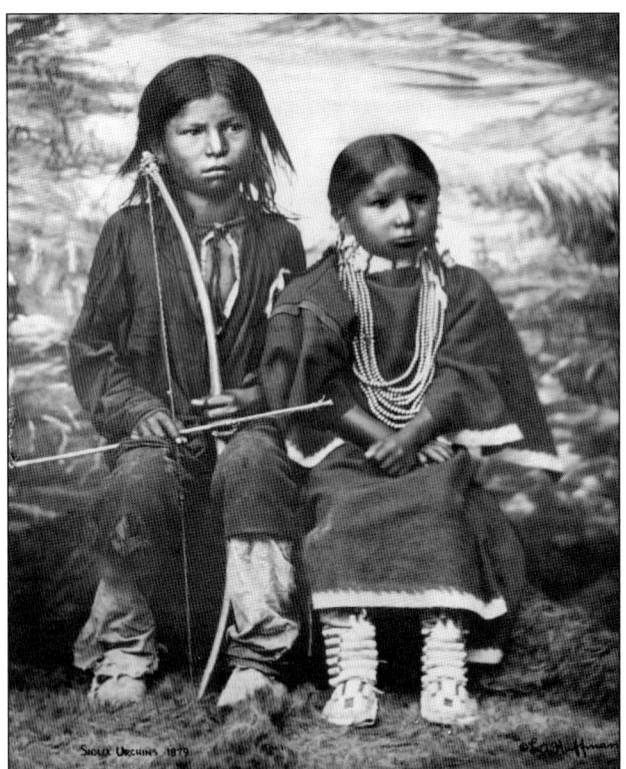

In the Lakota legend of Devil's Tower, a band is camped near the Black Hills. Each day a red eagle swoops down and carries a little girl to the mountaintop. Fallen Star hears the people's prayers and kills the eagle. He then places the spirits of the seven abducted girls in the sky, where they become *Wicincala Sakowin*, "Seven Little Girls," of the Pleiades. (Courtesy Coffrin's Old West Gallery.)

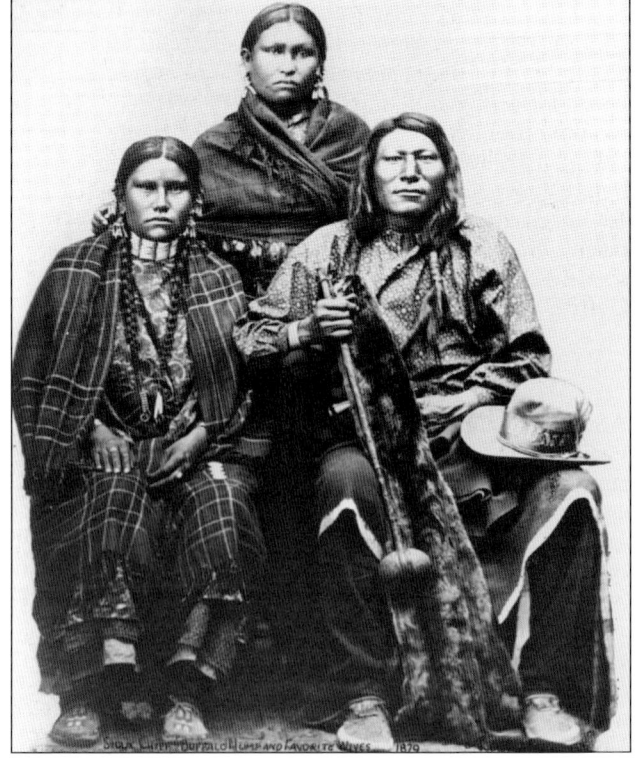

Fidelity was highly valued in marriage. This could be difficult, as it was common for a man to have many wives. A woman who was married only once and was faithful was held in higher standing than her peers. Sometimes these women prepared a feast for one another where, as evidence of their virtue, they would "bite the knife" of truthfulness. (Courtesy Coffrin's Old West Gallery.)

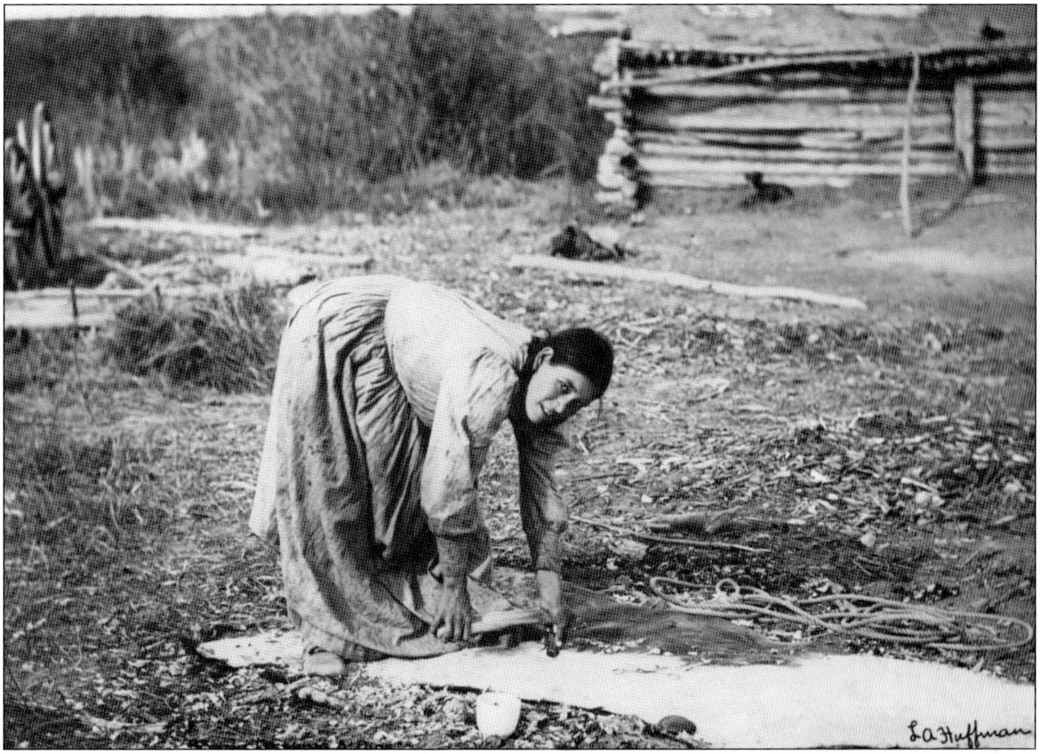

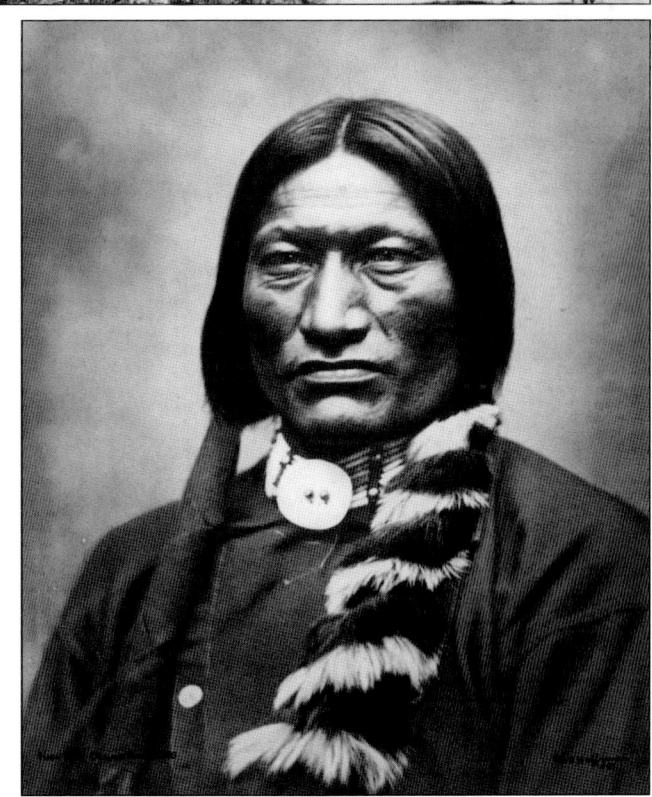

Lakota women turned their backbreaking labor into a contest. Each time they tanned a buffalo hide, they placed a black dot on their elk horn scraping tool, like the one this woman holds in her right hand. When a woman finished 100 robes, she was entitled to place a circle at the base of her scraper's handle. (Courtesy Coffrin's Old West Gallery.)

Among Lakotas, the greatest virtues were fortitude (bravery), generosity, and wisdom. Their warriors sacrificed themselves for the people each year in the Sundance ceremony. As Luther Standing Bear so eloquently stated, "True civilization lies in the dominance of self and not in the dominance of other men." (Courtesy Coffrin's Old West Gallery.)

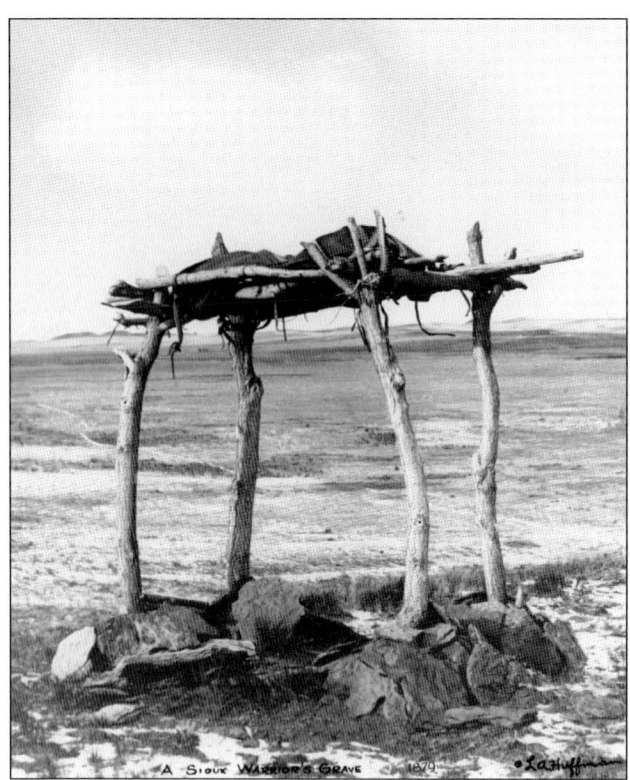

When a warrior died, his body was wrapped in a buffalo robe along with his personal items. Spirit moccasins, with beaded soles, were placed on his feet for his journey to the spirit world. His best horse was killed to carry him on this passage. His family then placed his body on a scaffold on a hill. (Courtesy Coffrin's Old West Gallery.)

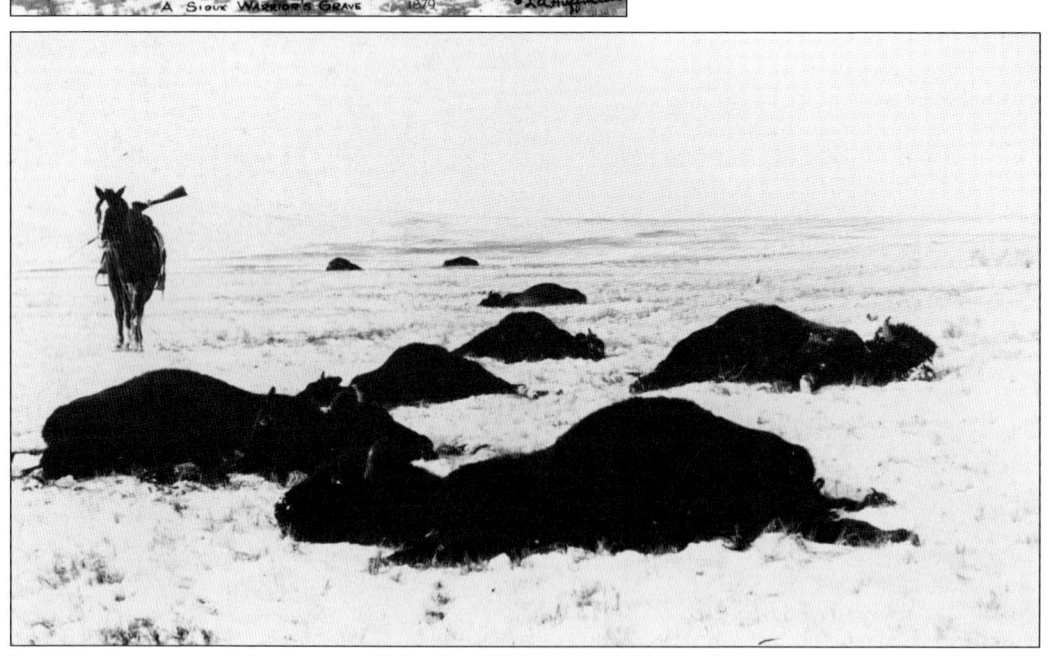

In 1873, Secretary of the Interior Columbus Delano said, "I would not seriously regret the total disappearance of the buffalo . . . in its effect upon the Indians." To this end, the army routinely supplied free ammunition to buffalo hunters. Gen. Philip Sheridan noted that "[these hunters] have done [more] . . . than the entire regular army. . . . Let them kill until all the buffalo are exterminated." (Courtesy Coffrin's Old West Gallery.)

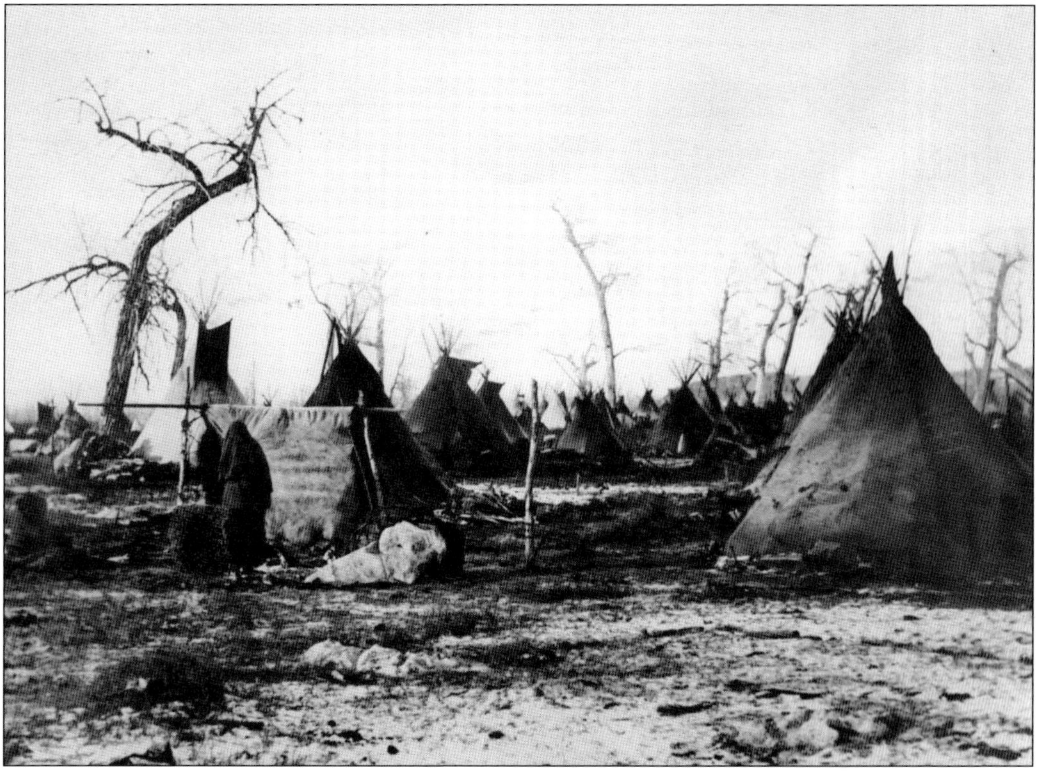

Buffalo hides, such as this one drying on the rack, were used for recording seminal events of the Lakotas. These hides were also painted with maps of the earth and the heavens. Stanley Looking Horse reported that "One hide was a star map, the other hide was an earth, 'maka,' map—buttes and rivers and mountains even creeks clear out to [Pikes Peak] Colorado Springs." (Courtesy Coffrin's Old West Gallery.)

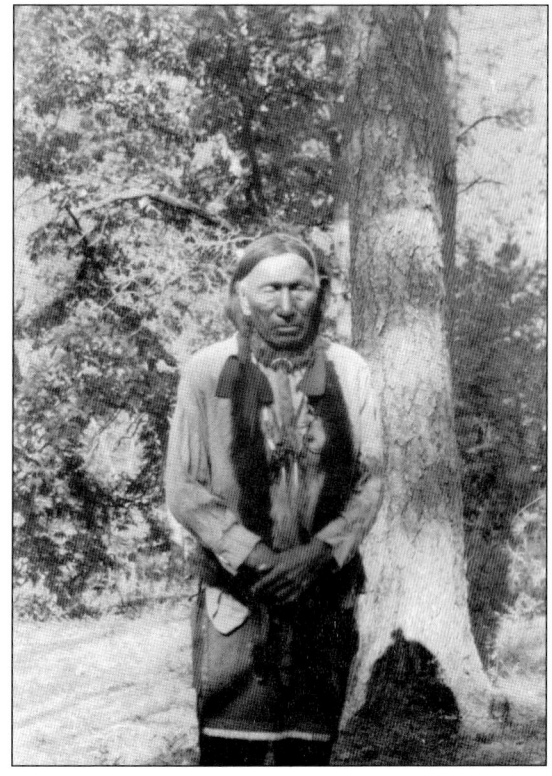

Around 1873, spirits took a nine-year-old Lakota boy to the top of Pikes Peak, where he was given a great vision. Black Elk's vision was immortalized by John Neihardt in *Black Elk Speaks*, even though the author changed the location to Harney Peak. The grandfathers told Black Elk that the Sacred Hoop of all life will be healed in this decade. (Courtesy DPL.)

Selected Bibliography

Cassels, E. Steve. *The Archaeology of Colorado*. Boulder, CO: Johnson Publishing, 1990.

Coel, Margaret. *Chief Left Hand: Southern Arapaho*. Norman, OK: University of Oklahoma Press, 1987.

Goodman, Ronald. *Lakota Star Knowledge*. Rosebud, SD: Sinte Gleska University, 1992.

Grinnell, George Bird. *The Fighting Cheyennes*. North Dighton, MA: JG Press, 1995.

Haley, James L. *Apaches: A History and Culture Portrait*. Norman, OK: University of Oklahoma Press, 1997.

Hassrick, Royal B. *The Sioux*. Norman, OK: University of Oklahoma Press, 1964.

John, Elizabeth A. H. *Storms Brewed in Other Men's Worlds*. Norman, OK: University of Oklahoma Press, 1996.

Kroeber, Alfred L. *The Arapaho*. Lincoln, NE: University of Nebraska Press, 1983.

Mendosa, Patrick M. *Song of Sorrow: Massacre at Sand Creek*. Denver, CO: Willow Wind Publishing, 1993.

Prucha, Francis Paul. *The Great Father: The United States Government and the American Indians*. Lincoln, NE: University of Nebraska Press, 1986.

Robinson, Charles M. *Bad Hand: A Biography of General Ranald S. MacKenzie*. Austin, TX: State House Press, 1993.

Simmons, Virginia M. *The Ute Indians of Utah, Colorado, and New Mexico*. Boulder, CO: University Press of Colorado, 2000.

Smith, Anne M. *Ethnography of the Northern Utes*. Albuquerque, NM: Museum of New Mexico Press, 1974.

Swanton, John R. *The Indian Tribes of North America*. Washington, D.C: Smithsonian Institution Press, 1969.

Tiller, Veronica E. Velarde. *The Jicarilla Apache Tribe*. Albuquerque, NM: Bow Arrow Publishing, 2000.

Wallace, Ernest, and E. Adamson Hoebel. *The Comanches: Lords of the South Plains*. Norman, OK: University of Oklahoma Press, 1986.

Discover Thousands of Local History Books Featuring Millions of Vintage Images

Arcadia Publishing, the leading local history publisher in the United States, is committed to making history accessible and meaningful through publishing books that celebrate and preserve the heritage of America's people and places.

Find more books like this at
www.arcadiapublishing.com

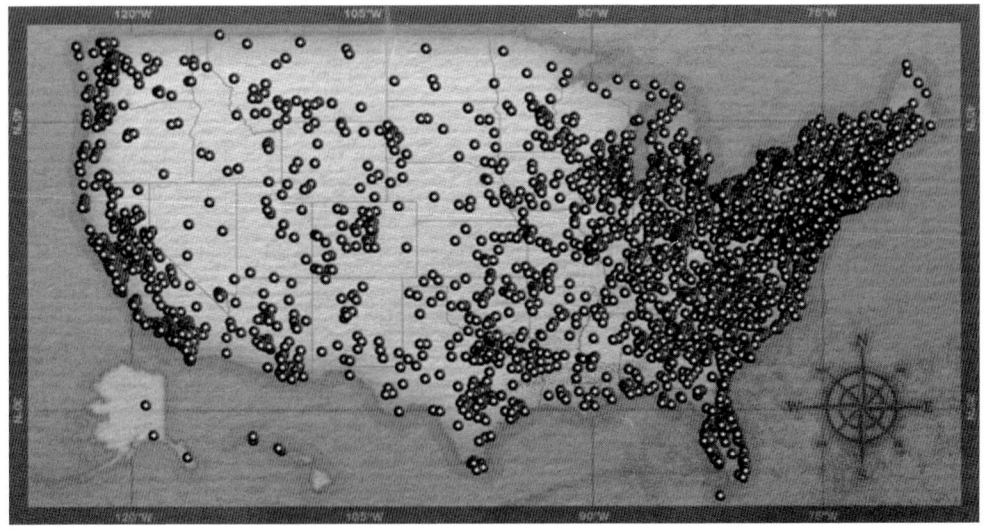

Search for your hometown history, your old stomping grounds, and even your favorite sports team.

Consistent with our mission to preserve history on a local level, this book was printed in South Carolina on American-made paper and manufactured entirely in the United States. Products carrying the accredited Forest Stewardship Council (FSC) label are printed on 100 percent FSC-certified paper.

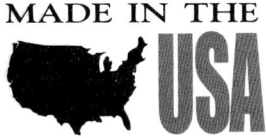

INDEX

Air Force Academy, 7, 11, 16
Anasazi, 8, 12, 15
Apaches, 8, 16, 19, 23, 34, 63–74, 77, 104, 107, 112
Arapahos, 8, 32, 57, 87–100, 104, 110, 112, 115
Aztec, 8, 17, 75, 114
Bent, George, 101, 102
Bering Strait, 8, 64, 88
Big Foot, 120
Black Elk, 8, 115, 125
Black Kettle, 90, 99
Buckskin Charlie, 2, 27, 42
Capote band, 17, 19, 27, 30, 51, 52, 68
Cheyennes, 8, 32, 87, 89, 90–93, 97–112, 115
Colonel Dodge, 87, 115
Colorado City, 8, 37, 97, 115
Colorow, 20, 23, 37, 60
Comanches, 8, 57, 63, 66, 75–86, 104, 107, 109, 111, 112, 115
Cuerno Verde (Green Horn), 67, 75
Fort Carson, 7, 11, 15
Garden of the Gods, 2, 7, 9, 11, 13, 16, 31, 32, 35, 59
Howbert, Irving, 8, 24, 35, 115
Ignacio, 25, 30, 31, 62
Jicarilla Apaches, 8, 63–74
Jimmy Camp Creek, 11, 15
Kiowas, 8, 32, 75, 80, 81, 104, 107–115
Lakotas, 8, 97, 107, 109, 115–125
Left Hand, 87, 90
Little Raven, 91, 95
maps
  Apache, 64
  Arapaho, 88
  Cheyenne, 98
  Comanche, 76
  Kiowa, 108
  Lakota, 116
  of the 1600s, 65
  of the 1700s, 66, 76, 77
  Ute, 18
Medicine Lodge Treaty, 8, 87, 92, 97, 102
medicine trees, 9, 46
Moache band, 17, 26, 53, 67
Navajos, 8, 63
Ouray, 21–23, 29, 38
Parker, Quanah, 79, 81
Piah, 24, 25
Pike, Zebulon, 107
Pikes Peak, 7–9, 11, 17, 28, 36, 43, 45, 46, 48, 63, 76, 87, 97, 107, 115, 125
Pleiades, 43, 44, 106, 113, 122
prayer trees, 9, 46
Purcell, James, 107
Rain-in-the-Face, 118, 119
Red Cloud, 117
Sand Creek Massacre, 87, 90, 97, 100
Satanta, 109, 111
Shoshones, 8, 76
Sioux (*see Lakota*)
Sitting Bull, 103, 118, 119
Tabeguache band, 17, 21, 24, 28, 29, 31, 37, 60, 62
Two Moons, 103
Utes (Nuche), 2, 7–9, 14, 16–62, 67, 68, 70, 75–77, 79, 101, 108, 115
Ute creation legend, 7
Ute forts, 9, 16, 35, 36
White Wolf, 82, 84, 110